In the
Service
of the Lord

In the
Service
of the Lord:

THE AUTO-
BIOGRAPHY
OF BISHOP

Otto
Dibelius

Translated from the German by Mary Ilford

 HOLT, RINEHART AND WINSTON

New York   Chicago   San Francisco

Designer: Ernst Reichl
81836-0114
Printed in the United States of America

Contents

FOREWORD 3

VOCATION 5

THE WORLD 19

THEOLOGY 37

TEACHER 55

PREACHER 77

PASTORAL COUNSELOR 89

ADMINISTRATOR 99

SUPERINTENDENT-GENERAL 113

RETIRED 135

BISHOP 171

COUNCIL PRESIDENT 215

PRESIDENT OF THE
WORLD COUNCIL OF CHURCHES 249

CONCLUSION 277

CHRONOLOGY 279

In the
Service
of the Lord

A FOREWORD
INTENDED TO BE READ

I DO NOT like forewords. A book which has anything to say needs no introduction. This time, however, I have to make an exception.

While I was still Superintendent-General of the Kurmark (1925-1933), I was asked to do a book on the pastoral office based on my personal experiences. A book, that is, along the lines of Büchsel's *Reminiscences of a Country Pastor,* from which whole generations of pastors had drawn aid and encouragement in their ministry.

The idea appealed to me, and I began to jot down notes on various aspects of the pastorate.

Then came National Socialism, and the whole project went by the board. For National Socialism wrought such fundamental changes in so many aspects of the pastoral office that an account of bygone days could no longer have evoked much interest.

But when I became again Bishop of Berlin in 1945, people both at home and abroad began to ask me to write my autobiography. I was reluctant to do so. An autobiography always includes many things that are not important enough to be told. At the same time, the personal things, particularly one's family life, should not be exposed to the public gaze. Some men can, perhaps, describe their reactions at the deathbed of a loved one or at the collapse of their country, but I cannot.

I had to concede, however, that some might find it useful to learn how a man in a position of responsibility within the church conceived of his office in times of appalling upheaval, and tried to carry it out.

So I took up the thread where it had slipped from my fingers years before. I condensed the chapters on the parish ministry, and added some chapters on my later activities.

Since my purpose is to give typical instances rather than a continuous account, the reader may be confused if I speak now of my ministry in a small town and then suddenly of my ministry in the city, or of the monarchy and then of the republic. I have therefore appended a chronology showing at a glance the various offices I have held at different times in my life.

What I have tried to describe is not a life but a ministry.

I have been credited with saying that a Christian is always on active service. I am not clear when or where I made that statement. But I have learned from Adolf Harnack that legends can be authentic historical sources. Perhaps that is the case here.

My personal feelings as I look back upon my life are hinted at in the conclusion. Merely hinted at. More I cannot say.

DOCATION

I HAD INTENDED to do something altogether different.

As far back as I can remember, it had been decided that my two brothers should go to the university. I, considering the limitations of my father's purse, was to choose a career which would allow me to stand on my own feet without delay. My parents had not urged this course on me; at least, I do not remember their ever speaking to me about it. It was entirely my own idea, and no doubt it arose from my instinctive horror of having anyone make a sacrifice for me.

I resolved to enter the postal service. In those days, when a young man went into the postal service as an apprentice, he received a small salary right from the start. After that, by taking a couple of examinations, he gradually worked his way up from the lower and middle echelons to the higher ranks. It was the kind of thing Bismarck called a treadmill. But it had been my father's career, and it was to be mine too.

I saw no reason to study. I was not interested in the sciences. Our high school at Lichterfelde had a very low standard at the time. We learned little and resented whatever was taught us at school. This was true of me, in any case. And much as I admired the intellectual vigor of my brother Wilhelm, who was later to be a professor at the University of Berlin, I felt no urge to emulate him. All I wanted was to be a solid citizen—and that did not require academic training.

I already regarded myself as a civil servant. I knew the civil service manual and the manual for higher officials by heart. I knew about every official—his rank, his salary, the distinction he could look forward to. I knew the secrets of bureaucratic government. I knew the difference between cosignature and countersignature, between an ordinance and a writ. I knew the difference between a *Wirklicher Geheimrat* (Acting Privy Councilor) and a *Wirklicher Geheimer Oberregierungsrat* (Acting Senior Privy Councilor to the Government). Indeed, I could never get over the fact that my good mother had no feeling for titles. To her last day she was unable to distinguish between an *Oberstleutnant* (Lieutenant Colonel) and an *Oberleutnant* (First Lieutenant), and she was completely indifferent whether a man called himself *Rechnungsrat* (civil servant with seniority) or *Regierungsrat* (Councilor to the Government), provided he was an honest man.

Then, just as I was entering my senior year at high school, the post office career was closed. There were too many applicants. Moreover, the senior postal officials, just because they had never seen the inside of a university, had an inferiority complex about the academically trained members of other departments. From now on, academic qualifications were also to be required of senior postal officials. And for a year or two there were to be no new admissions.

So my chosen career had come to nothing. What now? Should I study law? Should I go into business? Should I become a doctor? an officer? a pastor? I weighed each of these possibilities for some time. I would have preferred to go into the army. But here again I was concerned about my father's finances. So I finally decided to study law, as most people did in those days when they could not make up their minds what profession to pursue.

But shortly before my final school examination, a lecture by old Professor Beyschlag of Halle threw me completely off keel.

This was all very strange. Beyschlag was not at all the man to fire youth with enthusiasm. As a theologian, he favored accommodation. That, to begin with, had no appeal for the young. Nor did he have any great academic luster. He had originally been a pastor at Trier. There he had come into serious conflict with the Roman Church. When he became a professor at Halle, he conceived it his mission in life to call German Protestantism to vigilance against Rome. And as so easily happens when a man devotes himself to polemics, he laid himself open to attack and his reputation suffered even among many of his friends.

But at the time I knew nothing of all this. I saw a venerable old gentleman with white hair who radiated kindness and friendliness. And it flashed through me that such a man would have clear answers for the things that were filling my own heart with questions and doubts. Clarity, certainty, peace! What greater thing has life to offer than the chance to explore the world above us, to penetrate to the final verities, to arrive at peace oneself and then help others to arrive at clarity and peace in their turn?

Suddenly I was sure: I must study theology.

This certainty had, of course, been maturing for a long time, all unknown to me.

I came of a family where a firm Christian faith was the accepted basis of life. The picture of our grandfather, who taught religion at the Prenzlau high school, had looked down upon us all through our childhood, filling us with awe. His straightforward, profoundly Christian personality had earned him extraordinary respect. We had his large illustrated Bible in which were inscribed the names of those of his students who had gone on to the study of theology. There was a great number of them. We treasured this illustrated Bible.

We did not talk much about religion at home. My father, as a matter of fact, never discussed religion at all. But it was taken for granted that one attended church regularly, that one prayed, and that the day began with family prayers. It was a Christianity without problems, a conservative Christianity resting simply upon its own evidence.

My mother came of an intellectually alert Silesian family. Her father was a pastor. It was one of those parsonages where the externals were very simple, sometimes positively insufficient. There would be a cow in the barn and chickens in the yard, but the butter and eggs would have to be sold. The numerous children got neither butter nor eggs, and this told on them in later years. On the other hand, the family would speak English and French alternately at meals; they were at home in German literature, and to her last day my mother had a better head for the important dates in world history than her sons. She was more inclined than my father to reflect on religious matters and sometimes even to speak of them. But for her, too, it was axiomatic that one must not give way to doubt, and that the truth lay only where the pious men of Reformation times had found it. A dark memory remained in her family: her maternal grandfather, Court Chaplain Kauffer of Dresden, had made a profession of faith before his congregation upon his retirement, which was said to have been like a defection from scriptural truth. We learned nothing more detailed, but we knew that as a result, our mother harbored the secret anxiety that one of her sons might also fall victim to doubt and eventually to disbelief.

We youngsters felt ourselves to be children of a new age, indeed, of a critical age. What troubled us was nothing definite. We were ignorant of modern "higher criticism." We knew very little of the assault of materialistic natural science upon Christianity. We learned no more about such things at school than we did at home, and books on the subject were not readily available to us. It was quite simply the air we breathed, the spirit of our time, which gave us this feeling of inner uncertainty.

Those years before the turn of the century were years of fer-

8

ment. There was a groping and a searching in every field. There was a social question and a national question. There were questions of economics and questions of art. Everywhere questions and uncertainty. And as for the meaning of life, religion, morality, and eternity, there were queries upon queries.

We were under the spell of those times. All around us, people had stopped going to church. Everywhere we saw people who set store only by the tangible. We were quite sure that this was a miserable philosophy of life. But how were we to deal with it? It seemed to us impossible to settle every problem with a simple "I believe," as did our father. One must make use of reason and construct one's own philosophy of life. At the same time, our mother's fear was also, very secretly, our own: that in the end these questions might lead us from our Christian faith. And that must not be!

Not far from our house lived Eduard von Hartmann, the philosopher of the unconscious. We were friendly with his children. He had not allowed them to be christened. We always felt a little uncomfortable when we saw him lying on his couch, a man with a black beard and bright, piercing eyes, a man who had turned his back on Christianity. How could he go on living? To lose one's faith—did that not mean to lose everything? Did it not mean to plunge into the abyss?

The "quest of the times" lay in our blood. But we did not flirt with it in the fashion of those days, as though the highest aim was to be a "seeker after God" all one's life. We wanted not only to seek but also to find. We were, and remained, sure that the truth must lie in the Christian faith. But to comprehend this truth, to overcome the doubts raised by reason, to arrive at personal certainty—that was the problem.

We turned to the theologians who had achieved certainty. We had the great good fortune to have an ideal parish pastor, Max Stolte, who later became a superintendent-general. There was both youthfulness and distinction in his manner, and a physical and intellectual harmony that could only be described as classical.

9

He could be gay with young people to the point of exuberance. And a delicate humor flavored his friendly conversations with everyone. At the same time he always remained completely dignified and Christian. In the pulpit, too, he was perfectly natural, with a noble presence. His sermons were thoughful and direct. Professors, politicians, generals—in short, all churchgoers of name and status in Lichterfelde, which at the time was still a better-class neighborhood—gathered under his pulpit. Even young people, so prone to criticize, yielded to his preaching. He understood what it was that stirred in us, for he himself was still young. He wrote this verse by Emanuel Geibel in my autograph album:

> Study without respite!
> Your conclusions will not bring you far.
> This is the end of philosophy:
> To know that we must believe!

I was grateful to him for those words. But I felt that one could not accept this kind of counsel from another; one must learn it from one's own experience. And that was just how he had intended it.

One of Stolte's sermons helped me even more. The text was John 7:17: "If any man's will is to do his will, he shall know whether the teaching is from God, or whether I am speaking on my own authority." I do not remember what he said, but the text remained henceforth imprinted upon my mind—and this is the whole purpose of a truly Evangelical sermon. I clung to it. "If any man's will is to do his will"—that must be the liberation from all doubts of reason. To do God's will—yes, that was always possible. Only haltingly, of course, and often one did just the opposite. That I knew only too well. But one could always start again. Here was something solid, something absolutely certain. For generally speaking, it was not possible to doubt what God's will was. At least, not for us in those days. This did not, of course, dispense with the need to recognize the truth and make it one's own. On

10

the contrary. But there was no need to worry any more. The target could no longer be missed.

All this I had experienced without realizing its significance for my life.

And then there was our Uncle Franz, my father's only brother, later first chaplain in ordinary at Dresden. Every year, after preaching on Easter Sunday in his Kreuzkirche at Dresden, he would come to Berlin to recover from the exertions of the confirmation and Holy Week ceremonies. Other people, when they wanted a rest, would go off to some secluded place like the forest or the sea, but our Uncle Franz would go to Berlin. He felt rested when he saw as many people as possible around him, whether in the Friedrichstrasse or at the theater or wherever he was. He was a man of extraordinary vitality, and a powerful preacher. With his strong inner conviction he captivated his listeners and made a tremendous impression on us children. In him we had a living object lesson that it could be a wonderful experience to be a preacher of the Gospel.

Why had I not long before thought of becoming a pastor?

I felt that one had to be called to the pastorate. And I had not been aware of a calling. That was the reason.

I was right to think that one had to be called. I was right in a far deeper sense than I realized at the time. One cannot become a pastor as one becomes a businessman or a lawyer or an engineer or a doctor. To become a pastor means to take a risk.

The man who becomes a doctor knows that his choice of a profession is sound and sure. Later he might realize that he would have been better suited for another skill, or perhaps, for some reason, he wearies of his profession. But he will never doubt that sick people need help and that it is right and important to bring them such help.

With a pastor it is different. His duty is to preach the Gospel. He is not supposed to be an expert on religion in general or to engage in abstract philosophical discussions. His business is to

11

preach the Gospel, this single, quite specific Gospel contained in the Bible; to preach it as the eternal truth which holds the key to salvation and beatitude. This he can do only if he is himself permeated with this truth. If he begins to have doubts, or if he ceases to feel that it is really of the utmost importance whether people embrace the Gospel or not, then he can no longer be a pastor. Yet who is sure of his heart and his mind for his whole life? Who knows if what he believes at the age of twenty he will still believe at the age of fifty?

Nor is that all. The pastor must be sure that he speaks in the name of his Lord. He comes before men not as one who expresses his own opinion, nor as the representative of an association or a movement or a party: he speaks as the servant of the Church, whose Lord and Master is Christ Jesus. If he is not sure that he has been commissioned by this Lord, if he is not sure that when he preaches the Gospel he has this higher authority behind him, he cannot be a pastor. Will this certainty be his to the end? Will it come to him with constant renewal? He does not even have to fall away from scriptural truth—he has only to lose the savor of his zeal—and all is over.

Young people still at school cannot be expected to realize fully the magnitude of this risk. As yet they can know nothing of the grinding and sometimes harrowing temptations that beset a pastor, both from without and from within. Nor should they know of them. When people dare great things in life they never know all the dangers that lurk on the way. That is the way God orders things. But they must know that they are taking a risk.

In times when the Christian faith was taken for granted the risk was not as great as it is now. Only in such times, indeed, could the pastorate have become a profession—a career, that is, on which a man decides in his youth and on which he is then launched by the aid of a carefully organized program of studies.

In the early centuries of Christianity it was not so. A man entered the ministry because the community trusted him as a righteous guide. The great Ambrose of Milan had studied law and had

12

just become the very youthful governor of northern Italy when he was suddenly proclaimed bishop. His contemporary, Augustine, was a teacher of rhetoric when he became a Christian and soon after a priest. And in the three preceding centuries it had been taken as a matter of course that the spiritual leaders of the Christian communities should come out of the communities themselves. They were men from the most varied walks of life. They had been captivated by the Gospel. They lived with the community, and the community trusted them and chose them as leaders. In those days one did not say at the age of eighteen: "I want to be a pastor." One did not study theology. One was called to the ministry as a full-grown man. And when one was called, there was hardly any risk. For a man who came to the faith in maturity did not easily fall away—although that, too, sometimes occurred.

The real risk arises when the ministry becomes a profession, a career on which one has had to decide in one's youth. If the beginning of the ministry coincides with a time when the Christian faith is no longer taken for granted—a time of great spiritual crisis—the young minister may succumb to the prevailing atmosphere. He may be seized with doubts about the Gospel, at least about the Gospel as the church of the German Reformation understands it. That is what happened, for instance, with Christoph Schrempf in Württemberg. Schrempf had to give up his ministry when he was only thirty-one because he no longer shared the belief of his church. Several years later he left the church, and sought, unsuccessfully, to establish an independent congregation. He was a man of great earnestness and depth, but a tragic figure. The same thing happened with Paul Gohre. As a young theology student at Chemnitz he spent three months working in a factory in order to equip himself for missionary work among modern workers. He fell increasingly under the influence of Marxist thought. At the end of his life he was a Social Democratic Secretary of State, and wrote a weary, hopeless book about the "unknown God."

And there are many more whose names are unknown—men who destroyed themselves in solitary combat and finally left the ministry, quietly and wearily, or men who, without scruple, carried on in an office in which they had long since ceased to believe. At Lauenburg in Pomerania, I had an older colleague who claimed to be a "liberal" theologian, though he hardly ever read a book of theology. He did his duty till the normal age of retirement. Then— this was after I had left Lauenburg—he retired from his post. He stopped attending church. In his will he directed that no clergyman officiate at his cremation. He had become completely alienated from his own preaching of forty years, though his doubts had begun while he was still active in the pastorate. A wretched fate!

To become a pastor means to take a risk. Only a man who is sure that God has chosen him should take that risk. For when God calls a man, He graciously leads him unscathed through the temptations that assail him.

I have known ministers who never worried about such matters at all. They became pastors because their fathers and grandfathers had been pastors before them, or because it was the ambition of lower-middle-class families to give their sons a higher education, and theological studies were the cheapest to be had. When I was Superintendent-General, an application for a stipend passed through my hands, in which a young man naively confessed that he really wanted to be an official in the middle echelon, but that since that career was overcrowded, he had decided to study theology. He felt no inner call. Nor was he gifted. But he did not hesitate!

The upheaval of 1933 ejected some of these ministers. A few discovered that preaching the Gospel was not important enough for them. Politics or money beckoned. And when the opportunity was offered to gain an assured livelihood away from the ministry, they grasped it with both hands. Other men discovered to their dismay that the ministry did not give them the security and status they had expected. They withdrew from it at the first favorable opportunity. Others remained, though they should not have remained.

14

Perhaps in the church of the future there will no longer be a pastoral profession on which one has to decide at the age of eighteen or twenty, at least not as the only means of ensuring that the Gospel is preached in the name and service of the church. The harder the Christian faith has to contend for its standing, the greater will be the risk a young man incurs in becoming a pastor. To such a risk, only a few can ever be called, far too few to satisfy the need for clergy. God will not leave them unblessed, those few who dare to accept His call, bravely prepared for any sacrifice. But a profession cannot permanently be founded on risk. Reinforcements will have to come from the other professions.

That is a question for the future, however. Half a century ago, it was impossible to be a pastor without taking a risk. One had to be assured of a vocation in order to justify that risk.

Did I have a vocation myself?

When I was about to graduate from high school, I would not have dared answer that question in the affirmative. Nor did I yet know whether I would actually go into the ministry. I might become a professor like Beyschlag, or a teacher of religion like my grandfather. At that point I knew no more than that I must study theology,

I still had hours of uncertainty. Was it really enough to want to explore the truth oneself in order to help others arrive at the truth? Was truth the only thing involved in theology? Were there not many other things—religious obedience, sin, grace, salvation— to which I had not yet achieved the right approach?

I consulted Stolte. He told me in his friendly, reserved manner that for a young man, my position was a normal and legitimate starting point for the study of theology.

That was enough for me, at least for the first phase. I was now sure that God meant me to study theology.

Had anyone asked me how I conceived of the pastoral calling, I would probably have answered: As it is written in Isaiah 6 about the calling of the prophet, or in the first chapter of Jeremiah: "Now the word of the Lord came to me saying, 'Before I formed you in the womb I knew you, and before you were born I consecrated you; I appointed you a prophet to the nations.' Then I said, 'Ah, Lord God! Behold, I do not know how to speak, for I am only a youth.' But the Lord said to me, 'Do not say, "I am only a youth"; for to all to whom I send you you shall speak. Be not afraid of them, for I am with you to deliver you, says the Lord.'"

I would have thought that a man would have to experience something of this sort in order to be a pastor. Or if not that, then something similar—perhaps like Peter, at the draught of fishes, crying out: "Depart from me, for I am a sinful man, O Lord." And then receiving the solemn calling: "Do not be afraid; henceforth you will be catching men."

At all events, I would have thought of the call as an act of awakening and conversion, of some extraordinary event of the inner life.

Assuredly there are pastors who experienced something of the sort in their youth and, as a direct result, entered the ministry. But there are not many. I know of hardly one outstanding preacher who has had such an experience. One might perhaps cite Bodelschwingh, who was reading a little missionary pamphlet for children when he suddenly arrived at the certainty that God was calling him to be a pastor and to preach the Gospel. But Bodelschwingh was much more mature than a high-school graduate; he had gone through a variety of experiences already as a student, soldier, and farmer.

God does not reveal Himself only in storm and earthquake and fire. He also reveals Himself in a still, small voice; not only in exceptional experiences but also in the slow process of growth and maturation. For a young man it is normal that the certainty that God wants to use him in the service of the Gospel should come to him through a peaceful inner development. There is no harm in a pastor's son playing at being a pastor from earliest childhood, with no other thought than to follow in his father's footsteps—provided only that he has the certainty that behind the human desire is the will of God. The way this certainty is achieved and when it is achieved will differ with the individual. The Spirit of God has no fixed patterns. And no one is entitled to set himself up as a judge of the hidden experiences of another. The important thing is that the certainty should exist.

However, when the officiant, after administering the oath of ordination, says: "The Lord God sends you by order of the Church to work among His congregations," this must be no empty form of words; the young pastor must be able to say in his heart: "Yes, that is how it is; God is sending me!"

When Superintendent-General Faber ordained me in the Nikolaikirche in Berlin on December 23, 1906, I had that certainty. As a high-school graduate I knew only that God was calling me to study theology. That was sufficient for the time being. It is always sufficient if one is certain of the next step in the faith.

THE 𝔚ORLD

A YOUNG student at the university, thirsting for the final verities, might be expected to throw himself immediately into the study of systematic theology or the philospohy of religion. I did not.

At the university, in those days, everything receded before the new overwhelming sense of freedom, the sense of unlimited possibilities that lay open to the student. He had escaped the constraints of school. His only obligation was to register and pay for a certain number of lectures. No one cared which lectures he registered for, whether he attended them, how he spent the rest of his time. Somewhere on the horizon lay an experience called an examination. But what student worried about examinations in his first semesters?

The student purchased a lecture schedule. He noted with satisfaction how many learned men were prepared to serve him with their knowledge. The University of Berlin was in full flower at the time. The lecturers included Wilamowitz and Virchow, Dilthey and Kahl, Gierke and Erich Schmidt, and many others whose names are remembered to this day. The student could choose his lectures from an overwhelming abundance and satisfy his heart's desire. He was not bound to any faculty. He could attend lectures on law, medicine, theology, philosophy—whatever he wished. He could attend lectures from early morning to late evening. Or again, he did not have to attend any at all if he were not so inclined. There was something intoxicating about such complete freedom in the presence of such abundance.

Perhaps some young people were harmed by this freedom. But I have met very few of whom that could truthfully be said. For the vast majority of students, academic freedom is a wonderful gift. The eye and the heart can expand. One can acquire an education, a real education, not merely the specialized knowledge of the future expert.

All my life I have been opposed to compulsory programs of study, intermediate examinations, and all other restrictions upon freedom of choice in regard to studies. I have always considered it absurd for examiners to check in detail whether the examinee actually registered for all the lectures which normally belong to the particular course of studies. Give students their freedom and, when the time comes, let them answer for what they have or have not learned.

I had originally intended to go to Tübingen or Heidelberg, but this became impossible and I remained in Berlin. I lived at home. But my mother realized that her student sons wanted their independence. She did not make us keep any special hours. She never asked us how late we came in. And when we arrived hungry, whatever the hour, she always had something for us to eat. She certainly worried a lot about her children. That is the way of mothers. But she trusted us, and we were grateful to her for her trust.

As for money, that tiresome preoccupation of every true German student, I soon had more freedom of action than I would have dreamed. My small allowance could not have taken me very far, but I began to give private lessons and to write little articles for newspapers. At the end of my fifth semester I received the Royal Prize for a research paper. As a result, I was granted the Junken

20

Stipend for a number of years, like my brother Wilhelm before me. This was the only sizable stipend granted by the University of Berlin for scholastic achievement rather than need. So I had 900 marks a year, and something more from other sources. In those days that was a lot of money for a student who did not have to pay for his maintenance. Now I could buy books, I could travel, I could do as I pleased, without asking anyone's permission.

It was a wonderful but certainly not an irresponsible freedom. As the son of a German civil servant, I had the sense of duty in my blood. In my senior year at high school I had helped our pastor, Stolte, in his work with confirmants. I kept this up all through my student days. Every other Sunday afternoon and on specified weekday evenings I would be with my boys. I played football with them, and once a week I did gymnastics with them, so that belatedly I became a reasonably good gymnast, as I had never been at school. It was not always easy to fit this work in. But I would never have dreamed of reneging on a duty, even one undertaken voluntarily, with no question of remuneration.

The university meant freedom. The young German's drive for the limitless could develop unchecked—till experience taught him that a fruitful life lies not in the limitless but within the specific confines traced by his chosen career.

With all this I did not lose sight of my aim. But it seemed to me that one could not attain to the eternal truth of God by the study of theology alone. Is not God far too great to be compassed by church, theology, Christianity? Does not everything that is and was come from His hand? Must not His seal be found on everything living, and everywhere in history? To penetrate the truth, one must embrace everything living. That was what I felt and what I desired.

I found that one thing—and a very vital thing—was lacking if I wished to cultivate the universalism of a Goethe. I knew nothing of the natural sciences, not to speak of technology. We had not studied those subjects at school, and Berlin was not the place to open one's eyes to nature, its life and its laws. I was confined to what are known as the intellectual disciplines. But I wanted to learn about everything, and not just by means of lectures. Extracurricular activities are sometimes more important than anything else.

First of all, there was the academic reading room, under student government, but rich and varied. Here one could literally feast on German literature. At school we had read only the traditional classical dramas, and perhaps also Leisewitz's *Julius von Tarent*. That a German literature existed after the year 1810 we had not suspected. Our bookshelf at home had been as modest as was customary in those times. The nineteenth-century German certainly read books, but he did not buy them. To combat the dreariness of Greek and Latin classes, I had begun to read the German romantics during my last years at school: all of Tieck, E.T.A. Hoffmann, Platen, Arnim, Brentano. But that was all.

Now, in the academic reading room, I had the whole of German literature spread out before me, and needed only to stretch out my hand. I read the poets who even then were beginning to be regarded as semiclassics: Hebbel and Raabe and Storm, Fontane and Keller and the rest. I came to know others, too, whose stars were already on the wane—Spielhagen, Hopfen, Anzengruber, Heyse. But the authors I read most eagerly—like every other student—were those who appeared to be heralding a new era.

For the new generation was acutely aware that the year 1890 constituted a turning point in the history of German thought. It was the year Julius Langbehn's *Rembrandt als Erzieher* ("Rembrandt as an Educator") was published, a book which ran through forty-two editions in three years. It was also the year Sudermann's *Honor* was produced. In 1892 came Gerhart Hauptmann's *The Weavers,* which provoked strife and dissension from the Kaiser's palace down to the humblest homes in the provinces. Chamberlain's *Foundations of the 19th Century* had already appeared. Then came Elisabeth von Heyking's *Briefe, die ihn nicht erreichten* ("Letters Which Did Not Reach Him") and many other works which aroused passionate discussion, just as seventy-five years earlier, students had talked their heads off about Kant and Hegel and Fichte. And perhaps even more than German authors, foreign authors were the focus of debate: Tolstoy, Ibsen, Björnson. And behind them all, slowly but steadily gaining ascendancy, loomed the figure of the luckless solitary who was even then pining away at Weimar—Friedrich Nietzsche.

It was but a short step from literature to the fine arts. Berlin had many museums, both public and private. How often did I stand in front of Klinger's "Beethoven," exhibited at the time in the Potsdamer Strasse! How long did I gaze at Leistikow's pictures of the Grunewald, and at every new painting by Max Liebermann. I could not cultivate a taste for the classical art of antiquity, but I was at home in German painting of every century. I followed eagerly whatever was published by the Dürerbund (Dürer Society), or the *Kunstwart* (an art journal), and I identified myself with the campaign against the juvenile style and false pomp of the Wilhelmine era.

I lived for music too. I had put aside my violin, which had accompanied me through my school years. I could no longer practice for hours at a time and I suffered because I was losing my skill. I had to content myself with the piano. I took singing lessons and familiarized myself with the mysteries of counterpoint. And if I acquired only a scanty knowledge of symphonic music, I was very much at home with the German *Lied*, up to Brahms and Hugo Wolf.

And then there was the university proper. It was not my style to attend lectures regularly. I learned my lesson at the outset. In my first semester I wanted to learn something about the history of music. The only course I could fit into my program of studies was a lecture series by old Bellermann entitled "Music History up to Franco of Cologne." I did not know who Franco of Cologne was, but I was prepared to find out. So I registered and at the appointed time set out for the first lecture, which was to take place in Beller-mann's apartment.

I was shown into a dark room on the ground floor. It was so dark that at noon on a brilliant spring day the gas lamp had to be lit. On one side of a long table sat five students, and opposite them old Bellermann. He began to read something from a yellowed manuscript. Often he was unable to decipher his own handwriting. Then he would lift the manuscript to the gas lamp. And on the cover we could read the year of publication—1859. I did not go to any more of his lectures. Just before the close of the semester I returned with the effrontery of which only a young student is capable, to have the professor attest that I had regularly attended his lectures. The maid who opened the door asked in surprise what I wanted. When I said that I had come for the course, she said: "But that was over long ago! None of the gentlemen ever came back!" Only decades later did I find out who Franco of Cologne was.

That was not the only disappointing lecture. And yet there was a staggering abundance of fine things available, especially if one attended seminars as well as lectures. I studied philosophy and history, the history of music, the history of art, political history. I attended courses with Wilamowitz and learned more from him about Plato and Horace in a single hour than in a whole year of school. I went to Greek seminars, seminars on Kant and Fechner, seminars on the history of war based on Clausewitz's immortal work. I studied German law and the principles of economics. I learned something about anatomy and rather more about the history of literature.

In brief, I delved as deeply as I could in whatever this world offered the student in the way of intellectual life. At home I pored over Plato and Treitschke, Hegel, Marx, Lamprecht, and Rudolf Sohm. I did it all on my own, without direction, without counsel from any friend, always longing to broaden my horizon, to grasp the life of the intellect as a whole, confident that everything noble

24

and great and beautiful must somehow lead to God and be in harmony with the eternal truth I sought.

The real relationship with God I did not yet see. None of us saw it. We did not see the abyss which had opened up between the intellectual life of our time and the Gospel. We regarded Fichte's *Way Towards the Blessed Life* as a Christian work. We believed that Goethe's *Faust* and Theodor Storm's novels were compatible with the Christian religion even though we sometimes had to admit with astonishment that these poets had used very ugly terms for the essentials of Christianity. We thought that the Christian religion would come into its own once it threw off its blinkers and took possession of everything noble and beautiful in the world, according to the principle "All is yours!"

I remember once sitting with Wilhelm Schneemelcher in his apartment. (He subsequently became Secretary-General of the Evangelical Congress on Social Problems.) He read me something of Goethe's with great enthusiasm and said that once the pietistic orthodoxy of the older generation had been finally set aside, a new generation of pastors could speak to the educated with Goethe in one hand and the Bible in the other, a new age would dawn for the church. I was not altogether convinced. But something of this optimism reigned in all our hearts.

Of course, in all our fields of learning we barely touched the surface; there was no serious, exhaustive study. I can still see the look of consternation on the face of Professor Schmitt, who taught the history of war, when I replied to his question as to the time required to move an army corps from St. Petersburg to the Crimea. We were speaking of the year 1901 and in my innocence I guessed three days. The idea of introducing guesswork into his exact science horrified him.

But it was the German Student Association rather than my studies which plunged me most immediately into the life of the times.

During my first semester I did not become active in the association. I hesitated to commit myself too soon. At the beginning of the second semester, I continued to keep to myself. The student clubs with their colors held no attraction for me. The German Christian Student Association had not yet entered our orbit. And I did not want to join a theological society for fear of finding narrow-mindedness and one-sidedness.

Then in January, 1900, my brother Wilhelm took me along to a big anniversary celebration commemorating the foundation of the Reich. It was organized by the German Student Association and such a celebration was always an event in the life of the University of Berlin. The picture was calculated to appeal to a youthful heart. The huge Kroll hall was jammed with young people, all in festive mood. The officers of the association wore their attractive uniforms. The guests of honor included many prominent persons—professors, generals, members of parliament. Even a man like Dryander came to these occasions whenever he could. The speeches were on a high level, including the toast to the ladies, which on that occasion was given in verse by Hans Schmidt, later professor of Old Testament at Halle, a truly resplendent figure in his student regalia.

I joined the same night.

The German Student Association had been founded at the beginning of the 1880's, as a student reaction against the public demoralization produced by the spate of financial companies which had been floated during the bogus boom of 1871-1873. Many ardently patriotic theologians had taken part in the movement, Friedrich Naumann at their head. Stoecker and Adolph Wagner, the economist, were sponsors of the association. Treitschke was an honorary member from the start. Now every college had its German Student Association. The members wore neither cap nor ribbon. Dueling, which played so great a part in the student clubs, was avoided. The primary purpose of the association was to benefit the nation, not the students. Its objective was to combat freethinking, Marxism, and the Jewish influence in public life, and to inculcate patriotism among students. Bismarck was the hero. A greater Germany was regarded as the obvious political goal. The army and navy were given enthusiastic support. But social thinking, too, found a ready echo. At Kyffhauser, where the German Student Associations gathered for their annual rallies, a memorial was raised in tribute to the social message delivered by the old Kaiser in 1881.

When I became an active member, the German Student Associations were no longer quite the same. In the small universities, where the color-bearing clubs dominated student life, and where there were few of the stimulations of a city like Berlin, students wanted a regular club with ribbon and cap. The big Berlin association held fast to its old ideals, but not in the spirit of the early days. The motto was still "With God for Kaiser and Reich." But "with God" had been watered down. Only a minority still wanted to be avowedly Christian. Social thinking, too, had receded into the background. For disciples of Bismarck, it was felt, political realism must be the order of the day. This meant that one should believe only in blood and iron, and perhaps a little in economics, in potash and coal and iron ore—oil had not yet come upon the scene. Ranke's phrase, "The State is power," was the favorite slogan. This phrase was taken as the alpha and omega of political wisdom. Everything else was romantic or liberal. That was the position of the *Deutsche Zeitung*, the organ of the Pan-Germans. And the young editors of that paper were all members of the German Student Association and played a leading part in it.

Those of us in the association who were studying theology held other views, of course. We had long discussions with our fellow members, and it became clear to me that power for its own sake was not a morally justifiable aim either for the individual or for the nation. Power must always be merely a means to an end, otherwise it becomes demonic. But what is the end? What is the aim which the State should set itself? The well-being of its citizens? But when are the citizens well off? When they have as much as

27

they want to eat and drink, and can pursue their pleasure at will?

No, the aim must be something higher.

I was increasingly drawn to the idea of the Christian State. I knew, of course, that such an idea had become discredited. Both at this time and later, many protested that the Christian State was a romantic illusion far removed from reality, a museum piece from the woeful times of Friedrich Wilhelm IV and his "non-Aryan" professor Friedrich Julius Stahl. How could a State presume to exemplify Christianity and thus become a kind of pseudo-church? Let it remain what it was supposed to be—the temporal authority, the mold in which a nation's natural life is cast.

Needless to say, I wanted no part in Friedrich Wilhelm IV's romanticism either. But I argued that even if the State is to confine itself to the temporal and leave the spiritual to the church, it must still take a certain stand on questions central to Christianity. It must have a standard for its action, for its judiciary, for its judgment on social conditions. This cannot be dismissed with the glib retort that morals are self-evident. Morals are far from self-evident. Such matters as marriage or the position of women are variously viewed in Europe and in America. And the Communist's view on private property differs from that of the big industrialist. And there are many other questions on which the State must take a stand. What is just and unjust must not depend on the attitude of those who happen to be in power. Neither should it depend on public opinion. For public opinion can be manipulated at will by those who know how—at least in Germany and certain other countries.

The State's purpose depends on the standard it sets for the life of the people. This purpose can vary. It may be the material well-being of all nationals, or the domination of a particular class, or the unity and self-sufficiency of the nation. It may be world domination or individual freedom or national honor or the efficient organization of material life or a host of other things. In any case, the State must know what it wants. There must be a purpose in its action. And the nation must know for what it is fighting, for what it is making sacrifices, why its sons' blood is demanded.

It was my opinion then, and it has not altered with time, that there is only one criterion which is permanently valid: the will of God as proclaimed in the Christian Gospel. I was and am of the view that there is only one thing worth risking one's life for—the establishment of a regime in which people are free to live according to the Christian Gospel. And the State which decides upon the establishment of such a regime—and it has to decide, either for or against—I call a Christian State.

Such a State also has the moral right to use force and to fight for the freedom of a nation thus oriented. And no sacrifice is too great for such a State to demand.

That is what I thought as a student. And that, basically, is what I think today. Those were the issues which exercised us in the German Student Association. We discussed them and analyzed them very seriously.

We did not altogether neglect student merrymaking. Indeed, we often paid tribute to student tradition even more generously than we needed. But we also studied. We did not seek to cultivate an emotional patriotism; rather, we wanted to learn about the vital issues affecting the life of the nation. At hazings, freshmen were questioned not only about student regulations but also about the Kaiser's eastern policy, about Friedrich List, about the German settlements in Rumania and South America. This was not politics, and it was certainly not Pan-Germanism. It was simply a sense of responsibility for all who spoke German in the world.

Party politics, as such, interested us students not at all. And however concerned we were about foreign policy, we did not presume to pass judgment on it. For all our youthful conceit, we knew our limitations, and we knew when to keep our mouths shut. We wanted to show that our hearts beat for the fatherland because we understood what a fatherland meant, but that was all.

Bülow had just been appointed Reich Chancellor (1900). No

one could then have foreseen where he was to lead Germany. He was considered an intelligent man and an experienced diplomat. After the eighty-year-old Hohenlohe, young Germany regarded him as a deliverance. The first time we students heard him speak was when we had to take official part in the dedication of the Bismarck memorial in Berlin. It was not a significant speech. But the words he found for the genius of Bismarck did our young hearts good. "May the great man's name go before our people like a pillar of fire! May his spirit be with us forever!" Those were Bülow's concluding words. We believed the helm of the ship of state to be in good hands.

I often spoke at student meetings and demonstrations. My favorite memory is of the day at Friedrichsruh when we laid the foundation stone for the column which the student body was erecting as a memorial to Bismarck. The preparations had been made jointly by the Alemans of Bonn and the German Student Association of Berlin. One of the Alemans spoke at the actual ceremony, and I spoke at the related rally in Hamburg, earning the embrace of Kreis, the architect who had designed the column. I headed the university group of the All-German School Association, which later became known as the Association for Germans Abroad, and took part in a number of other activities open to a nationalistically-minded student.

Thus I stood with both feet firmly planted in the life and action of the world.

Was I too firmly rooted in the world?

The Christian is a citizen of two worlds. With all his senses he is held captive by earthly things. But at the same time he lives in an everlasting world, a world of whose realities this world is wholly ignorant. What should it know of guilt and grace, of salvation and freedom, of purity and love, of prayer and holiness? What should this passing world know of eternity and of God?

The two worlds are intimately related. Both belong to God. And the Christian belongs to both. Never should he plunge into one and exclude the other. He should not retire as a hermit into the desert, in order to live wholly in pious contemplation—and incidentally the desert need not be in Egypt, but in a German living room with pious pictures on the wall, and the text: "Love not the World!" But neither should he immerse himself in the things of this world and become dulled to the eternal.

The theologian, be he pastor or professor or teacher, is thrown upon the eternal world in a special way through his profession. He is supposed to be at home in the eternal. He has to give testimony to it. He has to understand its manner and its effect. If he sinks into the things of the temporal world, then he falls not only from his faith but also from his profession.

This danger is great, for the temporal has a demonic attraction. Schopenhauer said that gold is like sea water—the more one drinks of it, the thirstier one becomes. That is true not only of money and material goods; it also applies to the nobler aims of earthly life. A young man, especially, is easily swept away by the torrent and hardly notices that he is drowning in it.

I was in that danger. I would have had to be more firmly rooted in the Gospel than I was in order to escape it. I was still a seeker. I was inwardly uncertain. I had not yet learned that such spiritual poverty, seen in the light of the Gospel, can be riches. The first beatitude: "Blessed are the poor in spirit, for theirs is the kingdom of heaven," I had not yet understood. I was merely poor.

But I was also aware of my poverty. I struggled not to lose myself in worldly affairs. I remember as though it were yesterday an incident that took place in my fifth semester. The question had arisen whether the over-all leadership of the German Student Associations, which rotated annually among the individual associations, should again fall to Berlin. Had it done so, the leadership of the whole association would have fallen to me. Then I would have been absorbed in student and fatherland affairs for a whole year. I would have enjoyed the work, but it would not have been good for me; I saw that clearly. I gave a sigh of relief when the choice finally fell upon one of the smaller associations.

In the midst of the multiplicity of external things, I tried to stand firm in the faith. Slowly I began to realize that the God I sought is not to be found in the things of the world: neither in nature nor in history, neither in the ideals nor in the demonic forces that move men. In none of these can He be found if He has not already been found where He has revealed Himself in majestic radiance, in Christ Jesus. I knew now something of the great and beautiful creations of the human spirit. I saw something of God in a Rembrandt, for instance—but only if God came into the museum with me and looked over my shoulder. And whether God's anger or His grace was revealed in the events of history could not be learned through history but only through faith, schooled by Jesus Christ.

I began to realize this. And yet I did not regret having wanted to plunge into the stream of the world.

Had I studied forty years later, I should have reacted differently. Then there could have been only one watchword: Leave the things of the world to others and let the future pastor concentrate in deliberate solitude on the things that pertain to his calling.

But our times were different. The doors of the world stood open and invited those who wished to preach the Gospel: "Come in and help yourselves to everything!" Who troubled about the young in those days if the pastors did not? And could the pastors be content with bringing youngsters together for Bible study? If they wanted to be really effective, did they not also have to concern themselves with the way young people used their leisure? Did they not have to show them how to train both mind and heart, how to reject the untrustworthy and dishonorable and to cultivate the true and noble? Who taught the people in the villages and small towns to preserve the traditions of their fathers instead of casting longing glances at the big city, as though it held the key to earthly bliss? Who acted as intermediaries and conciliators in the bitter disputes between capital and labor? Who gave the simple man of the people an idea of the meaning of fatherland and State? Who concerned themselves with nationals dispersed abroad, or with sailors in foreign ports? Who, if not the pastors?

The doors stood wide open, and the world called the pastor. And the pastor was able to go into the market place in the name of his Lord sustained by the joyous conviction: "All are yours, and ye are Christ's"; or again, "the love of God compels us."

When I was pastor of my small town congregations, of course I tried to make the Gospel central to everything. Nor was I content simply to preach it at church services. I gathered small groups in the most unlikely places to study the Scriptures. Social evenings were organized, at which we would use song and word and pageant to bring home to the people the meaning of Christian family life in Germany, or of the German fairy tale, or of work or profession or fatherland or the world of children. We sought to draw people away from the false sentimentality of dance tunes to joy in good and authentic music. And if there was building to be done— and I was responsible for a great deal of building—we tried to show that even a very simple house could be built well, with true craftsmanship.

Later, in Berlin, it was my task to write a weekly "Sunday Mirror" in one of the big newspapers; this column dealt with questions of the church and the Christian religion in relation to current events, and aimed at forming a Christian opinion. This "Sunday Mirror" received considerable attention.

When I became a member of the Supreme Ecclesiastical Council and held the portfolio for schools, I was very concerned to find that the intellectual level of those responsible for the Christian education of youth left a great deal to be desired. It seemed to me important to do something about this in order to win back for the Gospel the place in education that was its due. The result was the foundation of the Institute for Religious Pedagogy, which introduced trained theologians to educational theory. I planned something similar on a national basis.

When war broke out in 1914, it was the pastor's duty to lead his congregation in intelligent devotion to the fatherland. (The same

33

duty became incumbent upon him, though in a different form, when revolution swept Germany in 1918.) The ecclesiastical authorities would not allow me to go to the front, so I had to do what I could at home. During the first year of the war, when I was still at Lauenburg, my chief concern was to give material assistance to the families of soldiers. In Berlin, where I lived during the remaining war years, the city took care of such matters, and this gave us all the more scope to work for the morale of the country, reaching beyond the strict confines of the congregation. I can still recall the great demonstrations which my friend Max Braun and I were able to organize in the Schöneberg churches. They were patriotic demonstrations, but obedient to the word of God.

All this had its roots in what I had learned and done as a student. Should I regret that, like so many of my contemporaries, I had plunged into the affairs of the world?

Time has left all this far behind. But every period is immediate to God, as Ranke says. Ours, in which the doors of the world stood open to the preachers of the Gospel, was immediate to God too.

Posterity may decide that our endeavor was vain, that it was not given to us to penetrate the life of our time with the spirit of the Gospel, and that the church, because it sought after the unattainable, suffered the penalty it deserved.

Posterity may so judge. How God judges we shall find out hereafter. We bow to His judgment in the clear realization that a great deal of guilt lies upon us. And He will decide whether the guilt lies only with us. The real question is this: whether separation from worldly affairs, which in other circumstances would have been the order of the day, was in fact God's final will for His church; whether the time will not come when in Germany, too, the doors will again be open and the world will call to the preachers of the Gospel: Do not leave us to ourselves any more, but show us how life can be penetrated and purified by the Gospel—not only in the heart of the individual but also in the conditions which men create for themselves and for others! Will not the words: "All are yours," apply again? Will not the theologians of the future have to remember that in this passage from I Corinthians 3, the Apostle specifically includes "the world" among the things the Christian is to possess? All is ours—even the world? Each single truth of the Scriptures has its appointed time, Luther said. And when the time comes again for the truth which was our watchword then may God grant His church His Spirit, that it may yield a fruit that endures!

Theology

Archbishop Söderblom liked to say that in two respects the German Evangelical Church was quite inimitable—in its deaconesses and in its theology.

The deaconesses I came to know later. But theology captivated me from my third semester at the university. For however much I sought to broaden my vision, I was still a theology student and I did not want to be anything else. I was quite convinced that theology and only theology must lead to the sources of eternal truth.

If I did not immediately plunge into theology, it was for a practical reason. I did not as yet know Hebrew. And without Hebrew one cannot study theology. Of course one can be a good pastor without Hebrew. Nowhere is it laid down that a man cannot preach the Gospel if he has not studied the Bible in the original. But scholarship ends where one has to work with translations.

I took the lecture schedule and looked for something that would help me, but I found nothing. So I began to study on my own. At the last moment a notice appeared on the bulletin board: Friedrich Delitzsch, newly appointed to the chair of Assyrian, would lecture on Hebrew grammar four hours a week. In the innocence of my first semester, I registered and went to the lecture.

In fact, it was the only lecture series that I really attended during my first semester.

It turned out to be something quite different from what I had imagined, as any student of philology could have told me beforehand.

What Delitzsch offered was a scientific grammar based on the history of the language. Such lectures were customary among philologists of all languages. They still are today. But they had not previously been provided for Hebrew since that language had been abandoned to the theologians. The theologians had written Hebrew grammars, but without any scientific method. They had simply recorded the language of the Old Testament as they found it, and systematized it. They offered no light on the why and whence of the language.

Now, for the first time in Berlin, a philologist of note was teaching Hebrew grammar scientifically. He took Assyrian as the base, brought in other Semitic languages wherever necessary, and thus was able to impart a real understanding of the nature and spirit of Hebrew.

It was something of a minor scholastic event that I had stumbled upon. At least for Berlin it was an event, although it attracted very little attention—least of all among the theologians. We were a mere handful attending the lectures—perhaps a dozen. I knew none of the others, and did not get to know them, as is so often the case in Berlin. So I did not know whether there were any other theology students there besides myself.

And now I realized to my horror that Delitzsch assumed—necessarily so—that we all knew Hebrew. The others probably did. I did not. At the first classes I did not know how to write the words which were selected as examples. As for their meaning, I had no idea.

Then I experienced for the first time what I was often to experience later, and it gave me a kind of method for all my work: if one sets his aim a good way beyond the strictly necessary, the necessary comes almost of itself. Because I was trying to master a course which went far beyond what was normally required of a theology student, I learned the language *incidentally*, shall we say? Later I could never understand how so easy and transparent a language as Hebrew could have caused anyone difficulty.

In the following semesters, I continued to attend Delitzsch's courses. I was grateful to him for what I had learned. And I remained grateful even after the great agitation started up about "Babel and Bible."

At a gala meeting of the German Oriental Society attended by the Kaiser, Delitzsch gave a lecture entitled "Babel and Bible." He drew a number of interesting parallels between the newly discovered cuneiform texts and various passages of the Old Testament. He pointed out that certain figures who had only a shadowy existence in the Bible now put on flesh and blood. He cited Kings Sargon and Sennacherib, for instance, who had waged war on Palestine at the time of the prophet Isaiah, and who could now be seen in alabaster reliefs talking to their field marshals or sitting enthroned before their tent. Their palace could also be seen, and the great State seal with which they had sealed their official documents. And also, according to Delitzsch, various obscure passages in the Old Testament were now at last made clear—for instance, references in the psalms and elsewhere to a battle between God and a primeval monster. What is the meaning of: "Thou hast broken Rahab in pieces, as one that is slain"? Or of this passage from Isaiah 51: "Awake, awake, put on strength, O arm of the Lord; awake, as in days of old, the generations of long ago. Was it not thou that didst cut Rahab in pieces, that didst pierce the dragon?" A Babylonian legend, Delitzsch pointed out, told how Marduk, chief of the gods, slew the primeval monster and created the world out of its body. The monster's name was reminiscent of the Hebrew word used in the above passage from Isaiah. Was there not some connection between the two? Delitzsch also recalled that the story of the flood was to be found in the Babylonian tradition too.

For those who had any knowledge of these things there was nothing unusual in Delitzsch's theories. The lecture was delivered in popular language; it was a little rationalistic, but dignified and scholarly. It would probably have attracted no public attention had not the Kaiser been present when it was delivered. The Kaiser, impulsive as he was and interested in everything, had the lecture repeated in his palace. Then he had Delitzsch discuss his theories at length with the chief court chaplain, Dryander, in his presence. And finally he wrote a letter to Admiral Hollmann, giving his own views on the issue. And he permitted the letter to be made public.

This was the bombshell. All the newspapers carried big head-lines: "Babel and Bible!" "Bible and Babel!" All church periodicals contained articles on the subject. It was discussed at pastoral conferences and district synods. Resolutions were drafted. Pious Christians felt that the authority of the Bible was being endangered and flew to defend the things they held sacred. Delitzsch was subjected to many attacks.

He could not be blamed for not keeping silent. The pamphlets and articles which he published remained at first on a fairly high level. But gradually a change set in. He began to think of himself as the trail blazer of scientific enlightenment against the clerical obscurantists—always a dangerous state of mind, less for the obscurantists than for the trail blazer. The success he met with in certain circles heartened him. He wanted to please his following. A deterioration set in. His final essay, entitled "The Great Deception," was something like the later Ludendorff pamphlets. He argued, for instance, that Israel's Yahweh was a rather miserable deity: he had promised his people the whole of Palestine, but in fact the Israelites had conquered only a part of it; Yahweh had fallen short by so and so many square kilometers! This kind of thing was unworthy of a German university professor. Now it was clear that Delitzsch was basically lacking in any understanding of the Christian religion, or indeed of the religious life altogether. He was a philologist, that and no more. As for the spirit of the subject which he explored with great philological acumen, he had not caught a breath of it.

Exactly the same thing happened to Ernst Haeckel, whose *Welträtsel* ("World Enigmas") ran through one edition after another. These "enigmas" contained hair-raising statements. One, for example, was that God, as conceived in the Christian faith, was a "gaseous vertebrate," and that there could be no such vertebrate. There were other fantastic assertions, even about facts which could be checked by anyone. Haeckel claimed, for instance, that it was the belief of the church that the four gospels had been selected in A.D. 325 from forty documents in the following manner: The bishops at the Council of Nicea had placed all these documents under an altar slab, then they had prayed, whereupon the right books had jumped of themselves onto the altar! In vain did the professors in the other faculties tell Haeckel that he had swallowed an old wives' tale. Neither indignation nor quiet, factual exposition availed. Haeckel simply had no capacity for anything that lay outside his materialistic natural science. Edition after edition of his book flooded the country, but nothing in his fantastic assertions was ever changed.

The case of Wilhelm Ostwald, the famous founder of modern chromatics, was not very different. A great scholar, certainly, but a great scholar who published his views on many things that lay outside his province. He decreed, for instance, that Esperanto should become the common language of mankind, because to learn foreign languages was a useless waste of time, and that mankind's highest moral law should read: Waste no energy!

Friedrich Delitzsch had now passed into the ranks of men like this. We now saw that one can be a great scholar and at the same time a complete Philistine. We learned, not without sorrow, that science of itself does not lead men to the deep things of the mind, let alone the deep things of Christian truth; other faculties are required for that. And those faculties can be completely atrophied in great scholars. For a young man this may be hard to believe—his respect for learning is too great—but he has to realize it sooner or later.

In any event, now I knew Hebrew and could apply myself to theology.

Although theology actually concerns only one book, the Bible, it nevertheless embraces a wide field. There are Old and New Testament studies. There is dogmatic theology and ethics. There is church history and practical theology, not to speak of a mass of auxiliary disciplines. Where should I begin?

As a young student, one's thinking on the subject is not particularly systematic. One feels instinctively that he cannot begin with dogmatic theology, and that practical theology must come, if at all, at the very end. Moreover, one is less concerned with the particular field of study than with the professors themselves.

The chair of Old Testament studies at the university was not filled at the time. For the New Testament there was only one professor-in-ordinary, though other professors lectured on the New Testament too. Weiss was already an old man. He had done solid scholarly work in his day; his treatment was always sober and detached, without brilliance, but arising out of a genuine personal relationship to the Gospel. He had written long and short commentaries on every part of the New Testament. He had written textbooks on all the usual questions pertaining to his subject. He had set views on every line of the New Testament. For him, new problems could no longer arise. What point, then, was there in attending his courses? One could read everything he had to say, once, twice, and three times over. If he nevertheless drew a tolerably large audience, it was because he was feared as an examiner. To go to his lectures was considered a kind of life insurance. I dutifully signed up for some of his lectures, but I did not attend any.

As a result—I realized only later what this meant—in all my years at the university I had no teacher who could really guide me through the New Testament. Perhaps I should mention Professor von Soden, whose lectures I occasionally attended. But von

Soden's academic lifework was to establish the best available Greek text of the New Testament, and to this end he drew upon every ancient manuscript he could lay his hands on. That was assuredly important, but it was not interesting for a young theology student who hungers for the content, not for the linguistics, of the Gospel.

Thus the very kernel of theological studies was lacking. It is a sin against the church and its youth if there is no teacher capable of bringing students into intimate relation with the New Testament on both a scholarly and a spiritual level. In other subjects one can, if he must, put up with dull or inadequate teachers, but for the New Testament the right men have to be available.

One of the prominent professors at the time was Reinhold Seeberg, whose field covered systematic theology, the New Testament, church history and the history of dogma. He was a lively and stimulating teacher, a man of great vision, the head of what was known as the modern-positivist school. He had a considerable following, but I could not bear the rhetoric and pathos of his lectures. For me it was axiomatic that the genuine must always be simple—an axiom which, like every other, is not without exceptions. But I have never believed a word of anything spoken with pathos.

Though I could not go to Seeberg, the way was still open to another man of great eminence, Adolf Harnack. He was my teacher of theology.

Harnack was now at the apex of his career. The controversy stirred up by his appointment to Berlin, in which the Ministry of Culture, supported by the Kaiser, had triumphed over the Supreme Ecclesiastical Council, was already forgotten. And nearly forgotten, too, was the dispute about the Apostles' Creed, as a result of which Harnack had finally fallen out with the traditional church circles, although his position at the university was not jeopardized. In 1900, he was not yet fifty years old but he was already the recognized authority on church history.

The radius of his activity widened from year to year. In the winter semester 1899–1900—it was my second semester—he gave his memorable course on "The Essence of Christianity," which drew a tremendous audience. Soon after, the Kaiser made him one of his intimates. Sometimes, when we were waiting for him in the church history seminar, a lackey would be patrolling the long corridor to hand him a sudden invitation from the Kaiser. Of course, that impressed the students, but it also annoyed us, especially when Harnack had to shorten his seminar in order to get to the Kaiser on time. We felt that in such cases he should have sent back a message: "Your Majesty, I am happy to come, but first my seminar!" We were denied the opportunity of finding out whether that is how we would have acted in like circumstances.

Then came the semi-centennial of the Academy of Sciences. For this occasion Harnack, in the midst of his theological work, had written a two-volume history of the Academy—an extraordinary achievement. He also took on the direction of the royal library, the first and only time an eminent scholar was charged with this office. He became the first president of the Kaiser Wilhelm Society, which was founded at this period. The church historian had become a representative of German scholarship as a whole, in a manner unprecedented since the days of Alexander von Humboldt.

When Harnack began a lecture, he would stand quietly for a moment on the dais behind a high lectern on which he had placed his open notebook. He was tall, with features of great spiritual refinement and a sharp profile. His eyes were compelling, despite his glasses. He would begin speaking in a slightly husky voice, soberly and simply, referring occasionally to his notes. Gradually he would grow more animated. Then he would put his notes aside, stand to one side, rest his left forearm on the lectern, push his right hand through his hair, pick up a pen and play with it mechanically. At the same time his manner would become progressively easier, warmer, more insistent. And although he did not always address the students directly—in fact he often looked out of the window as he spoke—his contact with his listeners became closer. When he spoke of one of the great men in church history, one with whom he felt a particular inner affinity—Augustine, for instance, or Francis of Assisi—his lecture would take on a forcefulness which no one could resist. Absolute quiet reigned in the big lecture hall till the bell rang. Then, when the last sentence had been concluded, the spell would be broken, in accordance with the student custom, by noisy stamping.

But the seminars were even more impressive. At those times we would sit together over a text which he would explain, after which there would be questions and answers. Here we could see how, in the middle of a painstakingly accurate weighing of each single word, something would suddenly flash through his mind—an idea, an analogy, a parallel out of the contemporary scene, something he had not thought of before—and light would be thrown on the whole text.

That was Harnack's way: to combine the most careful attention to detail with astounding intuition and thus to make the material completely alive. As with all great scholars, his scholastic achievements were based on exceptional industry, aided by the capacity to work fast and to grasp at essentials with a sure hand. He did not shrink from attending to irksome minutiae himself, pen in hand, even at the peak of his career and right up to his old age—the kind of thing others would have left to an assistant. When necessary, he would go deeply into every detail, but he would never lose himself in detail. He did not practise archeology. In everything he saw life. He it was who taught us that Greek antiquity survived in the Orthodox Church, and the ancient Roman State in the Roman Catholic Church. His book on the second-century Gnostic, Marcion, became a topical work in which, among other things, he developed the question of the validity of the Old Testament in the church.

Whether we read Cyprian with him, or Eusebius, or Augustine's *Confessions*, we were right at the center of that pulsating world where nothing really repeats itself but where the great problems of life always crop up again, because through all vicissitudes the human heart remains ever the same.

For two semesters I was a member of Harnack's seminar, and then for five semesters a senior. Finally I graduated under him as a licentiate of the Preachers' Seminary, with a paper on Valentine, one of the Gnostics. Thus for years I was in constant contact with him. I came to know and to respect him both as a scholar and as a man.

There was another lecturer who appealed to me, not as much as Harnack, but enough to induce me to go to all his courses and seminars though ordinarily I was not much of a lecture-goer. This was Hermann Gunkel.

Gunkel was certainly not the kind of interpreter of the Old Testament that a Christian theology student would wish for. He was first and foremost a critic, and much given to irony and sarcasm. That the Old Testament was in any way a revelation of God to man was not something one learned from Gunkel. For him, historical criticism and aesthetic inquiry were everything. Nevertheless, as Harnack once said to me, he had a touch of genius. He was able to portray the mysterious and incalculable in the experiences of the ancient prophets with something like empathy. For instance, one saw how Elias was driven hither and thither by the Spirit, so that he could tell no one where he would be the next day; how, after the slaughter of the priests of Baal, he sat, his head between his knees, waiting for the rain which was to put an end to the terrible drought; and how, as the downpour suddenly began, he jumped up and raced down from the heights of Carmel to the plain before the fast-trotting horses of Ahab. Or how the prophet Isaiah saw the heavenly throne of Yahweh, with the six-winged seraphim above it; and while the mighty "Holy, Holy, Holy" thundered from the seraphim's lips, smoke rose from the offered cup drawing a veil before the things the prophet had been permitted for a moment to see; and how the prophet, coming

46

to himself, lamented: "Woe is me! For I am lost . . . for my eyes have seen the King, the Lord of hosts!" Once you heard Gunkel describe this kind of thing, you never forgot it.

But even more important were the occasional methodological suggestions which he threw out in the course of his lectures. One of his best-known illustrations of the importance of the historical approach was this: "At the back of your gowns, gentlemen, you have two buttons. [In those days we wore the long flowing gowns later known as cutaways.] If you ask your tailor why those buttons are there, he will tell you that that is how it has to be. But you, as students, must not be satisfied with that. You must realize that when something is customary but does not have any apparent reason, then it conceals some historical process. And if you investigate further, you will learn that men's civilian clothing developed from the military uniform. The officer had button holes in his coat tails, and when he rode, he buttoned the tails on the two rear buttons. And that is why those two buttons are there to this day."

Whether this explanation was correct I never checked to find out. But one such illustration helped more than whole books to inculcate a critical historical approach.

Each faculty organized annual competitive projects which were to be worked on during the winter semester and delivered by May 1. One of the projects selected during my second year appealed to me. It was to show why certain twelfth-century German commentaries on the Lord's Prayer agreed almost word for word with what Martin Luther wrote in his Small Catechism on the individual petitions of the prayer. It soon turned out to be a wonderful subject for a beginner in research work. I was able to show that a firm tradition had existed in this regard since the third century, and that Luther had adhered to it. I wrote the paper and received the award.

This award, founded by Friedrich Wilhelm III, was a gold

medal. But instead of a gold medal one could accept a bronze medal and 250 marks in cash. I do not know whether any student ever chose the gold medal. For my part, I took the bronze medal and spent the 250 marks on a four-week vacation on the North Sea. I decided, moreover, to take my doctorate of philosophy on the strength of this paper. This I succeeded in doing by making a few revisions and various additions, so that I garnered a doctorate of philosophy in my seventh semester, long before my first theology examination.

At the university I learned to work systematically. But I felt very keenly that I still did not possess what is central to the theologian. Moreover, I had not yet decided whether to be a pastor or a teacher. And if I were to decide in favor of the pastorate, was all this academic training on which I had set my heart really right?

Lagarde once said that the more a pastor steeped himself in theological studies the more useless he became for service in his church. That was hyperbole; Lagarde enjoyed such hyperbole. But was there not—is there not—a grain of truth in it?

In the first place, when a theologian leaves the university he usually can no longer speak German properly. Nor, for that matter, can the others—the doctors, jurists, philologists. All their speech is patterned on the Latin construction; they use substantives where the German forms whole sentences. They talk in abstract concepts, not in words of flesh and blood. To cap it all, young theology students are taught, quite rightly, to begin by writing out their sermons, word for word. But in the process of writing, the sermon becomes anemic, abstract, un-German. And when the written text is memorized and presented on Sunday from the pulpit, it descends like a leaden cloud on the hearts of the listeners. In time, some learn to speak German again. But others never do. Had they not studied, they might never have forgotten their language.

Many a young pastor, fresh from the university, will preach on problems altogether remote from his congregation. In studying theology, he has forgotten that the Gospel turns on something very simple, that it proposes a choice, a very simple but also a very serious, practical choice. Often the whole sermon is so dialectical and so labored that even a theologian has difficulty in following it.

But all these are merely external considerations. The deeper considerations weigh much more heavily. Like every other branch of learning, theology is a critical study. Of course it is also much more than that. After one's original view of Scripture has been shattered into a thousand fragments, an authentic theology shows how those fragments can be reassembled to convey a new and clear picture of the nature of God's message to men. But first comes the task of criticism. And sometimes this is the only aspect that really sticks. But what the pastorate requires, what the Gospel preaches, is absolute certainty. Is it right for future preachers of the Gospel to busy themselves with criticism during their formative years?

Indeed, there is something in Lagarde's dictum.

There have always been pastors in Germany who have not received an academic training—missionaries, for instance, who for some reason or other have been unable to return to their mission field and have now been incorporated in the domestic pastorate. Some have turned out well and some have not. But on the whole the good results have outweighed the bad.

Nor should we forget the pietist preachers, whom the academically trained pastors are all too prone to despise. "Sect preachers," they call them. Yet every war has shown—the First World War perhaps even more clearly then the Second—that the soldiers at the front who, of their own volition, read their New Testament came either from college Bible classes or from the pietist congregations with their sect preachers. That is plain fact, and it gives food for thought.

In Russia, for instance, the German Evangelical congregations all had their precentors. There were few pastors with a university education, and those few could rarely come to the scattered settlements. But the precentors were on the spot. They taught in the schools. They worked their farms. They did the administrative work. And on Sundays they conducted divine service. They were quite simple men, but many of them were true witnesses to Jesus Christ.

I had never been in Russia. But I saw the Russian Evangelicals who arrived in Berlin in 1931. For months they had camped on the outskirts of Moscow, in the open, waiting for the authorities to allow them to leave the country. And finally they had received permission to go. Others, who followed them, were refused permission. Those who arrived in Berlin were quarantined at Prenzlau, some 1,500 men, women, and children, before going on to South America. I went there to greet them in the name of the church.

It was a misty December afternoon. The old infantry barracks, where they had been quartered, looked even more uninviting than usual. The people were assembled in the courtyard, the precentors in the front. Everything was grey on grey: the women with their heads swathed in shawls, the boys in their big fur caps and thick woollen scarves, the older men with their beards. All of them serious, their faces marked by years of want. A mute, grey mass.

And then we filed in a long procession into the great drill hall for divine service. One of the precentors said a few words on Psalm 124: "We have escaped as a bird from the snare of the fowlers; the snare is broken, and we have escaped!" Two four-part choirs sang. Then I spoke. We prayed together and for each other. And afterwards I talked with some of them.

During the service their faces came alive. Joy came into their eyes. The grey mass turned into living people. Not people like ourselves, stereotyped, practical, always calculating and concerned with material things, but open, natural, unspoiled, borne up by a firm, unquestioning faith, the legacy of their fathers and mothers. And for generations this faith had been taught them by their precentors, those simple, uneducated precentors!

Should the Evangelical preacher have been through a university?

If one consults the New Testament in the matter, one finds both learned and unlearned men preaching the Gospel. The first apostles were fishermen or tax collectors or something of this kind. And then came one who had studied theology—Paul.

And so it has remained. Besides the erudite pastors there have always been so-called laymen who have preached the Gospel. However, in the churches of the Reformation, the pastors—that is, those who officially conduct divine service for the congregation and give instruction—have all been to a university. With a Catholic priest, one cannot immediately tell whether he has had academic training or not. The same is true of the Methodists and Baptists. But an Evangelical pastor is almost bound to have received a higher education.

The question is, then, whether this uniform type will and should remain in the Evangelical church, or whether here, too, there will be a development of the situation as there was in primitive times, and as there is in most other churches. Such a development will surely take place, and it will be no misfortune. The pastor without university training will get closer to his people in many a country village and workers' parish than one who has been highly educated.

Unquestionably, however, an academically trained clergy is also necessary. There must be preachers who have learned to investigate and organize the riches of Holy Scripture, so that all aspects of life are illuminated by the Gospel. There must be preachers who have learned to distinguish between the inspiration of the Gospel and its pragmatism, who do not delve into the Book of Revelations or the writings of the prophets for omens for the future but who know that there, too, the living Christ and His eternal word are to be found. There must be preachers who have learned to understand the history of the Christian church, who do not interpret things according to a passing whim—this as bad and that as good, this as the work of the Holy Ghost and that as apostasy and the work of the devil—but who base their judgment on Holy Scripture with all the humility becoming to a Christian, but also with the unshakable determination not to regard the religious idealism of men as either divine revelation or spiritual sophistry. All this requires academic training.

Such preachers are needed. The Christian community needs them. It needs them to preserve the integrity of the Christian message. It needs them, too, when Christianity is attacked. To take one example out of a myriad—when the Nazis suddenly announced with great fanfare that Charlemagne, the scourge of the Saxons, had imposed Christianity on the German tribes by brute force, then it was not enough for the pastors to say that they had learned otherwise, and that such and such a professor was of a different opinion. There have to be enough pastors who can go to the sources themselves, who can read them and sift them and then demonstrate, with the sureness of an expert, that the facts are thus and so and not otherwise. As far as Charlemagne is concerned there is hardly a word in the records about force or compulsion, and whoever claims there is, is prompted either by malice or by sheer ignorance.

Highly educated pastors are needed. The future pastor must have learned to work scientifically, even if independent research is not a part of his subsequent functions.

And what of the eternal truth of God which I had set out to find? Had theology brought me any closer to it? When I began my studies, I had just perceived, very faintly, that the world, in the language of Schopenhauer, is will and imagination; that the will is the first and dominant force and that the imagination follows it and is usually no more than its reflection and tool. That became increasingly clear to me in the course of my studies. What I did not find was a discipline such as I had imagined, leading, so to speak, from alpha to omega along a path marked by facts and compelling conclusions.

At first I was desperately disappointed. For instance, when I took up a manual of dogma, thinking that it would conclusively demonstrate the reality of eternity and the divine Sonship of

Jesus Christ, I would read in the introduction that the work took its stand on the creed of the Lutheran Church. I would angrily close it again. If everything was already settled, if not the slightest attempt was made to prove that the Lutheran creed was right, why did I need the book?

I realized more and more clearly that eternal truth cannot be fathomed by intellectual speculations, but only by an act of will, and that one simply has to decide in favor of something definite. As Ernst Moritz Arndt put it, one has to set one's candle down somewhere, so that it can shine out into the dark places.

I understood that now. And in any case I was not in doubt that he for whom I must decide was Jesus Christ and no other. For whom else should I have decided? I could not understand how one could base one's whole philosophy on a totally diseased mind such as Nietzsche's, or on the teachings of an unmannerly hypochondriac like Schopenhauer. And how one could place his candle in his own hand and make his own unreliable "I" the measure of all things—that I could not understand at all. No, the measure could only be Jesus Christ.

That decision really required no theology. It required no advanced studies at all. What it required was the Bible and prayer. And it required those two things very badly, for the decision had to be carried out anew each day.

Yet it was precisely theology which had made me realize all this.

Prayer to God, asking Him to help me to do His will and to follow Christ, now became central to my life. When I was about to hand in my thesis and had to select a quotation for it, I chose the sentence out of Augustine's *Confessions:* "Give what thou commandest, and command what thou wilt!" That was the sum total of my experience up to that point.

ℭEACHER

AFTER PASSING my first examination in theology, I applied to Wittenberg for the two-year course at the Preachers' Seminary. Wittenberg had a reputation for postgraduate studies. That was just what I wanted. The fact that this was historical ground, that one could go in and out of the places where the Reformers had lived and worked, was an added attraction.

So I arrived in Wittenberg. But my experience was rather like the youthful Saul's who set out to look for his father's asses and found a kingdom. As far as scholastic advancement was concerned, Wittenberg had little to offer—or, more exactly, nothing beyond the small stimulation we seminarians could give one another.

However, we learned something that I had not expected: that in order to be a pastor one must first be a teacher. And that was an extremely important discovery.

The Luther School was housed, at the time, on the ground floor of the Luther House, which abuts on the stately seminary building in the direction of the old moat. It was a small elementary school comprising three classes, simple and unpretentious, of the kind one finds in a thousand country villages. It had been established because the country pastor also had to function as the local school inspector, and it was therefore good that he should have had some previous experience of this type of school. But for the seminarians it meant much more than that. For a year, for two years, they lived in close association with the children and the teachers. They steeped themselves in the atmosphere of teaching and the schoolroom, and they began to understand the significance of such education for the nation and the church.

At seven in the morning, or in winter at eight, the schoolyard would come alive. The children who had arrived early would be playing around the old well where Luther's children had played before them. Just before the hour, a hush would descend upon the schoolyard. The teacher would clap his hands as a signal for the children to troop into the schoolroom. As soon as the turret clock struck the first chime, the teacher would lead off with the morning anthem, the children joining in—from memory, of course, as befitted the pupils of a Christian elementary school. Then lessons would begin with a short morning prayer. The first subject each day was religion. On Saturday the Gospel reading for the following Sunday was discussed; in the afternoon a short devotion would be conducted by one of the seminarians.

That was the framework in which the life of the school was lived—a very happy life, incidentally, partly because the successive groups of seminarians provided a permanently youthful teaching staff. Something of the spirit in which the great Prussian kings had created the common elementary school still lingered here; indeed, Friedrich Wilhelm had once stayed at the Luther House.

During their first year at Wittenberg, the seminarians were required to teach in the school, under the friendly and discreet supervision of the senior teacher. Before a seminarian delivered his first address from the pulpit in the Schlosskirche, before he read his first scientific paper, he would have to sit at his desk preparing his next lesson for the Luther School in the sweat of his brow. And then he stood at the teacher's desk, saw twenty or thirty pairs of eyes directed towards him, and had to show whether he was capable of talking with children about the things of God.

However useful the teaching techniques which we learned in the process, they were the least of the benefits we derived from this experience. Of far greater importance, as we realized after a time, was the fact that this simple instruction of children was, as it were, the groundwork for everything a pastor is called upon to do.

For being a Christian does not mean that religious sentiment automatically takes possession of a man's heart. It means that something is accepted and affirmed and made the focus of one's life—something that God has done for men, at a particular time, in a particular place, and in a particular manner. It means faith in Jesus Christ, who came into the world to save sinners. Moreover, what Jesus Christ Himself said and did must be related to the rest of divine revelation as it is contained in Holy Scripture. A man must know something of all this if he is to be a Christian. And to know it, someone must teach him. Just as in the primitive Christian congregation the Apostles joined with those who were willing to believe in the Risen One, and recited to them what they had learned from Him—passages of the Scriptures which had been fulfilled in Him, and then His own words—so one generation must pass on to the next the teachings necessary for salvation.

There is nothing complicated about this, nothing of the problems which exercise German theologians when they prepare their classes. It is simply a matter of passing on the doctrine. Obviously this cannot be done mechanically, with so-called objectivity and detachment; a heart must be behind it which has itself been captivated and penetrated by the Gospel. But the basic task is simply to pass on the knowledge which is the condition of faith.

In former days, at least in Germany, this was the responsibility of the school, and on the whole the school carried out that responsibility very well indeed. So well, that the pastor did not have to concern himself with such teaching at all. The school passed on to him well-instructed candidates for confirmation. And when the pastor went into his pulpit to preach, he could assume that his congregation was not unfamiliar with the Scriptures, and he could make scriptural references in his sermon. If one had been through school in Germany during the first half of the nineteenth century, one had a sound knowledge of the Bible.

Since then, things have changed; indeed, they have changed very considerably. It is no longer unusual for children to present themselves for confirmation classes without knowing so much as the Ten Commandments. The church has been forced to realize that it must once again assume entire responsibility for teaching the Gospel. Of course the pastor cannot cope with the problem singlehanded. He would be unable to do so even if he had only children to deal with. But there is not merely the rising generation to instruct but the older generation as well. Adult Christians have become increasingly aware that they should know more about the fundamentals of the Christian faith, and especially the Bible. The pastor needs many helpers. But he must put his own hand to the plough too. He must be a teacher himself.

A pastor should not consider such work beneath him. He should not say to himself that he has not become a pastor in order to play the schoolmaster; that he should be preaching the Gospel to great crowds, or, if he has to address smaller circles, he should be discoursing brilliantly on religious questions; that it is not for him to prepare the material, read the Bible with his class, and give endless explanations till the text is clear to everyone.

There are pastors who take that view. But they should not have become pastors. A man who does not want to be a teacher is not fit to be a pastor.

Teaching and preaching, of course, are two wholly distinct operations, and the same man cannot be expected to excel equally in both. That we realized even as seminarians in Wittenberg. One of our number, Johannes Hoffmann, was a born teacher. When he gave a lesson, the teacher who was supposed to direct him would stand with clasped hands, at a loss for words. The young seminarian stood in front of his class with complete calm and warm friendliness; whatever his subject, he always made it crystal clear and vivid to the children, who hung on his words. And when the lesson was over, one felt that something had really been accomplished. Yet as a preacher he lacked fire and broad design; in that field, he was surpassed by others.

Teaching and preaching are two different things; nevertheless, if a man fails as a preacher, he fails also as a teacher, and where confirmants complain about the instruction, the congregation nearly always complains about the sermon.

The Luther School, where we garnered our first experience of teaching, did not survive the Weimar period. A superintendent came to the seminary who considered the museum, which occupied another part of the Luther House, as more important than a living, patriarchal type school. He wanted to turn the whole building into a museum and to oust the school. The bureaucratic school administration was perfectly agreeable to the plan; with its striving after conformity it had already destroyed much productive educational autonomy. A three-grade school conducted in a religious atmosphere was undesirable in a town whose four thousand school children were provided with only the best of school facilities. The educational value of the cheerful companionship of seminarians and children simply did not count. The school had to move out of the Luther House and was reorganized at the other end of the town in a new, enlarged form. A school idyll had come to an end, and with it a unique teacher-training opportunity for future pastors.

Twelve years after I left the Preachers' Seminary the revolution broke out, "our revolution," as the teachers' journal called it. The collapse of the monarchy brought with it the collapse of the system of local school inspection which for a long time past—at least as far as the Evangelical Church was concerned—had become a form without content. Now the pastor was no longer needed in the schools, and his educational work was henceforward to be confined to the instruction of confirmants and the children's service.

It is both a solemn and wonderful experience to instruct confirmants. Prior to 1933 (the point must be made, because in no sphere of religious action did the year 1933 mark so deep a cleavage as in the character of confirmation classes) such instruction was very much a schoolroom affair. The pastor stood in front of his class and taught as school children have to be taught. And yet the instruction was unencumbered by considerations of curriculum, transfer, school discipline, or any of the things which are really just as wearisome to the teacher as to the students. The sole consideration was to open young hearts to the Gospel, to that Gospel which had set the pastor's own heart afire and which should mold the lives of these young people. The sacredness of the subject lent a sacredness to the lesson. What could be easier or pleasanter than to teach in such an atmosphere and on such a subject?

Of course children will be children. At the age when they attend confirmation classes they tend to be unruly. So there were sometimes problems of discipline. If these problems became serious—I refer to the period before 1933—it was always because the pastor did not know how to handle the children. Perhaps he was also ignorant of the simple techniques of such instruction. For instance, it is obvious that the pastor should arrive in the classroom first, not last as at school. If he allowed the children to assemble haphazardly and then he himself turned up a quarter of an hour late, the children had gotten so much into the spirit of play, they could hardly be persuaded to concentrate. Or again, if his teaching was lifeless and dull, he could not hope to hold the young people's attention.

In former times confirmation students were usually divided into two separate groups: the thirteen- and fourteen-year-old elementary-school children on the one hand and the fifteen- and sixteen-year-old high-school students on the other. Two years, at that age, make as much difference as ten later on. The elementary-school children regarded their pastor as just another schoolteacher. It hardly occurred to them that confirmation instruction could be something special and could give them something special—something quite different from what they learned in school. They came in order to learn what they had to, so that they could be confirmed. And if what they were taught did succeed in gripping heart and conscience, then that was the outcome of the instruction itself; the children did not come predisposed to any such result.

With the fifteen- and sixteen-year-olds it was different. They were no longer children but young people, and very interested in themselves. They tended to see problems everywhere. God and eternity, death and life, good and evil—all these were important to them. The uncomplicated certitude of childhood had been left behind. They were aware of an inner cleavage. One day I said to myself: Be ashamed of yourself! And at that moment I discovered that I was not *one*, but *two!* That is the young person. The young people to whom I refer were inwardly open to what the instruction could give them. They expected something to come of it, something of advantage for their inner life.

What is most wonderful is when the confirmation instruction leads to an inner transformation, a turning to God, a sense of responsibility, a joy in the faith. Occasionally parents would tell me that toward the end of the year of instruction, something of the kind had been evident in their children. When the pastor prays for his confirmants—and what true pastor would not?—that is what he prays for. I have had confirmants come to me later to say that during the instruction, they received the decisive impetus to faith. A former confirmant once told me: "It was you who taught me how to pray." And I shall not forget the look in the eyes of a youngster who came to see me a few weeks after I had spoken to him very seriously about a temptation to which he had been constantly giving way and who now called from the doorway: "I'm free of it!"

For the pastor this kind of thing is each time an occasion for endless thanks to God, and compensates for a thousand disappointments. And if it happens only very, very seldom, then the pastor must remember that young people of that age do not easily reveal what is going on in their hearts. When we were confirmants, we did not confide readily in our pastors either.

Yet we should be deceiving ourselves if we denied that this wonderful experience takes place in only a small percentage of confirmants. Does that mean that our sights are wrongly set? Perhaps they are. Perhaps we are still, parents and pastor alike, too much influenced by the pietism of our forefathers, the kind of pietism which was altogether alien to Dr. Martin Luther. Perhaps we have to learn to think more soberly and more in the spirit of the Reformation. Perhaps we should simply try to impress something of God's word on the children, and then leave it to God when and how His Holy Spirit will bring this word to life in their hearts.

On the other hand, the psychologists tell us that very little of the material taught during the period of adolescence is carried over into later life. Consequently what we teach the confirmants must be quite short and effective, so that they will not forget it. For instance, I sometimes told my confirmants that they must retain at least three words of the instruction. If they forgot everything else, those three words they must remember—at every opportunity I would say them, over and over: "God is present." This was the gist of the whole confirmation instruction and of all five parts of the catechism. And confirmants—I remember two in particular—told me later that they had really retained that thought, and that it had given them a foothold in life.

Is this goal still too high and too personal? But is it enough simply to introduce young people to the religious life of the congregation, as is too often the case nowadays? How many of the confirmants really enter the life of the congregation? It is hard enough just to get them to come to church regularly during the period of their instruction!

These are difficult and grave problems. They trouble every pastor, today even more than thirty years ago. Perhaps they

62

should trouble him and not simply be shrugged off. If tragedy is eliminated from the profession of the teacher, he becomes no more than a technician. And a pastor who does not mourn for the souls entrusted to him is not a true teacher of the Gospel of a crucified Saviour.

Confirmation instruction in my day was almost always instruction *against* the family. It was bad enough when this was openly admitted. On two or three occasions in Berlin I instructed boys who came to me against the express wishes of their parents. At home they were not allowed to breathe a word of what they had learned, and they finally came to be confirmed entirely alone. They were among my best confirmants. What was far worse (and this was the rule) was when parents were "in principle in favor of religion"—not of very much, but of some—though the home showed not the slightest trace. Everything the pastor told the children about prayer, churchgoing, faith, and sanctification of life was contrary to the spirit of the home. And how could two short hours of instruction a week prevail against the spirit in which they had grown up and in which they lived and breathed every day? Even so, confirmation instruction is among the most rewarding duties of a pastor. How can he help loving this crowd of young people who come prepared to listen to the Gospel? He will not idealize them. He will see them as they are—the boys with their proverbial laziness and boorishness, the girls with their dose of silliness. And yet in all of them is something that can be reached, some good will directed toward what is honorable. Sometimes when such a youngster stood before me, still innocent of all conscious piety, but fresh and honest, the words of the story of the rich young man sounded in my ears: "Then Jesus beholding him loved him." Is it not part of the imitation of Jesus for the pastor to love his confirmants from his heart?

I can still see a sixteen-year-old high-school student standing in front of me, the son of a prominent theologian in the church administration. I had set the class to learn a psalm; each youngster

63

could choose his own. Now I called on him. His eyes lighted, half mischievously confident, half expectant. And then he rattled off Psalm 117, which consists of just three sentences: "Praise the Lord, all nations! Extol him, all peoples! For great is his steadfast love toward us; and the faithfulness of the Lord endures for ever. Praise the Lord!" And down he sat, beaming. All the others were beaming too. How could one help loving such a boy? I joined in the laughter, and then I told him: "That is excellent! Except that Psalm 117 actually goes together with Psalm 118. So you will have to learn that one too. And so that we don't forget, report with it next time at the beginning of class!" A few years later the boy was drowned in the Rhine.

A pastor in the west end of Berlin frequently came upon unusual confirmants. Once a young dancer requested instruction. She was still in training but had already performed in public. A few years later she made a great name for herself. She was exceptionally earnest about the instruction. Then there was a young woman of over twenty who had lived in Turkey for many years, far from anything resembling an Evangelical church. The fact that she had not been confirmed had given her no peace; now she wanted to make up for the deficiency. Or again, there was a high-school senior who had had no opportunity of attending confirmation classes at his private school. I asked what had been discussed in the religion class and he promptly replied: "We are doing the Egyptian monuments." "And last year?" "We discussed the Babylonian monuments." But the monuments had not satisfied him after all. He was as receptive as parched soil, and I could confirm him in good conscience.

Then came the year 1933. And with it, for many a pastor, came the end of joy in preparing youngsters for confirmation. It now became the fashion for confirmants to denounce their pastor to the Party for this or that statement. Generally they did not do so on their own initiative. In the country it was usually the schoolteacher who was behind it; in the city, a member of the Hitler Youth.

64

Dozens of pastors were arrested as a result of such denunciations. Some were tried and condemned to long prison terms. No court evinced any understanding of the disastrous consequences of having children systematically trained in breach of confidence. In the proceedings against Pastor von Lutzki in the Lichterfelde section of Berlin, two boys lodged the damaging information. At the very same time, those two boys were taken into police custody for roaming the streets at night and deliberately ringing apartment house doorbells in order to get people out of their apartments. The public prosecutor said that that was just why these boys should be given greater credence than the others in the class who had heard nothing of the allegedly damaging statements; by doorbell ringing they had both proved that they were not informers but full of life! The pastor got a two-months' jail term. And the two boys were confirmed by a neighboring German Christian pastor. This is but one example among many.

Some confirmants hesitated to open the Old Testament; it was a Jewish book, they said, and they wanted to have nothing to do with it. In many places they could no longer be persuaded to come to divine service at all, if only because they had to attend the Hitler Youth drill every Sunday morning. And the times of classes were constantly being upset by political events.

Confirmation classes became a constant, nerve-shattering struggle with the anti-Christian powers. Many pastors considered suspending confirmation in their congregations altogether, because they felt that under such conditions it was a farce. If they did not do so in the end, it was only because they realized that this would simply be playing into their opponents' hands. For this was precisely the Nazis' aim—that religious confirmation should cease and be replaced by a political youth consecration. And most pastors refused to believe that these intolerable circumstances could continue.

I conducted only one series of confirmation classes after 1933. That was when Niemöller was arrested in 1937. I had promised to deputize for him should anything happen to him. It was a joy to instruct those confirmants. Not for nothing had they gone to Niemöller or been sent to him by their parents. Trust was there, and spiritual vitality. It was the kind of instruction I had been used to. Both the classes and the confirmation ceremony were marked by a special earnestness. One of the confirmants was Niemöller's eldest son, who later fell in the war.

Under Communist rule, confirmation classes became an out-and-out battlefield between State atheism and Christian faith. But we shall have more to say about that later.

The children's service, as it existed up till 1933, was the sunshine of the pastor's life.

A merry crowd around the church. Shining eyes. The older boys a little more reserved, but happy too. Then the doors of the church are opened. The children have learned that they must be quiet in church, but from time to time they have to be reminded. Yet, despite the hush, the church seems to throb with life.

The service begins. It has a definite form, but the pastor has wide discretion in adapting it.

In this freedom lay the charm of the proceedings. It was a community of joyful singing and praying and listening. It was the Hosannah shouts of the children on the first Palm Sunday translated into modern idiom. And upon them lay the blessing of Him who expressly sanctioned such songs of praise, as St. Matthew tells us in the twenty-first chapter of his gospel.

Of course there was a gravity about all this which is never absent from the things of God, but a gravity permeated with the great joy which has come to every people. If the Christian community were ever to forget that the Saviour's Christians are a merry people, then the children's service should remind them of it.

But even in those days one could not conduct a children's service without thinking of all the other children who could not be reached, despite all the efforts of the church workers. At

Lauenburg, for instance, when I was there, there were 1,700 children of the ages for which the children's service was intended. Of these, some 400 to 500 attended regularly. During Advent there were more. And at Christmas there would be some 900. This was considered a "flourishing children's service." Yet only half the children were reached from time to time.

The children's service was the really popular church activity in those days. It was quite a recent innovation; it had begun in the 1860's. My Uncle Franz delighted in telling me how, as a very young pastor, he had introduced the children's service at Dresden —over the opposition of teachers and pastors, and under the protection of no less a personage than the Catholic King Albert! That was in 1874. At Crossen and Lauenburg I, too, introduced the children's service, and experienced similar opposition. I can still hear the long, indignant tirade of the good rector in the church council: children will lose every reverence for the Saviour if they go to church every Sunday! Once a year on Christmas Eve—that was right! As for finding church workers, men and women, to attend the children's service every Sunday that might be possible somewhere else but not in our parish. But the workers were quickly found. They were to be found everywhere. And once the children's service had taken root, the whole congregation rejoiced in it. The children's service excursions were like public holidays; so were the Christmas festivities and a number of others.

There were even children's service experts. They wrote in the papers. They laid down rules for the conduct of the service. They explained scriptural texts for children and advised on the training of church workers. They published books on child psychology and related subjects. There were excellent men among them, but I always preferred to show them my respect at a distance. For I thought in my heart, Does one really have to study psychology and the rest before one can talk to children about the Lord? O thou pedantic Germany!

Only once did I agree to have a well-known children's service

67

expert talk to my children. That was at a big Gustav-Adolf celebration at Crossen one Sunday. First there was a welcome ceremony for the guests at the town hall. Then the bells rang. And while the guests, accompanied by the local notables, solemnly marched across the market square to the neighboring city church, the children formed a cordon on either side, the little girls in white dresses with forget-me-not wreaths in their hair. It was a glorious summer day, and the children made a delightful picture. After the procession of elders had disappeared inside the church, the children went singing over the bridge to the hillside church on the other bank of the Oder where their service was to be held. The great expert got up in the pulpit and preached a lengthy sermon, very correct, very ingenious and redolent with psychological theory. Boredom, like a grey cloud, descended upon the children, and I had a hard time bringing them back to a cheerful frame of mind afterwards.

Children must be given things to do. A truth is retained only if it has been experienced. The children's favorite "good works" at the time were connected with the missions. Nor was this simply on account of the aura of adventure which clung to the missionary who had lived in far-off Africa, or China, and who now talked to the children about life and customs in those lands.

For a whole year the Lauenburg children saved up for a bell to be sent to the mission field in East Africa. After the necessary sum had been collected, the bell was brought to Lauenburg and hung in a simple belfry in the church. There it was solemnly rung in by the children themselves. Perhaps the first peals disappointed them a little—a bell which has to be carried across the African veldt must necessarily be small, and a small bell does not have a deep tone—but the longer it rang, the more radiant became their faces. The crossbeam had been engraved with the inscription: "The Master is come, and calleth for thee." This provided the text for the service. The children did not forget that hour. And the parents—the big church was crowded to capacity—did not forget it either.

We also collected slates for the East African schools and wrote a greeting on each. The Bethel mission was particularly inventive in setting projects of this kind.

The annual flower service, which I had first come across in Scotland, brought solace to the members of our own congregation. On a summer Sunday, the children brought flowers to service. The flowers were arranged over the altar by means of a cruciform wire grating. Then the children sang: "Go forth, my heart, and seek delight" and other hymns containing references to flowers. The text was from the nineteenth psalm, or from the Sermon on the Mount, concerning the lilies of the field. And when the service was over, the children and the workers went off together to the hospital and the infirmary, where they gave flowers to the patients and sang hymns for them. This always gave everyone great pleasure.

But the center of the children's service was the group instruction, prepared by the church workers at evening conferences. How they carried out the instruction the following Sunday was their affair. I was always convinced that some workers were better at the job than the pastor. What distinguished, highly educated women we had at our children's service, looking after their groups in truly motherly fashion! Young people helped too, and they knew just how to handle the older boys. And if in spite of the preparatory conference, the actual group instruction did not always conform exactly to prescription, what did it matter? I remember passing by a group once where a woman factory worker was teaching. The group was discussing the parable of the wicked servant. She was making her point with great enthusiasm. And I heard how she ended the story: "And then, let me tell you, that servant got a good licking!" That was language a pastor could not have used. But the children's eyes were shining. Could I have asked for a different language?

The main thing about the preparatory conference was that here was a group of people growing in knowledge of the Bible, not simply for their own advantage but in fulfillment of a responsibility

69

which they had assumed in the name of the Lord Jesus Christ. For it is a mistake to hold that the study of Holy Scripture is most fruitful when the individual studies the text only in relation to the message it contains for himself, for his own faith and his own obedience. However necessary and important these may be, the Christian must also sometimes stop thinking about himself. In order to prepare properly for the children's service, the workers will always endeavor, first of all, to place themselves quite personally in relation to God's word. And since the children are central to their responsibility, a motive enters the Bible study which makes it all alive and fruitful.

And what was the fruit of this whole labor?

If any of those who pioneered the children's services in Germany believed it would produce a new generation, devoted to the church and rooted in Holy Scripture, they must necessarily have been disappointed. Only a small number of the children who attended the children's service subsequently became faithful churchgoers in their congregations. The children's service did not affect the movement away from the church.

But that is not a proper way to put the problem. We do not have to see the results. We have simply to do God's will. God Himself will determine the results. His will, however, is clear and peremptory: "Suffer little children to come unto me." Where the family does not carry out that command, or perhaps is unable to, and where the school does not carry it out either, the church is called upon to do so. Nor can the church evade its responsibility for the children in regard to the commandment to keep the Lord's day holy. In how many families would Sunday be a holy day for the children were there no children's service?

Today attendance at the children's service is far smaller than in the past. Yet it is often at the children's service that children are first introduced to Bible history and to many other things which they formerly learned in school. The children's service is thus developing in the direction of the English Sunday school. But something from the past has come over into the present. Instruction and worship are interrelated. And this relationship of teaching with worship is what places Christian instruction in a soil where it can grow and mature.

In every parish to which I was assigned, I also had to teach in the schools—high schools, girls' schools, teachers' colleges, private schools. During the First World War, I gave twelve hours' religious instruction weekly at the Steglitz high school, in addition to eight confirmation classes.

This instruction, too, I enjoyed very much. Of course the school lacked the special atmosphere which marks the confirmation class. And then there were syllabuses to adhere to. In my day the syllabuses were all bad. They bore the stamp of a religious idealism for which Christianity was only a special form of the religious seeking and groping common to all mankind. A teacher of religion who was unequivocally a Christian could not possibly teach in accordance with such notions.

My instruction was doubtless poor and amateurish as regards method. Although I myself later founded a religious teaching institute, I have always tended to regard pedagogy with something less than reverence. I believed—and I believe to this day—that what is needed is to present a real, living faith to young people. For a man is effective only through that which superabounds in him. I believed that my students, both boys and girls, sat up and took notice when they were confronted by a pastor for whom "religion" was not just one cultural asset among many but the heart and lodestar of his existence. And this impression was confirmed when a number of students who had never thought of it before, now decided to study theology.

A minister has to be a teacher—not only a teacher of youth, but of adults too. The place for this is the Bible class.

I had never attended a Bible class. At home there had been no such thing, and even if there had been I would assuredly not have attended it.

When I came to the Preachers' Seminary in Wittenberg, I found that to conduct a Bible class was a part of my training. Each seminarian had to take his turn once a year. The classes were held in the long refectory of the Luther House on a weekday afternoon. They were announced in the church bulletin in order to give any member of the congregation a chance to attend. But no one did. Or rather, there was always one old man, but nobody knew his name or who he was. This "Bible class man" was celebrated among whole generations of young seminarians.

The seminarians sat about on the benches and the housekeeper and the director of the seminary joined them. The seminarian whose turn it was to conduct the class would begin by leading the group in a hymn. Then he would explain a passage of the Bible rather in the manner of an exposition in a sermon, but more informally and in somewhat more detail. Afterward we all sang and recited a prayer. That was all.

We did not really see the point of such Bible classes. All we knew was that we might some day go to parishes where Bible classes were customary, and that we should know how to conduct them. That was all there was to it.

In fact, many of us did go to such parishes.

For me, it started with the villages near Guben, where I was the assistant pastor. Then, in the autumn of 1907, I was appointed pastor or, as it was still called at the time, archdeacon of the small town of Crossen on the Oder. There I found just the kind of Bible classes we had conducted in Wittenberg, not in the town itself but in the surrounding villages. I was responsible for three of these villages. They were incorporated in the urban parish, and had no church of their own. From time immemorial, Bible classes had been held in these villages during the winter months, once every two or three weeks. And what my predecessors had done, I naturally did too.

So once or twice a week I went out in the winter darkness to

72

conduct my Bible class. It was always held in the schoolhouse; there was nowhere else to hold it. There they sat, the sturdy peasants, both men and women, on the little school benches, squeezing their knees under the narrow tables. They had set their tallow candles and hymnals in front of them on the tables. The glow of the candles cast a flickering reddish light on the wrinkled faces of the old people as they carefully adjusted their glasses and sang lustily out of their hymnals. The schoolroom was always packed with old and young. The older children often had to stand. The air would gradually thicken. If we did not end the class on time, the candles would go out because all the oxygen had been used up.

That is how it was in those days in thousands of other villages too. Every old country pastor knows it.

The people came gladly to these Bible classes, much more gladly and in greater numbers than to Sunday service. Who could blame them? The church was some distance away; in winter it was cold; they did not really feel at home, scattered in the big church among people they did not know. But it was only a couple of steps to the Bible class. They could sit on the school benches, not very comfortably, to be sure, but in warmth. And they were close together. They did not mind the bad air; country folk never mind bad air. On the contrary, it was when the candles began to go out that they really began to feel just right. The word of God was physically close.

Of course, those who had attended Bible class on some week-day evening did not go to church the following Sunday. They had had their divine service. For that was how they looked upon the Bible class—as a service for which the pastor came to the village. They were entitled to consider it as such. In every village there were people who could hardly make their way to church any more. Through the Bible class, the pastor came into real contact with the individual village, and the village with him. There was real fellow feeling in these gatherings.

In the town of Crossen itself, as I said, there was no such Bible class. I did not want to conduct classes on the village model, so I announced that there would be an informal discussion of scriptural questions, and everyone might bring his Bible. We did not have a parish hall so I invited the parishioners to come to my parsonage.

I had counted on an attendance of some ten to twelve persons. Little tables had been pushed together, and chairs set around casually. But over fifty people turned up the very first evening. The little tables had to be taken out again quickly. A couple of ugly yellow benches were brought over from the church. The whole careful arrangement went by the board. In the end they all sat crowded together, and the air was not much better than in the village. As for informal discussion, there was none. It was quickly apparent that the people were too varied in type and education for that. Had I had a little professional experience I would have known that beforehand. It ended with the pastor giving a lecture. And yet it was different both from a church service and from the usual Bible class. It was what people were beginning to call "confirmation classes for adults."

In 1915 I was called to Berlin as assistant pastor of the Heilsbronnen parish, at the Bayrischer Platz. Hardly had I preached my first sermons than I was asked by members of the congregation to organize a second Bible class; one Bible class already existed under the direction of my able colleague, Pastor Geest.

I had a sheet printed giving the theme and text for every Monday evening from October to Pentecost. I announced that each Bible class would be made up of three parts, two short and one longer. First I would always discuss the most important problems in the life of the parish. Then I would answer any questions submitted in writing. And finally—this would be the principal part—I would comment on the scriptural text.

It was my uncle, the first chaplain in ordinary at Dresden, who had drawn my attention to the value of written questions. He had found that most people hesitated to speak before a large gathering. If they did overcome their shyness and ask something, then the pastor's reply, being necessarily extempore, often proved unsatisfactory. People were much more likely to state what troubled them in writing, especially if they were assured of anonymity. Foolish questions, unsuitable to a Bible class, could be passed over in silence. Sometimes the pastor might devote half the period of the Bible class, or the following Sunday sermon, to some of the questions submitted to him at the class. In brief, by this method something could really be accomplished.

This is what I announced, and this is how I conducted my classes for nine winters, as long as I was pastor at Heilsbronnen. At first the attendance was small, but each winter it grew larger. After a few years our little hall, which at most might accommodate 200 persons, was filled to capacity. Sometimes people stood in the doorway, and it was repeatedly suggested that we move to the church. But this I could not bring myself to do; the Bible class would have filled only a relatively small part of the church, and half-empty places are something a pastor should avoid like the plague. So we stayed where we were.

In all those years there were, of course, people who were not really serious about the Bible, but who came to the class simply for an hour of uplift—a kind of weekday service—just like my villagers near Crossen. Such visitors would bring along their hymnals and then sit back in their chairs in agreeable expectation of the pastor's elevating words. One just had to put up with them. The Bible class was held not for them but for the others—for those who really wanted to delve more deeply into the scriptures. These people had their Bibles with them. They had usually read the text beforehand and thought about it, and read it again afterwards at home.

We would begin by discussing the text very soberly, externally, so to speak. How did the particular incident take place? What was the original intent of the words in their context? This always led to a discussion of what theology and biblical criticism had to tell us about that particular text. Then we would try to understand the text as a scriptural text should be understood—as God's word to us, demanding something quite definite of us.

The class always followed very attentively. It was a very mixed group. Women were in the majority—wives of officials, wives of businessmen, teachers, nurses, titled ladies, students—reflecting the population pattern in the west end of Berlin. But there were a good number of men too—even men whom one would least expect to find at a Bible class. For instance, a producer from the Wintergarten would come whenever he was not on duty. There were also doctors and officers, students, officials, secondary-school teachers—but rarely elementary-school teachers. Some came and went again without my finding out who they were. The regular visitors one came to know personally, if for no other reason than because a Bible class automatically becomes a parish working group.

Many of those who came were really devoted to those Monday evenings. Certainly I was. If I sometimes had to cancel a sermon, either because I was sick or because I had to go abroad, it was quite a sacrifice for me. But to cancel a Bible class was simply unthinkable, and it happened very rarely.

Here, in the Bible class, the pastor was the teacher of the congregation. And that is precisely what a pastor has to be.

PREACHER

IT WAS IN 1910, when I was transferred from Crossen on the Oder to Danzig, that I really found out what preaching meant.

I had gone to Danzig very reluctantly. The Reformed congregation to which I was assigned numbered barely two thousand souls, scattered throughout the city and its suburbs. Of "reform" there was not a trace. People were prosperous and worldly, that was all. And the small congregation was lost in the huge church of SS. Peter and Paul. A magnificent musician, Professor Fuchs, sat at the powerful organ. But he was not interested in the service. During the sermon he read his Schopenhauer.

From the first day I realized that everything depended on the sermon. The members of the Reformed congregation were not to be counted upon—with a few exceptions, of course. Those who came to church did not come to take part in the religious life of the congregation. As for the non-Reformed, they did not want to have their children confirmed there, and they definitely did not want to attend the Communion service. Those who came, came exclusively for the sermon. There were no workers or members of the lower middle class among them; these went to their own parish churches. The only people who came were the well-educated, for whom membership in a congregation meant nothing, but who were looking for a preacher who had something to offer them. It was sheer coincidence if one of them happened to belong to the Reformed congregation.

I made few personal contacts. I had no idea who was at service. Some wrote to me after my sermons, and such letters occasionally led to contacts. But basically I was thrown back upon myself. I tried to put my time to good use. I began to learn to preach.

I always found preaching hard. Even as a student at Wittenberg I envied those of my fellow students who were glad when their turn came to preach in the Schlosskirche, over Luther's tomb. I was never glad. I felt too inadequate to be able to hand on to the congregation, with authority, the word of the holy God— for that is what preaching really is. This sense I have retained right up to my old age.

It was easiest, of course, to preach to the kind of educated congregation that was slowly building up in Danzig, or the kind I later had in Berlin, at Heilsbronnen. Sermons before such congregations certainly required the most careful preparation, but nevertheless one was addressing communicants from the same world as the preacher. They lived with the same issues, even if they did not arrive at the same conclusions. They listened to the words of Holy Writ with the same assumptions. They had read the same books. They were interested in the same events in public life. They understood quickly what the preacher meant, even if he did not always express himself with complete clarity.

Preparing a sermon was always hard for me. But once I began to speak from my pulpit at Heilsbronnen—with people standing all the way out to the vestibule, sitting on the altar steps, often on the steps leading up to the pulpit too, with the altar beautifully adorned by the skillful hands of members of my church societies, with many faces familiar to me from my Bible classes or from house visits—then it was easy to say what I had to say at the command of my God.

Nevertheless I would often go home from service depressed. For I could not preach as the strict Lutherans preached. Once, the president of the Westphalian church, who was a Lutheran of that stamp, was sitting in the sacristy during a festival service at which he was to preach the second sermon. He saw his young colleague who had preached the first sermon wiping the sweat from his brow as he descended from the pulpit. "You are sweating, my brother?" he asked in a tone of reproach. "Only falsehood brings out the sweat!" That was the Lutheran principle: God's word is efficacious of itself; the preacher should not try to make it more efficacious by his own efforts.

I could not preach like that. I had to preach with body, mind, and soul, as the Apostle Paul says, in intimate contact with the congregation. I had to demand something of the congregation. I had to be able to see in their faces whether what I said in the name of my Lord Jesus Christ was reaching them or not. And from the way the congregation said the *Amen* I had to be able to sense whether the sermon had gone home. With the *Amen* I was released from the inner tension in which I had lived during the preceding twenty-four hours.

Today it is not uncommon to hear it said that the liturgy is more important than the sermon, and that a feeling for the liturgy should be reawakened in the Evangelical Church.

I do not deny that these liturgical endeavors have their significance. How often have I longed for purely liturgical services myself! For instance, at sessions of the synod, after four to six days of incessant talk from early morning to late evening, I often found it intolerable to listen to yet another sermon at the close of the proceedings. Could we not for once have an hour of reflection at a liturgical service without human speech?

But it is not my own wishes that I have to consult, least of all at services which I am conducting. I have to think of the congregation. And in the present-day Evangelical congregation the sense of liturgy is largely undeveloped. The liturgists, who pride themselves on reworking the order of the Evangelical service in the

79

direction of the Roman Mass, usually have no real conception of the indifference of the overwhelming majority of the faithful to their undertaking.

I am the last to overestimate the importance of sermons in the inner development of the church and in the practical application of the Gospel to the life of our people. It should not be imagined that anything decisive can be given to people in a fleeting half-hour on a Sunday, especially when attendance is irregular. Something effective can occasionally happen, but each time it is the result of a special grace of God.

As for "famous pulpit orators," these are the worst, and their importance has been vastly exaggerated. In the 1880's, Berlin had more brilliant preachers than it ever had before or since. There was nothing unusual, in those days, in seeing dozens or, rather, hundreds of people waiting before a closed church door an hour and a half before the beginning of the service in order to secure their places. And it was precisely at this period that parish life decayed and Berlin became a worldly city. The Rhineland, on the other hand, always had remarkably few pulpit orators. But parish life flourished, both inwardly and outwardly. The same is true of the Moravians. Famous preachers, whether they will it or not, gather an audience rather than a genuine congregation. They attract people who care more about the manner than about the matter of a sermon, people who in running after a famous preacher evade their duty to their own parish.

The important thing in the Evangelical church is the sound, average sermon. But the average sermon requires diligence and concentrated spiritual power. That is the only kind of sermon which will carry conviction.

I was thankful that for years I could minister to quite unpretentious congregations. I was never tempted to try to preach like a Rittelmeyer, for instance, who always showered upon his congregation a veritable cornucopia of modern literary allusions and brilliant reflections, and made it quite clear that he was fully conversant with the problems of modern art and science. The rest of us, to be sure, might almost envy him the number of cultivated persons he drew to his pulpit. Yet the Gospel of Jesus Christ is a very straightforward affair, and it is this that everyone needs for his salvation, old and young alike and in every walk of life, however exalted and however lowly. I was happy if I chanced to notice a fourteen-year-old nudging his little brother at some point in my sermon as though to say: "Do you hear? That's meant for you!" Then I knew that the sermon would be understood.

When I was still a boy, a curious law suit took place in Berlin. A young officer had gone to church in Charlottenburg with a detachment of soldiers. They found themselves at a service conducted by Pastor Kraatz, a very liberal minister. The preacher's critical comments on the Gospel shocked the officer, who came of a very strict religious family. Finally he could stand it no longer. He signed to his men and they all left the church together—and their departure, as is customary with soldiers, was not altogether noiseless.

The liberal church council initiated proceedings for disturbance of a public religious service. The pastor was called upon to testify. The judge asked him to state what he considered to be the purpose of a sermon. The pastor replied that the purpose was for the preacher to "discuss religious questions" with the congregation. To those of us young people who had not rallied to the standard of liberalism, such a definition was quite shocking. But it was definitely a sign of the times.

The advent of the National Socialists in 1933 marked the beginning of the *Kirchenkampf* (church struggle), and with it a turning point in the history of the sermon.

The pastors who had accepted National Socialism were, at Hitler's behest, calling themselves "German-Christians." Many of these German-Christians—and important ones among them—let

81

themselves be carried away by their political enthusiasm, quite heedless of the scriptural text. For instance, on Good Friday, there would be a description of the arrest of Jesus. "Then all the disciples forsook him, and fled." To which the preacher would add: "Such a thing could never have happened to Adolf Hitler!" and he would go on about German loyalty, about the fighting courage which National Socialism had restored, and so forth. Or again—this was a particular favorite with the German-Christians as a text for sermons in 1933—"But thanks be to God, which giveth us the victory!" The words "through our Lord Jesus Christ" were suppressed. And the fact that the whole verse deals with victory over sin did not trouble them. The victory, as they saw it, was Adolf Hitler's victory of January 30, 1933, and the victory of the National Socialist movement.

Nor did they shrink from altering the text when it suited them. For instance, the opening words of the Gospel of St. John would now be cited as reading: "In the beginning was the people, and the people was with God, and the people was God!"

Now people began to open their eyes. Up till then they had felt unsure. A pastor tells this incident out of his life. In 1918, as a young soldier, he heard a sermon in Brussels on the parable of the fig tree; how the lord of the vineyard had wanted to cut down the tree after vainly looking for fruit three whole years. This parable the naval chaplain applied to the British and the French; for three years they had aroused God's anger and were now ripe for judgment; perhaps the extra year would be granted them which the gardener in the parable asks for his tree, but if they still felt no compunction or repentance, then inevitably the command would be given: "Cut it down; why cumbereth it the ground?" The sermon made a great impression on the huge soldier congregation. The future pastor felt that there was something not quite right about it, but he was not quite clear what it was.

Now it was clear to everyone. When Karl Barth called upon the theologians to "get down to essentials," his call found a resounding echo among both pastors and congregations. What people wanted to know was not what Pastor X thought about political, religious, or other problems, but what God's eternal word had to say to them in their need and temptations. Quotations from modern poets stuck in pastor's throats. Congregations no longer wanted to be told that they might believe this or that because Goethe or Wilhelm Raabe had said something of the sort—something more beautiful and impressive, even, than the New Testament. No, people now wanted to hear what the Church of Jesus Christ proclaimed to them as the word of God.

Overnight the collections of Rittelmeyer's sermons, which previously had gone through edition after edition, were discarded and forgotten. It was the substance that mattered once more, and that, generally speaking, is how it has remained to the present day.

One result of this new frame of mind was the renewed popularity of what theologians call the homily. This is a sermon in which the text is analyzed sentence by sentence, rather than as a whole, and in which not much time is devoted to its practical lessons.

I have never used that form of preaching. To my mind a homily has a purpose only when the members of the congregation have the text open before them and can follow the exposition verse by verse. This occurs in some British congregations, but not here, unfortunately. And only rarely is the text so well known—the parables of the Good Samaritan or the Prodigal Son, for instance—that the congregation can follow the preacher point by point. In other cases the precision and acuity of the homily are lost on them. The homily is suitable for the Bible class, not for the parish service.

I have the impression, too, that with this type of sermon the pastor tends to stick too closely to the text itself and fails to make the connection with the practical life of the congregation. Even if he tries to relate the text to present-day reality he will often not get beyond generalities.

83

I have always regarded the sermon as a vehicle for pastoral care. It should reach the members of the congregation in their daily duties and needs. That is why it has to be practical. For the parish pastor, the substance of his sermon is constantly supplied by his daily work of pastoral counseling. The pastor who has no parish has to search further for a subject. But no sermon should be without pastoral impact on daily life. During the sermon the listener should form resolutions. "He who does not have a God to thread his needle, does not have a God to give him salvation either," wrote Elise Averdieck in her old age. That is the spirit in which a sermon should be preached.

I remember an incident which took place at Lauenburg in 1913. We were having our big annual mission celebration. Dr. Axenfeld, the director of the Berlin Mission Society, was staying with us. In the morning I had to preach the regular Sunday sermon. It was certainly not a good sermon, for I had not had enough time or peace to prepare it. After the service, Axenfeld put his hand in mine and said. "I was so happy; you *demand* something of the congregation." I felt he understood.

My principle regarding a sermon has always been quite simple and straightforward. When the wife comes home and her husband asks her (or the other way round, as the case may be): "What did he say?" she should be able to reply quite definitely: "He said *this.*" Perhaps the text was so simple that she can repeat it. That is good. Perhaps the preacher gave an illustration or told a story which she can relate in her turn. That is also good. And it is also helpful if the pastor organizes his sermon under clear headings and recapitulates those headings toward the end. Then the listener can give an account of it, both to himself and to others. And what is remembered may bear fruit.

The pastor should prepare his sermon in writing. If he cannot do so because he is too busy, then he must make it an iron rule to write out at least every second or third sermon. Otherwise he will inevitably slip into monotonous chatter.

The art of preaching begins with the translation of the written word into living speech. The written and the spoken word are two fundamentally different things. The written word moves in relative clauses and paragraphs. The spoken word requires short sentences, clear associations. It uses emphasis to express many things which in the written word have to be explicitly formulated. Very few people have the gift of delivering a written text so that it comes alive. Sermons that are read are nearly always boring.

In our day, people will not tolerate the old-fashioned oratory in which every word was so polished that the text had perforce to be committed to memory verbatim. We have become too sober and realistic for that kind of thing. Today the only possible way to preach is to master both the over-all theme and the details of the written sermon, to memorize certain important phrases, but to develop the sermon itself from the pulpit. It is an art that comes naturally to very few. Most preachers have to acquire it laboriously over the years. The preacher who prides himself on jotting down brief notes and then speaking freely will soon show his superficiality. A sermon is not an address before a meeting. It is bound by its scriptural text. It undertakes to proclaim eternal truth in the name of God. The man who treats it lightly is not fit to be a preacher.

This truth, be it added, is the glad message of the grace of God which in Jesus Christ has become final reality. It is a message which includes moral imperatives. But sermons on morals, unrelated to the Gospel, should never be preached from a Christian pulpit. And if this glad message also contains words about God's judgments which man must ultimately face, it is still a message of joy, and that fact must emerge from every sermon. I rarely preached a penitential sermon. I could never get over what St. Paul wrote to the Corinthians: ". . . lest after preaching to others I myself should be disqualified." But the penitential sermon in which the preacher declares himself at one with those to whom he is speaking is actually no longer a penitential sermon, for it must of necessity end in a glorifying of God's grace.

Let those who feel themselves called upon to be prophets preach penitential sermons! We simple servants of God should preach in such a way that those who listen to us may always feel: "We are the Saviour's joyful people!"

In fifty years of ministry a pastor will have preached more than two thousand sermons. Most of them he has soon forgotten, but a few will remain fixed in his memory.

As far as my own sermons are concerned, I shall mention three of them here.

The first of these was the sermon of March 21, 1933, which the National Socialists and later the Communists held so strongly against me. To the end of my life in the ministry I abided by what I said at that time. I shall refer to it again later.

The second sermon relates to July 1, 1937, when Niemöller was arrested. The day was a Thursday. On the following Sunday I had to conduct the service in his place.

People streamed into the church. Two overcrowded services took place in succession. My text was from II Timothy, where St. Paul speaks of the sufferings he has undergone. The text was not deliberately chosen, but taken, I believe, from the Bible reading for the day. (The sermon is no longer in my possession.) In the sermon I adhered strictly to the text. Each word was carefully weighed. The congregation followed the sermon with palpable emotion. Niemöller's name was not mentioned till the final prayer.

The church was swarming with agents of the Gestapo who were immediately conspicuous by their irreligious and sometimes boorish behavior. A couple of courageous women stopped some of these "Stapisten," as we called them, after the service, and asked them what they had to say about the sermon. They could say nothing at all. They admitted that not a word could have been construed as hostile to the State—although of course everyone in the church sensed what was behind the words.

At first nothing happened. Ten days later I was arrested—for the third time. The sermon had been taken down by faithful members of the congregation and reproduced. They had meant well. They had not yet learned that under a totalitarian regime one should commit nothing to paper, at any rate not under the author's name or without his permission. Inevitably the notes of my sermon fell into the hands of the Gestapo. The desired grounds for prosecution had been provided, after all.

A couple of days later I was brought before the magistrate who was to determine whether the police custody should be followed by a bench warrant or not. To that extent judicial forms were still observed.

The judge had the sermon before him and now began to go through it sentence by sentence. "You refer to the Apostle Paul all the time," he said, "but in fact you always mean Niemöller!" There was a grain of truth in what he said. This is the way the congregation had understood the sermon, and I had known that they would so understand it.

Nevertheless I could in good conscience give the judge a little lecture to the effect that a sermon belongs to the service and must be interpreted within the framework of the service. If a National Socialist trial judge subsequently goes through every word with a blue pencil, an interpretation will emerge which does justice neither to the preacher nor to the congregation.

This seemed to make some impression on the judge. After a half-hour's talk, he suddenly informed me that he would not issue a bench warrant and that I was free. He signed to the policeman who was guarding me. The policeman readily conducted me back to my cell and told me to pack my things. In a short while I was outside in the street and could telephone my wife to tell her of my release.

Later I learned that the news of this unexpected release aroused something of a storm within the Party. But this time they did not dare rearrest me, as they had already done once before.

The third sermon was delivered on May 20, 1945.

On April 25 the Russians had marched into Berlin. For two weeks we had had to live in cellars, constantly threatened by hostile visits by day and by night. It was a terrible time.

In the meantime we began to rebuild our ecclesiastical organization. On May 7 the Consistory was reconstituted in Dilschneider's parsonage at Zehlendorf. We met every day. And one of our first decisions was to hold a big service in the church of St. Matthew in Steglitz on Whitsunday, May 20, at which the new church leadership would appear before the congregation. I was skeptical. Transportation facilities had not yet been restored. It was impossible to publish announcements. Who would come?

But as we made our way on foot from Lichterfelde to Steglitz, we saw our congregation flocking in the same direction—groups of people from Nikolassee, from Schlachtensee, from Zehlendorf, from the heart of Berlin. They were undaunted by the long trek, an hour, two hours, through the ruins of Berlin. They could not all fit inside the church. But the building, after all, had no windows, and the doors would not close. So I preached my sermon to the packed congregation and beyond it, to the many whom I could not see.

I have never experienced such an atmosphere before or since. The people's faces still bore the marks of the shock of the recent past. At the same time they were buoyed up by a new hope, a new resolve. Everything was destroyed. But the Church of Jesus Christ remained. With it and in it they were prepared to make a new beginning.

The text was taken from the second part of the Pentecost story: "This Jesus hath God raised up, whereof we all are witnesses." We recalled the Whitsunday, twelve years before, when Pastor von Bodelschwing, newly elected Reich Bishop, had preached in the Zion Church in Berlin, and all the sufferings the church had undergone in those twelve years. And then I called upon the community of the faithful to help the new church leadership: "Help us to trust in the Holy Ghost. Help us to pray that the Holy Ghost may come upon us, too! Help us to do the deeds of the Holy Ghost!"

Pastoral Counselor

In former times the pastor was the obvious person for a parishioner to turn to in every need, both spiritual and temporal. Whoever wanted advice came to the parsonage.

Those days are over. The pastor has been replaced by the doctor, the psychiatrist, perhaps the astrologer or the fortuneteller. The world has become materialistic, even that part of the world which combats materialism.

Formerly, as I have said, it was otherwise—with exceptions, of course. My Uncle Franz used to tell me that when he and Dryander were students, their teacher of practical theology at the University of Berlin would make a point of telling them: "Whatever he does, the pastor must not make house calls, otherwise the mantle of Elias will fall from his shoulders!"

That was the point of view of Lutheran orthodoxy. The pastor is a personage. It is not for him to go to his parishioners but for them, when they need him, to go to him.

I have known pastors who took the same view. Not to speak of those who had no Lutheran principles in the matter, but who acted thus in practice for convenience' sake. Most of those pastors officiated in Berlin.

When I took up my duties, the pastor was still by way of being a person of authority. I can still see the face of the state trooper who stopped me one day during my first weeks at Crossen as I was cheerfully cycling on the Oder dyke, unaware that I was infringing a regulation. Riding on the dyke was prohibited, he told me. I never found out why. Bicycles certainly could not damage the dyke. But in Prussia, things had to be prohibited. So the state trooper took out his notebook and asked my name, profession, address. "I am the new pastor at Crossen," I told him. The trooper's pencil fell out of his hand. "Oh, I must apologize! I had no means of knowing!" Then his official conscience began to prick him. "But of course that should make no difference! Well, then . . ." I comforted him. I told him I would take his warning to heart, now that I knew I must not ride on the dyke, and I picked up his pencil for him. We parted good friends.

Yes, that is how it was in those days. What the pastor said carried weight with people. But he must not only speak, he must act.

When I was assistant pastor at Guben, one of my confirmants was a poor lad who suffered from paralysis of the right side. His mother worked hard in a factory, and though she worried about him she did not reflect on what would become of him. His teacher had not bothered to teach him to write well with his left hand, and his writing was pitiful. I took him into our own household for a year, taught him to write tolerably well, and got him a job first with a lawyer and subsequently in the office of the district president. There he soon rose to the rank of assistant, married, and raised a family. He died a respected official and paterfamilias.

That was the kind of pastoral care which ministered to soul and body at once, and there were plenty of other opportunities for such "existential" assistance.

A young Oder bargeman, only recently married, came to tell me his sad story. He had come home after a long run to find the nest empty—his wife had gone home to her mother and taken the furniture with her. It did not take any special discernment to see what had happened. I got him to promise to take his wife along on his next trip, in two weeks' time. Then I drove to the village, assembled the wife's family, including her grown brothers, and said that the furniture must be taken back that very evening, that I would return the next morning, and that if they had not taken it back I would see to it myself. When I returned the following morning, nothing had been done. Probably they had not believed that I meant what I said. But when I made the gesture of getting hold of a couple of sturdy fellows to handle the move, the brothers capitulated, and the young woman was able to cook her husband's dinner at home again. And the trip on the Oder barge, far from the influence of the mother-in-law, took care of the rest. The marriage turned out well.

Such cases occurred repeatedly. Other marital troubles, both serious and absurd, had to be handled also. Foolish complaints could be disposed of if one was able to impress upon the parties the significance of the Christian prayer of penitence. Other cases were more difficult. The hardest of all was that of a young colleague beyond the Oder. He had not the slightest idea of money or budgeting, and had used official monies as his own. When he found himself hopelessly in debt, he took to drink.

I also had to minister to the dying. Certain hallowed hours at the bedside of the dying brought me untold benefit.

At Lauenburg, in Pomerania, where I was appointed in 1911 after a short interlude at Danzig, circumstances were similar. Here, too, there were neglected children to look after, marriages to be patched up, the sick and the dying to be ministered to.

When the war broke out, I had to stay at home. Assistant pastors and parish workers were obliged to leave on the first day of mobilization. Soldiers came to the town. We two pastors had our hands full. Certain episodes will remain with me forever: the Communion services attended by the conscripted soldiers and their families; the arrival of the East Prussian refugees, some of whom we put up in our own home; the news of the victory of Tannenberg, which reached me at night, and in honor of which I at once went down to ring the church bells myself.

The war also provided opportunities for greatly expanded "social pastoral care," if that expression may be used for action intended to produce both material and spiritual benefits. Our little town council had planned nothing and prepared nothing. It was completely helpless in the face of every necessity that arose. Initiative was never the Pomeranians' strong suit. The men had gone off to the war, the women and children remained behind with nothing to live on. My wife and I immediately set up a knitting parlor, and I bought up all the wool I could lay my hands on. But that was soon exhausted. And I could not permanently pay the ever growing number of women out of collection funds. So I traveled to the army authorities at Danzig, concluded a contract with them for the delivery of socks, then went to Berlin where I again bought up all the wool I could find, and instructed the church fund to pay six thousand marks. This thoroughly upset the city fathers, who had long observed my unconventional operations with suspicion. When I came home, the atmosphere was charged. Had I insured the wool? Was I sure about the estimate? I did not let their protests disturb me.

Time passed. The workers' apartments were without gas or electricity. All the kerosene in the town had been used up. There were no more candles to be had. The women, who now replaced the men in the factories, got up in darkness and came home in darkness. The children were uncared for. Apartments were neglected. I traveled to Swinemünde and got the navy to agree to let me have a dozen barrels of kerosene. And seldom have I been so happy as when I was able to station myself at the first of the kerosene barrels and supervise the delivery to the soldiers' wives.

There were also difficult individual cases. Once my attention was drawn to a hopelessly sick woman with three children. I went to see the family and found the woman utterly emaciated, the children dirty, the apartment in a terrible condition. The woman claimed that she could absorb no food. I talked to the doctor, who said that medically there was nothing wrong with the woman; she had simply surrendered to despair and had not much longer to live.

I took the head nurse of our hospital into my confidence—that wonderful woman, Ada von Kriegsheim, of the Elizabeth House of Deaconesses of Berlin—and the mother was transferred to the hospital. She was told that her particular illness required that she should not retire to bed before evening. Every day she had to get on the scales. Every day she was told that she had gained one or two pounds. She regained vital energy and began to eat. In two weeks she returned to her children, rested and cheerful and able to be a proper mother to them again.

In 1915, much against my will, I was appointed to the Heilsbronnen parish in Berlin. There, in the big city, everything was altogether different. All material needs were provided for, as far as was humanly possible. The pastor had to concern himself exclusively with the pastorate, and this meant, first of all, pastoral counseling.

The beginning was very difficult. At Lauenburg my doorbell had rung all day long, and on Sundays the church had been packed. In Berlin I went through the same kind of experience as Stoecker and Frommel relate about their early days in the ministry: I stood at the window and looked out into the street to see if anyone was coming to ask me for anything. But no one came. On Sundays the church was only partially filled, whereas my colleague, Pastor Geest, attracted an overflow. My confirmation class was very small. Never have I felt so superfluous as I did in those early days of my Berlin ministry.

I went to the chaplain-general of the army. I told him that I was available now, and that I wanted to join up in order to help with the tremendous pastoral needs arising out of the war. But the chaplain-general would have none of me. Why, I shall never know. I made a second appeal, this time to the Supreme Ecclesiastical

Council, but met with the same response. I had to resign myself to staying where I was.

And then, gradually, things began to improve. Wartime conditions provided many opportunities for making contact with people. I obtained the addresses of the soldiers from my district, sent them greetings to the front, and whenever I received an answer I went to visit the family. I announced from the pulpit that there would be open house at my apartment on certain evenings. People came—titled persons and housemaids, executives and minor employees. And I sometimes observed with joy how they suddenly realized, to their own astonishment, that they were all one family. The fact that they now began to greet each other in friendly fashion was in itself a minor pastoral achievement.

Then there were house calls to be made on the families of my confirmants. These I carried out scrupulously, even when the number of my confirmants rose to two hundred, and when the pressure of my other duties made it increasingly difficult for me to spare the necessary time. I never spoke to the confirmation students privately unless they came to me of their own accord—apart from special cases, of course. But I visited the parents, and I always announced my visits beforehand. This saved me useless trips and also prevented the embarrassment of my appearing just as the mother was in the middle of spring cleaning or some such chore. The conversation certainly did not always plumb any great depths. Nevertheless it was sometimes possible to break through the barriers of conventionality and speak of what is really essential.

As a result of my preaching, the number of those who came to seek advice gradually increased. Their problems usually concerned the inner life. Some were plagued by doubts. Others were toying with the idea of going over to Roman Catholicism or leaving the church altogether, but wanted to talk to an Evangelical pastor first. Young people came who had not been confirmed for one reason or another, and who now wanted to receive instruction. People came saying they wished to join the Evangelical Church. Toward such I was always more reserved, for they were usually impelled by extraneous motives. Where they were considering marriage to a member of the Evangelical Church, I gladly went as far as I could to help them, because it is always better for both spouses to belong to the same church, especially where children are concerned. It is very rare to find both parties to a mixed marriage remaining earnest Christians.

My hardest problem came when Jews asked for baptism. This was a common occurrence in the Bayrische Viertel, with its large Jewish population. Those who came all declared that they were moved by profound conviction and would do anything the pastor required. But in the end it nearly always turned out that there was some other reason. I therefore became increasingly firm and exacting in my demands. This gradually became known, and in the end I was spared such externally motivated requests for baptism. It did sometimes happen, of course, that a Jew desired to become a Christian out of deep inner conviction. In such cases I never refused to baptize·him, even in the National Socialist period when it meant risking one's life.

The most common form of pastoral counseling in the west end of Berlin was to assist people when their marriages had come to grief. Usually it was the wife who came to me, rarely the husband. Divorce proceedings had either been initiated or were to be initiated shortly. The pastor had to lend his ear to all the grievances which had led to such a decision. I always tried to listen without impatience. At first I was inclined to regard dissolution as the only course where a marriage had long ceased to be a marriage—though I never actually counseled divorce. But with experience I became firmer and more decided as the years went by. Finally I said this: "Divorce, except for adultery, is forbidden by our Lord Jesus Christ, and anyone purposing to seek divorce is guilty before God. If the other party has committed adultery, then the duty of love is to forgive. The marriage vow is binding beyond all estrangement. Separation, yes, if nothing else works; divorce, no." As a pastor I cannot say more on the basis of God's word.

I have often been reproached for narrow-mindedness, and I am well aware that there are cases which cannot be fitted into this scheme. But I have received so many expressions of thanks from those who have been helped by this straightforward, clear, and definite application of the scriptural command that I have been strengthened in my opinion. One helps people by placing before them a clear decision, not by trying to be as sympathetic and accommodating as possible.

For this reason I was particularly firm when I saw that the divorce plague threatened to invade even the parsonage. A pastor whose duty it is to say at the marriage service: "What therefore God hath joined together, let not man put asunder," should not be divorced himself, otherwise his whole teaching will be suspect. There may be exceptions, but such exceptions can be permitted only in very rare cases. The rule must be that the pastor who gets divorced from his wife is, at the same time, divorced from his office. At first very few of my colleagues in the Consistory shared this view. I have abided by it to the last.

I repeat: the minister as a pastoral counselor is being increasingly edged out by the doctor, the lawyer, the psychiatrist. And no one is trained in pastoral counseling. At the university, perhaps, or at the preachers' seminary, a couple of remarks may be made on the subject, and perhaps the pastor will tell his curate this or that incident from his pastoral experience. But that is all, and it is nothing.

In former days the curate was taught to visit the sick with a copy of the New Testament in his pocket, to read them a passage from it, or from the hymnal, and to end with a prayer. But the opportunity for such sick calls is becoming increasingly rare. Nowadays the permanently bedridden are placed in hospitals or infirmaries; there is no room for them at home. And in the hospitals there should be experienced clergy to dispense pastoral care.

Some say that the pastor should be trained in psychiatry, otherwise his counseling will be clumsy or useless. And best of all—he should make a thorough study of medicine.

I have always been against such advice. People who have studied two or even three specialities are rarely capable of exercising one of them. They do not really live in the one profession to which they are supposed to give their wholehearted allegiance. It is quite different, of course, if a man originally had another profession and then became a pastor. But to study law or medicine in order to become a better pastor is usually utter nonsense. The pastor should be a pastor through and through, and not play about with other branches of learning.

I used to think that the pastor should acquaint himself with popular custom and religious tradition. I do not hold that view any more. What there is to learn, the pastor will learn fast enough if he really takes trouble about his congregation. In the essentials, that is, in those things which constitute the specific task of the pastor, man is and remains ever and everywhere the same. A proper exhortation at a marriage service is essentially the same whether it is delivered in a princely mansion or in a workers' parish church. Similarly, the form of a confirmation class may vary between a private country school and a public school in one of the poorer neighborhoods, but in essence it must provide the same instruction.

For his counseling, the pastor need learn only three things. He must be completely available to those who come to him, and must be able to listen to them patiently. He must never for a moment forget that he is being consulted not as a man but in his capacity as a servant of the Lord, and that his advice must be grounded in the word of God. And, finally, he must observe absolute secrecy, which is the precondition of all pastoral trust.

Actual private confession does not occur as often as is sometimes believed, but it does take place at times. I have never done as some pastors do: put on a gown and lighted candles for private confession. Solemnity has never been my forte, and I have never noticed any longing for it in anyone else. But many a person has told me what was on his mind and which he had never disclosed to anyone else.

Pastoral counseling can be difficult, and in some causes haunt a pastor for days and weeks. But it is also a joyful thing in its sacred responsibility. And if one had only helped a handful of people to surmount their marriage difficulties and remain together, that would in itself be a justification for one's existence.

The pastor in a big city finds that he not only dispenses pastoral counsel to others but also receives it from his parishioners. To be sure, he is also likely to come across people who would rather criticize than minister to him. But criticism can be salutary, even if it is anonymous. As a bishop, I always threw away anonymous letters unread. As a parish pastor I used to read them, but have kept only one, which begins with the words: "Daily we supplicate God to shorten your days—yours and those of your kind." It does not hurt the pastor to see from such communications what people there are among those who surround and observe him. Thank God, in his ministry to souls he also comes upon Christians who have more to say to him than he to them, both orally and in writing. That I have experienced abundantly.

𝔄DMINISTRATOR

I was the son of a civil servant, but I was not cut out to be a civil servant in my turn. With all my heart and soul I was a pastor. And I have always regarded bureaucratically minded pastors—there are some—as unfortunate specimens of their kind. As a young pastor at Crossen I went to visit my colleagues in the vicinity, and came upon one who also functioned as the local royal school inspector. Very proudly he showed me his daybook in which all receipts and expenditures were neatly entered. "Look," he said, "today is February 7, and I am already at file No. 183!" I never visited him again.

Where the Gospel is preached in living fashion, regulations lose their authority and files their importance. A Christian congregation does not need to be administered but to be penetrated by the power of faith and love.

I am not saying, of course, that the pastor should arbitrarily set himself above regulations and neglect the administrative side of his work. The temptation to do so is great, and not a few succumb to it. What he should do is deal with administrative matters, as it were, with his left hand, and if they become too onerous for him to deal with alone, then he should recruit assistants to take them off his hands. He must be both inwardly and outwardly free for his specific task. Otherwise he should never have become a pastor.

First impressions stick, however trifling they may be. Of bureaucracy, I have two distinct initial impressions, one on the ecclesiastical, the other on the secular plane.

I had registered for my first examination in theology and had thus for the first time come within the purview of the Royal Consistory of the Province of Brandenburg. Two weeks later I received a communication from the Consistory stating that I must also file my army papers; it was signed by the president of the Consistory. In the army this kind of note is signed by the district sergeant. In the church it is signed by the Acting Privy Councilor to the Consistory, bearing the rank of first-class councilor, president and honorary doctor of theology! What can these people have to do?

I learned later that it was an old principle of ecclesiastical government that the president should see all incoming communications and, unless he was sick or on leave, that he should sign all outgoing communications. This was considered necessary so that the president should have complete control of the whole operation. There was great reluctance to depart from this principle. Even Dr. Kapler, who was the first in the Supreme Ecclesiastical Council to break with it, did so with a heavy heart. But it was absurd all the same, even as long ago as 1904.

My first experience of government bureaucracy came when I was pastor at Crossen on the Oder. I was also, very unwillingly, the local school inspector for three villages incorporated in the parish. In one of these villages the government wanted to build a new school. Very rightly; the school was old, the teacher's quarters wretched. It was one of the commendable features of the public-school administration of those times that it sought to erect new schoolhouses wherever it could, and each time contributed the lion's share of the costs.

100

Naturally the peasants were against it. As children they had sat in the old schoolroom on the old school benches. Why should this not be good enough for the new generation?

A meeting was scheduled. An elderly senior government official arrived from Frankfurt, accompanied by a surveyor. He sat down at the desk, mumbled something unintelligible, and then said: "I am now writing the record; in the meantime you can talk." While he wrote, the surveyor, who had seated himself with the peasants, was giving them some straight talk about "moving with the times." The peasants shook their heads disapprovingly. They had no wish at all to move with the times.

Now the government official was ready. "I shall read it aloud: 'According to paragraph X of the law concerning the maintenance of elementary schools of such and such a date, and according to paragraph X of the statutes, in conjuction with paragraph X of the law of such and such a date . . . '" And so it went. The peasants did not understand a word of it. "There, and now we shall all sign. First, the chairman of the district council." The chairman of the district council came forward, hesitant, confused. But he signed. Then the others came and signed too. Then the government official packed up his documents, said good-by, and disappeared with his companion. The school was built.

I saw and heard all this and thought: So that's how it's done! But I knew that I could never proceed that way.

As parish pastor I had very little to do with the ecclesiastical administration, except when someone occasionally complained about me, which usually earned me a gentle reprimand from the authorities. In any case, since I was generally the assistant pastor, administrative matters did not concern me. At Lauenburg in Pomerania I was chief pastor for four years, and therefore responsible for all external affairs. But the Consistory was nearly two hundred miles away, at Stettin, and we rarely heard from it.

For my part I avoided contact with the authorities as much as possible. I did a great deal of building. But I never built with

101

church tax money or in association with the parish council, which would inevitably have brought me into contact with the world of officialdom. I was on excellent terms with my church elders, but to propose, to plan, to do anything together with them was altogether out of the question. The parish councils were like that in those days, at least at home, in the East. I created my own organizations, and obtained the funds elsewhere. In that way I retained my freedom of action.

Only after I had been appointed to Berlin and had just begun to feel at home in my new congregation did fate catch up with me. I was to be, in part, a functionary after all!

It was just after the collapse of 1918. On the evening of November 30, I received a telephone call from Dr. Lahusen, the theological vice-president of the Supreme Ecclesiastical Council. He said that the political upheaval involved far-reaching consequences for the church; that the new church order should be erected on broad foundations; that a Mutual Trust Council composed of all ecclesiastical and theological tendencies was to draw up a new constitution and advise the Supreme Ecclesiastical Council during the transitional period, but that it would be ineffective unless it had an Executive Secretary and one, moreover, who was not connected with the church administration. Was I prepared to take on the job? I said I was, and the next day I received the appointment. But I was to continue in my pastorate as well.

When I turned up at the Supreme Ecclesiastical Council, I saw right away that I was a most undesirable intruder in the eyes of President Voigt, who was the very embodiment of ecclesiastical bureaucracy. For him the Mutual Trust Council was a revolutionary organ and he wanted no part in it. There was no office space for me, there were no clerks, no funds, no instructions.

So I had to fend for myself. I set up an office at home and worked there until offices were finally made available to me in the administration building many months later. I published printed information sheets in which we told the churchgoing public what

the Mutual Trust Council was doing. When the National Constituent Assembly convened in Weimar, it was our task to keep in
touch with the theologians among its members so that they might
duly press for action on matters of major concern to the church.
The same task faced us when the National Assembly was dissolved
and the first new Reichstag convened.

Not the least of our concerns was the school question—specifically, whether the Christian religion should continue to be at home
in our schools. It was obvious to me—to others too, of course—that
in so weighty a matter our parliamentary representatives must
have backing. So we organized a petition for the Christian school
throughout Germany. The petition received more than four million
signatures. It was the largest petition ever submitted to a German
parliament.

All this, of course, meant a lot of work. I was soon employing
three secretaries—women secretaries. In the hallowed precincts of
the Supreme Ecclesiastical Council this was something unheard
of; all the clerical work in the church government was done by
male clerks. President Voigt raged because I had introduced "fe-
males" into his male world. The only reason he took no action
about it was that he was just about to retire. The younger members of the Council sided with me, and it was not long before they,
too, were working with women secretaries.

I also had to attend the meetings of the various committees. The
best work was performed by the committee on the constitution.
Professor Kahl was on it, and former Secretary of the Reich Justice
Department Lisco, and former Cabinet Minister Sydow. Then
there were the leading jurists of the Supreme Ecclesiastical Council: Moeller, Kapler, and Karnatz. The theological aspects were
handled primarily by Dr. Lahusen. The debates were on a very
high level, and the draft church constitution which resulted was
masterly, at least from a legal point of view.

Later, however, in the constituent church assembly, the draft
gave rise to heated debate. The majority of the members wanted a

preamble paraphrasing the church's creed. The jurists cautioned against it—justifiably, from a formal point of view. The liberals and the moderates fought tooth and nail against any direct reference in the preamble to the principal confessions of the sixteenth century. They regarded it as an intolerable attempt to turn the clock back. When the majority insisted on such reference, they rejected the whole constitution.

The question of primary elections was also to play a great part. Here it became apparent how strongly the political atmosphere of those days intruded into ecclesiastical deliberations. There were those who wanted to play at democracy in the church, too, with proportional representation and the broadest concessions to every point of view. The conservative forces offered resistance. Finally a compromise was agreed upon: voting rights in the church were to be confined to those whose names were entered on a special electoral list; the only condition for such entry was that they had paid their church taxes. The electors would vote directly for the provincial synods instead of indirectly through district synods, as before, and they would vote according to a party list, on the model of the system now in force in the political sphere. The provincial synods would then elect the General Synod. In this way the liberal minorities, which thus far had scarcely been represented on the synods, moved into all the ecclesiastical organs.

This constitution was later blamed for facilitating the penetration of the National Socialists into the church by granting the same rights to those who supported the church and those who were indifferent to it. After 1945 every effort was made to remedy this defect. Only those who were loyal to the church, who went to Communion, who took part in the work of the congregation were to be permitted to vote. Condition upon condition was to be imposed to prevent any recurrence of what had happened in 1933. This action was very understandable. Nevertheless, it should be realized that if a movement of such violence as National Socialism sweeps over a people, constitutional provisions are powerless against it, whether of the State or of the Church.

104

Through this work in the Mutual Trust Council I came to feel at home in the Supreme Ecclesiastical Council. And that accounted for what followed. In 1921 two theological posts fell vacant, one full-time and one part-time. I was offered the choice of either and chose the part-time post; I wanted to remain a pastor and not an out-and-out functionary.

Now I had an opportunity to revise my not overfriendly opinion of administrative bodies. The Berlin Supreme Ecclesiastical Council was an outstanding body. This was not really surprising, for it recruited the best men from the seven consistories subordinate to it, in the middle as well as in the higher echelons. The work it did was therefore accurate and judicious. The addresses preparatory to decisions in plenary were thoroughly thought out and discussed. Of the elements required to form a judgment, none was lacking. Decisions made sense. And if a memorandum went out, it was often classical in style.

I soon realized that an administration must necessarily work with such care, for to an administration nothing is either given or forgiven. The individual can readily admit that he has made a mistake. One day he will resign, and his successor will not be held responsible for his errors. But an administration remains the same, even when its members change. For instance, around 1890 the Supreme Ecclesiastical Council had obediently subscribed to the new social and political policy initiated by the Kaiser and his ministries. At first it had appealed to the clergy to take part in social and political action; a year or two later it cautioned them against it. Naturally the Council denied that this was a reversal of policy; its second ordinance, it explained, was directed merely against exaggerations and abuses. But the public took a different view. Thirty years later, when all those who had been in office at the time were long since dead or in retirement, Professor Rade could still publicly tax the Supreme Ecclesiastical Council with vacillation and submissiveness to the State—the nineties had proved it! An administration must act with great care and deliberation, otherwise it is taken to task two generations later.

In the Supreme Ecclesiastical Council I assumed the portfolio held by Professor Kaftan, who had now become vice-president. It consisted of university matters, school matters, and "I" matters. The last named were the *Irrensachen*—"crazy things"—communications from more or less eccentric persons such as every office receives daily. For these I alone had the final power of disposition. At first I would write on these letters: "Wastebasket!" But then there appeared in my office the senior clerk who had been assigned to me—or I to him, according to the point of view—and very solemnly drew my attention to the fact that the wastebasket was not an officially recognized repository; I should write: "File." I had learned something again.

Understandably enough, Professor Kaftan would not give up the university matters. They concerned his colleagues. I remember only one occasion when, upon the decision of the Board, I was entrusted with a fairly important assignment in this sphere. The Greifswald faculty had proposed Pastor Elert, then director of the Old Lutheran Preachers' Seminary at Breslau, for a professorship. The Supreme Ecclesiastical Council feared that under Elert's influence Greifswald would become a stronghold of extreme Lutheranism, especially as it appeared doubtful whether Elert would even ally himself with the United Church to which Griefswald belonged. So it was making use of its right of veto. And I had to settle this in person. My conversation with the Minister of Culture was not pleasant but it was successful. The appointment was not made. Elert later came to Erlangen, to the Lutheran Church of Bavaria, which was surely the right solution.

By contrast, the school question kept me very busy indeed. The church's task in the matter could be either enlarged or minimized. I decided to enlarge it.

What purpose was there in fighting for the confessional school if the men were lacking—avowed Evangelicals—who could in good conscience be placed at the head of such schools? What purpose was there in the church concerning itself with the public school system if a purely secular attitude prevailed throughout the teaching body, if the handful of loyal Evangelical teachers were intellectually no match for those represented by the All-German Teachers' Association, and if the top posts in the school system fell to teachers who, for political reasons and also on grounds of competence, were indifferent, not to say hostile, to the church?

It was obvious that the Evangelical Church was in a position similar to that in which the Catholic Church had found itself thirty years before. Intellectually it had fallen behind, if one were to judge by its rank and file. The Catholic church had got the better of this situation by decades of tenacious, purposeful work, and was now beginning to harvest the fruits of its cultural policy. It was time for the Evangelical Church to embark on a similar process.

My idea was that gifted, avowedly Evangelical teachers should be assisted by the church government so that they might graduate from universities and embark on a teaching career with the prospect of obtaining supervisory posts. But above all I wanted to prevail on young theologians to graduate in pedagogy and then, if they were qualified, to aim at a professorship, so that an Evangelical pedagogy, an Evangelical way of life, might be brought to bear on the academic world. For it was this, precisely, that was lacking in the universities—outside the theological faculty, of course. When my brother Wilhelm took his English class on a Sunday outing and happened to stop in at church with his students, it was a unique occurence. The norm in the academic world was arrogant indifference to the church and to what it preached. The war and the collapse had not affected that attitude at all. I believed that this was a challenge to the church, and that it must try to effect a change, so far as that was humanly possible.

I founded an institute for religious pedagogy. And the Supreme Ecclesiastical Council (to its honor, be it said) showed understanding for my plans. With the 25,000 marks it allocated to me nothing very sensational could be done. But I was able to secure rooms, furnish a library, and set a small number of men to work each year, both elementary teachers and theologians.

When the German-Christians penetrated the Supreme Ecclesiastical Council, one of their first moves was to abolish the institute of religious pedagogy.

It became increasingly clear to me that it was not right that the church should be directed by a group of functionaries. According to our new constitution, the principal direction was no longer to rest simply with the ecclesiastical government. A church senate had been created, to which the Supreme Ecclesiastical Council was to send only a few of its members and the provinces each a superintendent-general. But who were the other members of this senate? At its head was Dr. Winckler, former district president and chairman of the German National group in the House of Representatives. Then there was von Berg, former Lord Lieutenant of East Prussia; Count Seidlitz-Sondreczki of Silesia; von Gersdorff, a former administrative district president; Preiser, chairman of the Senate; von Krosigk, general provincial director. There was only one representative of labor, Labor Secretary Hartwig. They were for the most part intelligent and educated persons. But a group so composed, and meeting only every other month, could not provide any stimulation. The direction still rested with the Supreme Ecclesiastical Council.

But here, absorbed in the painstaking routine of administration, one more or less by-passed the crucial problems facing the church. In four years, never once did I hear a meeting of the Supreme Ecclesiastical Council discuss the labor question, though this question must inevitably have been of decisive importance for the present and future of the church in so highly industrialized a country as ours. And again, no notice was taken of the theological trends of the time, though this was almost understandable in a group so predominately juridical in character.

I had already come across all types of ecclesiasticism abroad. Nowhere, however, had I found church administrations such as ours. As a result of the centuries-old association of Church and

State, jurisprudence had taken on an importance in Germany that was unparalleled in any other country. Must everything of validity really be legislated into being? Must everything be set down in legal provisions? Must everything that was to carry weight with people be backed by an anonymous administration, rather than by men of flesh and blood? Could nothing be official unless a church administration had laid down that it was?

The famous thesis propounded by Sohm, the canonist, that law was in contradiction to the Gospel, was still exercising many minds. Only in Germany could such a thesis have been propounded and discussed. Other churches had no experience of any such primacy of jurisprudence. And it was important to realize that this preoccupation with law did not belong to the essence of an Evangelical church; it was a German trait. We had to consider very earnestly whether we would not have to get away from it if we were to build a road for the Gospel into the future.

When I became Superintendent-General of the Kurmark in 1925, I entered a subordinate church administration and an exceptionally inadequate one—the Berlin Consistory. When a church councilor in some other consistory proved incompetent, he was transferred to Berlin. A large administration, so it was argued, could best absorb him. But if anyone in the Berlin Consistory happened to be above average, he soon became known to the Supreme Ecclesiastical Council, which was also located in Berlin, and taken over by it.

I took part only in the meetings; I did not concern myself with the internal administration. I did not wish to trespass on the jurists' preserves. Even during the years when I held the chairmanship, I left the daily business to the presiding councilor responsible for legal affairs. At first that created quite a sensation. Later it came to be taken for granted.

My only concern was to prevent the administration from becoming increasingly inflated as a result of progressive centralization.

Centralization, that universal phenomenon of our times, is a very curious thing. The person who advocates it is, in fact, always right. Tax matters *are* handled more smoothly and efficiently by a central agency than by the individual parishes, which often lack both the necessary knowledge and the necessary ability. Building operations, too, are usually more satisfactory if they are supervised by a central planning office than if they are undertaken by individual master masons of small towns. Decisions on the validity of elections are more unified and better founded when they are made by the central administrative board rather than by some district authority. And whenever someone in the Supreme Ecclesiastical Council shows annoyance at some action of a consistory, some other member can always say: "But naturally! This kind of thing cannot be left to a consistory! The central agency must take it over!"

Thus whoever favored centralization was always right. The only trouble is that as a result of overcentralization the congregations must eventually lose all sense of responsibility and all satisfaction in their work, and pastor and parish councils will finally regard themselves simply as the executive organs of superior authorities.

And that, for a church organism, is a sickness unto death. The church is not a business where a board of directors makes the decisions and stockholders are satisfied with those decisions if the dividends do not decline. The strength of the church depends on the individual congregations, on the faith and love which reign in the services, the instruction, the pastoral action. The church leadership can co-ordinate, it can give incentives, it can give assistance, but it cannot create life. A congregation can live without a consistory, but a consistory cannot live without congregations.

Hence everything depends on strengthening the sense of responsibility of the congregations. The church administration should, of course, say to itself, whenever new tasks and new needs become apparent, that this is a matter of concern to the church as a whole. The congregation must know that it must take responsibility in the matter. But it will do so only if it is always, and as a matter of principle, given as much responsibility as possible, if it is given the material and spiritual opportunities for autonomous action. Inevitably mistakes will be made in the process, and sometimes very irritating mistakes. But the strengthening of the sense of responsibility offsets a thousand such mistakes.

Consequently, I have encouraged decentralization, in all circumstances, and in all areas. And the more decentralization there is, the smaller will be the apparatus of administration. Of course, this must not be exaggerated either. The tremendous differentiation of our whole life also makes a certain broadening of the administrative apparatus indispensable. But before a new office is set up in an administration, it must be shown that the work cannot be simplified by referring some of it to the subordinate—in reality the superior—organs.

That was my fundamental principle, to which I have adhered to this day.

It was at that time that I wrote my book *Das Jahrhundert der Kirche* ("The Century of the Church"). The general public did not take any notice of it. In Germany the public never takes any notice of a book whose title contains the word "church." But the theological world was concerned with it. In a short time it had gone through six editions. Henceforward my church was to think of me in terms of the views I expressed in that book.

My purpose was to show that in the space of three hundred years Protestantism in Germany had not become a church, in the proper acceptance of the term, but had remained a department for ecclesiastical affairs within the secular government. Only since the middle of the nineteenth century had something like a "church" developed on Evangelical foundations. This new state of affairs must be accepted with joy at a time when the era of individualism was drawing to a close and social thinking was making mighty strides forward. A genuine church required freedom from the State; it required a real episcopal office, a definite social purpose, and many other things.

Today, thirty-five years later, I would not write such a book in so sanguine a manner. But in substance I would not say anything different from what I said then, not in the smallest particular.

It daily became more apparent that things really were developing as I had foreseen. What a difference from the days of my youth, when the center of interest was the "religious personality," whereas today it is the church and its attitude to this or that problem which newspapers and radio are always referring to.

To have seen this in 1924, when I was writing the book, would perhaps have required some small experience of ecumenical thinking, and of such experience there was not a trace in German theology at the time. The book was regarded as an arrogant trumpet call for a new Germany in which Evangelical bishops, crozier in hand, would govern the life of the community. Karl Barth poured the vials of his scorn on the "violet age"—the book had a violet cover—which was about to dawn. And all who were opposed to Evangelical bishops, especially the Reformed, applauded him enthusiastically.

I did not let this worry me. Books which arouse no opposition are not worth writing.

Niemöller once reproached me, twenty-five years later, with never having been a man of the Confessing church but only a man of the church. But what else should I want to be than a "man of the church"?

The book was written with my heart's blood—the same heart's blood that later went into my little *Bericht von Jesus von Nazareth* ("Note on Jesus of Nazareth").

SUPERINTENDENT-GENERAL

THAT DECEMBER DAY in Munich in 1924 was one of the happiest in my life. I was on my way home from Merano where I had been recuperating after a bout of typhoid, and I felt rested and well. My wife, who had contracted a bad case of phlebitis as a result of the devoted care she had lavished on me, had now recovered too. And just then a telegram reached me from Berlin informing me that the Church Senate had appointed me Superintendent-General of the Kurmark.

Oh, yes, I was happy. Not that I had been hankering after what constituted the episcopal office of my church; I had never sought to be "a personage." But it was a liberation from a situation which had become simply intolerable. For four years, my daily schedule had been as follows: From 8 to 9 A.M., work with my secretary. Then consultations, for which the two hours till 11 o'clock never sufficed. Then two hours of confirmation instruction. After lunch, official functions at the cemetery and in church. From 4 to 7 P.M., other obligations permitting, visits to parishioners. At 8 P.M., evening activities such as Bible classes, youth groups, preparation for the children's service, parish evenings, and so on. At 10:30 or 11 P.M. I would finally get to my desk to prepare my sermons or addresses, and to do whatever writing there was to be done. At midnight the assistant pastor would telephone me to discuss the schedule for the following day; this was the only time he could be certain of reaching me. At 1 A.M., and often later, I would retire to bed.

On Wednesdays and Saturdays, when I had no classes, I spent the whole day at the Supreme Ecclesiastical Council, partly at meetings, partly attending to my paper work. Sunday was the hardest day of all.

This was my schedule, year in, year out, without a break except for a none-too-long summer vacation. For some time, I had realized that I would not be able to keep up this pace much longer, either physically or mentally. I had promised in my ordination oath "to devote the powers of body and soul to the sacred ministry," and I took my promise very seriously. But that surely did not mean that at the age of forty-four one should be physically and mentally exhausted. Now an alternative had been offered.

My work in the Supreme Ecclesiastical Council, although important, had become increasingly burdensome to me. The school portfolio, which prior to 1918 had been without special significance, now demanded full attention and long-range planning. I could console myself with the knowledge that my work in this sphere had not been altogether fruitless. But what work it had been! Every little thing one set down in writing had to go to a legal assistant referee, from him to the vice-president and in certain circumstances to the president. Every important suggestion had to be discussed by the board. Everyone raised objections; in administrations there are always objections. And what eventually emerged from all this was often nothing at all or something altogether different from the original proposal.

I realized that it could not be otherwise, at least not in existing circumstances. The trouble was that I was not made for this kind of work—I liked to be independent. I did not want to draft papers but to go out to people. I did not want to act indirectly but directly

114

and immediately. As a member of the Supreme Ecclesiastical Council this was not possible. In the office of superintendent-general it would be possible.

My "greeting" took place at my beloved church of Heilsbronnen, where I was to continue to preach. Professor Kaftan, now theological vice-president of the Supreme Ecclesiastical Council, officiated. Solemnity was deliberately eschewed. Anything savoring of episcopal consecration brought deep misgivings. There was no blessing, no laying on of hands, no presentation of the pectoral cross—nothing. It was really a very sober occasion.

The elderly president of the Berlin Consistory, Dr. Steinhausen, almost fell off his chair when I informed him that I would come to the Consistory only twice a week and, for the rest, attend to my duties from home, free from any administrative routine. I would set up my own office at home. A house was soon rented for the purpose. Then I called together my forty-five superintendents and told them that I did not want to be bishop of an *ecclesia invisibilis* but of an *ecclesia visibilis*. I wanted to visit my congregations. For this I needed a car. I did not want to ask the Supreme Ecclesiastical Council for it; I wanted to be independent. They, the superintendents, should raise the funds from their church districts. They did so at once.

Between Easter and Pentecost I toured my diocese in my own car, a procedure unheard of in 1925. Every day I visited a different church district, talked to the congregation, to the pastor, to the patrons and the parish councilors. No pastor and no parish councilor would be able to say that they had never so much as laid eyes on their Superintendent-General.

The following experience shows how extraordinary all this seemed at the time. I had ordered that at these pastoral conferences one pastor should make a report which would be the starting point for a discussion. The further I went the worse the reports became. Finally I had it out with one of the superintendents. He

115

admitted, very shamefacedly, that none of the superintendents had believed that I would keep the visitations up for six or seven weeks; they had all expected me to stop halfway through. Consequently they had made no preparations for the second half of my circuit.

By Pentecost, all the contacts had been made. Now I had to see just what the work entailed.

The Kurmark was the administrative district of Potsdam, covering the area around Berlin. Big cities had never been able to grow up close to Berlin. Potsdam and Brandenburg, with their populations of 80,000 to 90,000, were the largest. The Kurmark was an agricultural diocese, dominated, for the most part, by the big estates of the old landed families which for centuries had maintained the most intimate ties with the House of Hohenzollern. In the most literal sense, they had been lords of the land. And now that the monarchy had been abolished, they regarded themselves as the guardians of the monarchical tradition. In particular, they regarded themselves as the tacit masters of their Evangelical Church, at least within their territorial jurisdiction.

They exercised their patronage, some with reluctance and in niggardly fashion, many with earnestness, piety, and devotion. Their forefathers had built the churches; they kept them in repair and from time to time built new chapels. They were concerned that prayers be offered for the patron at every service. No pastor or schoolteacher who fell out with his patron could keep his post. As for the superintendent-general, he was treated with all courtesy, of course, but he too was expected to conform to the wishes of the patrons and to take their part in any disputes. My predecessor, Dr. Axenfeld, an intelligent and zealous man, had permanently forfeited the patrons' friendship and esteem when he referred publicly to the great financial losses incurred by the church when the nobility took advantage of a complaisant legislation to appropriate church property which should have been theirs by hereditary tenure only.

116

It was clear to me from the start that I could not be a subservient tool of the patrons. The heart of the superintendent-general must belong to the pastors and the congregations; the patrons would be included only so far as they were active members of their congregations. When I had to spend the night away from home, I wanted to stay at the parsonage and not at the patron's castle. And wherever there was a dispute, the pastors must know that the Superintendent-General would stand by them to the fullest extent of his powers.

Politically speaking, I felt attuned to these aristocratic circles, and I had always honestly recognized what they had signified for the state of Prussia throughout the centuries. But the church, in which I was about to carry out the office of a bishop, must not become an auxiliary of the German National party, but must preach the Gospel of Jesus Christ. Its duty was not to foster the past but firmly to seek out the roads which a new age must travel.

It was increasingly necessary to find those new roads. With the revolution of 1918, the agricultural worker had dropped out of the church. The profession of the teacher devoted to the church was doomed to extinction. The new district presidents, with few exceptions, cared little for the church. Opposition—or at least indifference towards the church—was everywhere. The old patriarchal methods used by my predecessors, Kogel, Dryander and others, to carry out their functions simply did not work any more. New methods had to be devised.

With such views, it is understandable that I was not inwardly attuned to the world of the patrons. And I fell out with most of them after I had forbidden one of the Uckermark pastors to speak at political gatherings; he was a good speaker, and was constantly being used by the German National party, but spiritually he was going to pieces. Even Count Arnim-Boitzenburg, whom I esteemed most highly as a knight *sans peur et sans reproche,* now became hostile to me. As for the ladies, I incurred their displeasure when I showed that the Evangelical women's guilds which served

117

the parishes were more important to me as superintendent-general than the patriotic women's club which from its foundation was directed to wholly different ends.

The conflict came to a dramatic head seven years later, shortly before the National Socialist seizure of power. Pastor Wilm, whose especial function at the time was to work with the youth of the province and who also acted in liaison with the national youth associations, had persuaded me to have a frank discussion with the representatives of those associations. In order that the confrontation should not have too personal a character, my colleague of Neumark and Niederlausitz, Dr. Vits, was also invited. But in reality it all turned on me.

I faced them in the little reception room in the Hotel Prinz Albrecht: the Stahlhelm (steel helmet) leaders, the representatives of the Arnims and the rest of the patrons, and the Nazis, headed by Prince August Wilhelm. I said a few words about the fundamental position of the church. Then the attacks began to rain down on me: I was betraying the national will of Germany; I was siding with the Social Democrats; I had no understanding of the nationalist upsurge of youth; I was isolating the church; I had nothing of the fighting spirit of Jesus and Martin Luther. One of the Stahlhelm leaders called out rhetorically: "To me the most sacred words in the Bible are these, 'I have not come to bring peace, but a sword.'"

I stood there like St. Sebastian, pierced by arrows from every side. Not one of those present had a word to say in my defense. It was no good my asking the Stahlhelm leader to read over the tenth chapter of St. Matthew to see how these words of Jesus were intended. It was no good my pointing out repeatedly that political and national questions were only very indirectly related to my office, if at all; that my immediate duty was to see to it that no one was restrained from free access to the Gospel of Jesus Christ by reason of his political opinions. I added that no church which took

118

Romans 13 seriously could refuse obedience to a State headed by a man like Hindenburg. The mention of Hindenburg was greeted with loud guffaws.

No understanding was possible, and we parted unreconciled. The great struggle against the church was to break upon us all before the chairman of the patrons' association, von Arnim-Kröchlendorff, could publicly declare, much later, that they had misjudged me.

My concern was not for rural congregations alone. In the neighborhood of Berlin, at Brandenburg on the Havel, at Wittenberg, Luckenwald, Eberswald, lived hundreds of thousands of workers' families for whom I also bore responsibility. And to carry out this responsibility properly was endlessly difficult.

This, then, was my Kurmark. What could be done here to make a new religious start?

Little could be done from above; spiritual strength in the Evangelical Church grows only in the soil of the congregation. And the Superintendent-General cannot live in such permanent contact with six hundred and fifty pastors and their congregations as to produce any effect. He can make suggestions and encourage certain courses of action. He can try here and there to give assistance, to set an example. For everything else he must implore God's grace.

If the old aphorism that one time is no time applies anywhere, it is in the church. I realized that special events which had taken place once and were not followed up could achieve very little. My predecessors had renewed the practice of the general visitation, which had existed in the first half of the nineteenth century and then fallen into disuse. Occasionally in the parishes I heard of something Kogel had said, some subject on which he had preached. But all in all no lasting fruit had come of the fact that a commission of more or less distinguished gentlemen had come into each parish for one day and had spoken with the fathers of families, with the school children, the pastor, and the teacher. Single experiences, however exciting, remain without effect. Only something that is repeated becomes imprinted in the mind, and formative.

For this reason I dropped the general visitations and tried missions instead, which were to be conducted in each congregation of a church district for at least a week. It was not hard to elicit the support of pastors and missionaries. On one day in the course of a mission week I myself would preach, and visit the schools wherever possible. Probably nothing much was achieved by this. But occasionally, as a result of such a general mission, some activity would develop in the parishes—a Bible class or a women's guild, for example.

And then there was the Kurmark church rally. This was something new. Every year on Exaudi Sunday (the Sunday before Pentecost) I preached in the Garnisonkirche at Potsdam and afterward spoke to the youth. In the evening a big church concert under the direction of Pastor Kempff took place. On Monday I officiated at a morning service in the Friedenskirche and a public gathering in the Konzerthaus, the biggest hall in Potsdam. Here I would report on the preceding year and issue a general directive for the work of the next twelve months. In the afternoon the wives of the pastors met, and individual church organizations held separate meetings.

The purpose of all this was to arouse a sense of independence in the church. In the old days, when State and Church were still far too closely linked, such a thing could never have developed. Perhaps it was not even necessary. Now, however, it was very necessary. I felt more and more that it was my function in life to encourage it. We did not altogether fail in our goal. The church rallies soon became popular affairs, and attendance was limited only by the facilities available. The overcrowded Garnisonkirche, with the youth pennants around the bedecked altar, always afforded a beautiful sight, and the meetings on Monday were packed to danger point.

Potsdam, of course, contributed the main contingent of visitors.

The Crown Princess came to the services and sometimes to the principal meeting, although when I said something unacceptable her entourage would urge her to stay away. I did not invite government or municipal representatives; I wanted to be together with the pastors and their congregations. The authorities could come if they wanted to take part as members of congregations. Most of the diocesan pastors were always present—a noteworthy participation considering the distances involved. And those of the patrons and parish councilors who had any feeling for the church also came. People looked forward to the Potsdam church rally from one year to the next. And their joy filled all the events of the rally from start to finish.

Of course this general satisfaction did not obscure for me the numerical insignificance of a gathering once a year of 3,000 adults and 2,000 young people in a city of 80,000 to 90,000 inhabitants—with many of those attending coming from outside the city. Nevertheless, the annual church rallies did give rise to a strong nucleus of devoted parish workers who did not ignore the goals I set for the following year.

I would always point up these goals by circular letters addressed to all the pastors at intervals of about three months. In these letters I also discussed other questions, secular and religious, which concerned us.

This, then, was my organizational contribution to the renewal of the church. The superintendent-general, however, has to operate not only organizationally but also, in the proper sense of the term, spiritually.

The first thing to be done, therefore, was to have pastoral talks with the clergy. On this point let me say that the old adage that the superintendent-general is the *pastor pastorum* does not touch the heart of this office. It is the superintendent who is the *pastor pastorum*. He is the one who knows the parsonages of his church district. He notices when one of his pastors is upset about something.

He quickly finds out if there are any domestic dissensions. He knows when pastor and congregation are in any way at odds.

The superintendent-general, however, learns of such things belatedly, accidentally. He can only be a refuge when the superintendent is at a loss, or when the pastor does not wish to confide in his superintendent—which happens none too seldom.

"welfare" was very much to the fore in Germany. It was so much

My desire was that the pastors should have confidence in their superintendent-general. They must know that if they had been unjustly attacked, their superintendent-general would stand by them. Perhaps I sometimes went too far in my readiness to defend them. Sometimes it recoiled on me. The worst such instance was at Königshorst, not far from Potsdam, in the marshes of the Havel. Years before, someone had been shot in the parsonage. A rumor sprang up, and was seized upon by the press, that the pastor—or rather, the deacon who officiated as pastor—was the murderer. I knew the man, and I had always had a good impression of him. The following Sunday I was in the parish. I stepped before the altar and declared my confidence in the man. The press published that too. But a day or two later it came out that this same deacon had assaulted a young servant girl. The murder case itself remained unsolved. The whole anticlerical press of Berlin and the vicinity raised a hue and cry lasting for days against the superintendent-general who had interfered in a pending action and who wanted even unworthy clergymen to be shielded from justice. My Consistory disavowed me, naturally! I took it as a lesson, but I did not give up my principle of standing by the pastors of my diocese until such time as they were actually proved to be at fault.

This was not without its effect on the clergy. Years later, after the Second World War, when I was to speak before the clergy of another territorial church and the bishop who was my host began his introductory remarks to his pastors with the word "Gentlemen," I could tell myself that we in our Kurmark had had a more fraternal relationship.

122

Heinrich von der Becke

Bishop Otto Dibelius

Preaching in St. Mary's, East Berlin, the oldest church in the city.

The ruins of the Kaiser Wilhelm Memorial Church, Berlin.

Klaus Kindermann

At a meeting of the World Council of Churches in Vienna. Bishop
Dibelius, with Dr. Franklin Clark Fry, President of the Lutheran
Church in America, and Pastor Niemöller.

Planning postwar relief. Left to right: Dr. Roswell Barnes, Executive
Secretary in America of the World Council of Churches; Bishop
Dibelius; Dr. Paul C. Empie, Executive Director of the National
Lutheran Council; and Dr. Eugen Gerstenmaier, President of the
West German Bundestag, who is a Lutheran pastor and headed
Hilfswerk, the German relief agency, after World War II.

National Lutheran Council Photo (Hilfswerk-Weitmann)

At the White House. Dr. Fry, President Eisenhower, Bishop Dibelius.

Bishop Dibelius with Archbishop Iakovos, the Greek Orthodox Primate of North and South America and President of the World Council of Churches since 1961.

Bishop Dibelius, with Bishop Henry Knox Sherrill, of New York, and Dr. R. D. Paul, Church of South India.

Günther Metzner

The Kirchentag (Berlin, 1961)

Bishop Otto Dibelius

A church which glories in the name of Jesus Christ must give evidence of its faith in deeds of love. That, for me, was an immutable principle.

The State had begun to concern itself increasingly with the needs of the population. Since the revolution of 1918 the word emphasized, in fact, that my predecessor, Dr. Axenfeld, like other superintendent-generals, had allowed himself to be persuaded to set up an Evangelical welfare service in addition to the "Inner Mission," which sounded too old-fashioned and pietistic for the new age. The chairmanship of this welfare service fell to me by reason of my office, as well as the chairmanship of the Inner Mission of the province.

I regarded the welfare service as a secularization of our Christian aims. We could confidently leave welfare questions to the State. Our concern was with service to the needy, and withal a service to the needs of body and soul. So I reorganized the executive of the welfare service so that it was identical with the executive of the Inner Mission, and gradually ceased to use the secular title. It disappeared unnoticed.

For the work of the Inner Mission I soon found the right man in Dr. Wenzel. Anointed with a drop of pietistic oil, as our forefathers used to say, he soon gained the trust of pastors and parishes. He gathered a good number of zealous pastors with whom he did missionary work among the masses, particularly in church districts, such as those around Berlin, where fruitful contact had not been established between church and population. He founded a large number of old-age homes in the province. Such homes were urgently needed. The housing shortage after the First World War was appalling. The fortunes which would formerly have sufficed to ensure an independent old age, free from financial worry, were a thing of the past. Since the circumstances of the Kurmark did not permit old-age homes to be put up by the church districts, a central agency had to intervene. And since this central agency received a modest maintenance contribution from every new

123

home, it gradually became possible to undertake still other costly charitable works. All this was in such excellent hands with Dr. Wenzel that I did not have to concern myself with any of the details.

The Kurmark was a large diocese and required all my attention. I was not satisfied with traveling to the various parishes only on special occasions. Whenever I had a free Sunday, I would get into my car and drive to some church a couple of hours' distance away. In this way I would see the regular religious life of the congregation and hear the pastor preach as he preached on ordinary Sundays. Some were embarrassed when they saw me sitting in the church. Others remained unperturbed. I remember one Cantate Sunday (the fourth Sunday after Easter) when I drove with my wife and two children to a village near Potsdam. I was unaware that a big mission celebration had been held the week before, in which the whole village had taken part. Consequently on this Sunday the congregation consisted of ourselves, the pastor's wife, the sacristan and a couple of women. When I went forward to greet the pastor and his wife after the service, they came to me beaming: "How nice that you should have come just today and helped us sing; now it was a beautiful Cantate service after all!"

I decided to move into my diocese, that is to Potsdam. But it was hard to find a house suitable for a bishop's residence. And however attached I was to the Kurmark, I could not disguise from myself that its significance for the whole life of our church was small. It had no university, no preachers' seminary. Whatever it produced that was above average—pastors, doctors, teachers, lawyers, politicians—all were absorbed in the big cities, Berlin especially. The important decisions were not made in the Kurmark; and so much depended on those decisions, for the individual diocese too. Even had I moved to Potsdam, I would not have been able to by-pass Berlin.

124

Potsdam itself was a city to steal one's heart. The two slim towers of Garnison and Heiliggeist, flanking the lovely cupola of St. Nikolai, and finally the castle, the baroque buildings facing it, Sanssouci with its great park, the marble palace and all the rest —these were a sight to rejoice both eye and soul. I have not often wept in my life, but when I saw Potsdam again in 1945, with all this lying in ruins, my tears overwhelmed me.

But Potsdam was unthinkable without Berlin. And in Berlin I had to take care not to encroach on the prerogatives of my colleagues. Under the new church constitution, however, a superintendent-general always presided over the Consistory. If there were several superintendents-general in one province, as there were in ours, the presidency was to change hands every two years. And the man who held the presidency had a voice in Berlin affairs too.

At least one trace remains of my own tenure of office—the Martin Luther Hospital.

At the time, a scandalous situation prevailed in regard to religious ministrations in many of the public hospitals in Berlin which were controlled by Social Democrats and Communists. No Christian service could be held, either at Christmas or at any other time, if one patient in a large ward objected. If a patient requested Holy Communion, the only place he could receive it in privacy was the bathroom. Fresh complaints came in every day.

As president of the Consistory I persuaded the appropriate superintendent-general, Haendler, that we ought to waste no more time and effort on futile complaints, but that we must take remedial action. We should build a big Evangelical hospital in the west end of Berlin. If, as was to be expected, this hospital showed a profit, such funds would be used to build a second hospital in the east end, where no profit was possible.

We had no money at all. The Evangelical Church, apart from negligible collections, depends on the church taxes of its members, and these it does not—and in general, may not—make available for such purposes. But my plan was successful. A brilliant architect,

125

Kopp, designed the building for us—a model of functional design. It cost 4.5 million marks. Had the city of Berlin built it, it would have cost two and a half times as much. Pastor Siegert, whom I had summoned from Fraustadt, took charge of the organizational work. The Evangelical nursing association provided an excellent Matron, Lingner, and a splendid nursing staff.

Nothing came of the profit, however. For hardly had we started to build than the terrible economic crisis of 1930-31 set in. Big banks failed, industrial enterprises declared themselves bankrupt, fortunes were lost. We could be glad that the hospital was completed and put into operation on time. But it definitely did not become a "gold mine," regardless of the outstanding reputation of the chief physicians, Munck and Nordmann. The east end hospital was never built.

What was known as the Dewaheim affair occurred at this time, a consequence of the general economic collapse. The central committee of the Inner Mission, as was its duty, had undertaken the building of settlements to help meet the housing shortage. The Dewaheim, which it had founded, was a thoroughly sound enterprise, even if certain difficulties had to be expected from the outset. Building costs at the time were abnormally high. Loans could be obtained only at very high interest rates. Such contingencies were bound to be handicaps in time of crisis, and better precautions should have been taken at the start. But there was no question of the kind of irresponsibility which marked the operations of so many other building societies which were shooting up like mushrooms.

What happened was that the central committee fell under the spell of a man who claimed that it was the church's duty to help "break the thralldom of interest"—a slogan carried over from National Socialist propaganda. This man, Herr Jeppel, had devised a system whereby one paid a certain amount into a fund and in return could obtain a far larger loan at low interest. He wanted to by-pass the banks and replace them by a savings fund. Whether

126

Jeppel himself believed in his system, I was never able to find out. But he was certainly able to arouse the enthusiasm of all kinds of people. And in the central committee no one saw through the scheme. That was the most inexplicable part of the story. A banker's clerk of even average ability would have seen that this was a game with other people's money.

With the economic crisis, Jeppel's enterprise—called the "Deuzag"—collapsed. Those who had put their money in it lost all, for no real securities were behind it. The Evangelical central bank, which was connected with the Inner Mission, had to close down. A church building co-operative in the Rhineland declared itself bankrupt.

The administration of the Dewaheim lost both heart and head. At the first difficulties, it, too, declared bankruptcy. The decision was wrong. The houses which had been erected were standing and represented a much higher amount than could be obtained in bankruptcy proceedings. There had been no waste, no embezzlement, no irresponsible speculation. Even in the bankruptcy proceedings which, as always, ate up a great deal of money, those who gave up at once lost comparatively little. And those who waited patiently lost nothing to speak of beyond a few years' interest.

I had nothing to do with the whole affair. I did not belong to the central committee. But the thought that many thousands of people who had entrusted their money to a church institution were to lose it was unbearable to me. So I founded a committee of assistance to those who had suffered damages in the Dewaheim affair and persuaded the German territorial churches to raise a sum of six million marks which, had bankruptcy not been declared, would easily have sufficed to put the whole enterprise into smooth working order again.

As sometimes happens when one tries to help, I bore the full brunt of the Dewaheim group's fury: I had not raised enough money to indemnify every victim immediately and to the full. At a turbulent creditors' meeting under the chairmanship of Count Alvensleben of Saxony I had to swallow every kind of abuse. Some years later, when the affair was finally settled, Count Alvensleben made a public apology to me. He explained that psychologically speaking it had been impossible to do anything but open the sluices to the fury of the victims; now the time had come to thank me for jumping into the breach. I did not care about thanks; it was enough that I had been able to help reduce the effects of the disaster.

The central committee of the Inner Mission never really recovered from this affair. And the experience served to strengthen the organized church in its distrust of church-operated economic undertakings, a distrust which remains to this day.

While I was still at the Supreme Ecclesiastical Council, I was asked to write a weekly column for the *Berliner Sonntagsblatt,* which had a circulation of 100,000. In this column I was to inform the readers of what was going on in the world, but in such a way as to enable an Evangelical Christian to evaluate events and to form an opinion. I did so gladly. When I became superintendent-general, I wanted to hand over the job to someone else, for it had only an indirect connection with my specific sphere of responsibility. But when my intention was rumored, such a clamor arose on all sides that I finally gave in and continued my column to the end of my term as superintendent-general.

To this there was soon added a second duty of a similar but more exacting nature. Dr. Hinderer had come to an agreement with the Scherl-Verlag concerning the Berlin daily, *Der Tag.* Here I must interpolate a few remarks about Dr. Hinderer. Outwardly unremarkable, he was in fact enormously intelligent, energetic, and reliable, as Swabians so often are. He taught journalism at the university, and had created an Evangelical press service from scratch after the First World War. It was a comprehensive and altogether exemplary undertaking which he headed himself. It included press associations in the various territorial churches, a

128

national news service, Sunday papers, church papers, special literary projects, special departments for education, art, and other matters. No one knew how he financed it all. But a press needs freedom. When the Nazis came and freedom disappeared, Evangelical press work ground to a halt. Hinderer tried to weather the storm. His papers grew more colorless, more boring. Finally Goebbels put a stop to everything.

Hinderer died in obscurity. Posterity bestows no wreaths on the men of the press—not even the church press. Hinderer, then, had made an agreement with the Scherl-Verlag; *Der Tag* was to become an out-and-out Evangelical paper; in return, the press association would promote it throughout the Evangelical world.

The project did not materialize. An Evangelical daily needs avowed Evangelicals as editors. And of such there were none in Germany around 1925, not even in the Scherl-Verlag. Readers were constantly complaining of offensive advertisements and articles. Then Hinderer and I went to see the Director-General of the Scherl-Verlag, Klitzsch, and I suggested the following: Either the publisher should place a specific number of lines each week at the disposal of the church for articles to appear as editorials, without by-lines, as in the British press, or there should be a regular Evangelical commentary on current events every Sunday under the heading, say, of "Sunday Mirror." Klitzsch and the chief editor immediately chose the latter, but on condition that I write the column myself. I did not want the project to fall through, so I agreed.

The paper in which I wrote supported the German National party. My column could not have appeared anywhere else at the time. But I carefully refrained from any reference to the action of the political parties during those years, however apparent it might be that Germany's very fate hinged on political action. Consequently I never took a stand on the menacing growth of National Socialism. Only once did I write against Adolf Hitler. That was when he sent a telegram expressing his support of the National Socialists, who had brutally murdered a Communist innkeeper,

Potempa. Here the Christian conscience had to speak up. Murder is murder! I made that abundantly clear. The National Socialists made a note of it, as was to become apparent later. But they never dared refer to it again publicly.

Thus I had two weekly columns to write. This was no small burden. Whether I was working or on vacation, whether I was abroad or attending week-long meetings, the articles always had to reach the editor's desk on time. This very regularity seemed to make this work a service to the church.

I would gladly have done more. I proposed to my fellow super-intendents-general that we should form a working group and publish a series of books together in which we would take a stand on important moral, political, social, and religious questions. What I had in mind was an independent spiritual leadership in our church which would not commit anyone or infringe on the authority of other ecclesiastical bodies. They agreed with me, but in the execution of the plan they left me alone. The time for this kind of thing was not yet ripe.

What resulted was my own book, *Friede auf Erden* ("Peace on Earth"). Here I tried to show, first, that there had been many different kinds of war throughout history, and that Luther's book *Ob Kriegsleute auch im seligen Stande sein können* ("Whether Soldiers, Too, Can Be Saved) presupposed a wholly different kind of war from those of the twentieth century. I said that the Christian's duty to his country included the bearing of arms in defense against aggression. Nevertheless, if a man refused military service on grounds of his Christian conscience, the State must respect such refusal. And the church must profess its fraternal solidarity with these fellow Christians, even if it could not share their views.

In saying this I was stirring up a hornet's nest. Neither my clerical nor my political friends supported me. When the National Socialists came to power the book was not publicly banned but it could no longer be bought or reprinted.

Twenty-five years later I was to witness, not without emotion,

130

how an all-German synod at Berlin-Weissensee proclaimed my argument as the unanimous will of Evangelical Christianity in Germany.

For the rest I stuck to my position that as superintendent-general I had no business to engage in party politics. I was repeatedly asked to canvass for a seat in the Reichstag, not only by the German National party but also, later, by the Christian Socialists, who wanted to put me up as principal candidate for Berlin. I always refused.

But I was and remained a member of the German National party. I did not share the view of many of my colleagues that an Evangelical pastor, particularly when he occupied a prominent position, should not belong to any political party. I was convinced that the pastor, too, was a citizen and had to fulfil his civic duties. In a democratic form of government the fulfilment of these duties involves action through parties. But such parties—as I believed then, and as I still believe today—must have a nucleus of members on whom they can count. A party which always has to fear that the voters will desert it will not have the courage to take occasional unpopular decisions. Consequently I always remained loyal to the party on which I had once decided, even when it followed policies which I could not endorse.

That was the case, for instance, with the German National party under the Hugenberg regime. I did not attend political meetings and wrote no partisan political articles. But I paid my dues, to the extent that they were requested. There was no regular assessment. The "bourgeois" parties found it far too laborious a task to mobilize their followers in the manner practised so successfully by the Socialists and the National Socialists. They expected to swing the elections with the capital of their friends in industry. That was and remained their weakness.

Inevitably, in the exercise of my functions, I had frequent occasion to meet persons in the public view, from Hindenburg to Albert Schweitzer. But I had no conversation with them worth recording. Only with Stresemann did I once have an encounter which might be noted here.

It was in Geneva, where I had gone because I wanted the League of Nations to do something for our Evangelical brethren in Poland. I was unaware that on that particular day a meeting of the League Council was being held under the presidency of Stresemann. After a long and arduous day's work, Stresemann came to a dinner given by the German Consul-General, Aschmann. When he saw me he came up to me and said in his vivacious manner: "You can think what you like of me. But one thing you must concede, that my career has given me a sense of what a people's psychology will take and what it will not. And I tell you: the Evangelical Church will never be popular so long as its highest spiritual office retains the unspeakable title of 'superintendent-general.' You should say 'bishop'!" I could only answer that this was precisely what I thought too.

At table I sat opposite Stresemann. It was a heavy meal, as was customary among diplomats. One wine after another was offered. Stresemann set the glasses before him without touching them. He was nervous. Finally he got up and made a short after-dinner speech. Obviously relieved, he sat down again—and now proceeded to drink up one glass of wine after another. At midnight he took his leave, in order to prepare the next day's work with his staff.

I was surprised that a short after-dinner speech should have been of such anxiety to a man so accustomed to public speaking. But I was not surprised that Stresemann's health did not stand up to the strain of such a way of life.

Those were rich and also dark years which I spent in my office as Superintendent-General of the Kurmark. Politically the position in Germany was becoming daily more bewildering. The moral devastation wrought by war and revolution was bearing its fruit. The religious forces which might have stemmed the tide were not in evidence.

132

I had neither the time nor the opportunity to reflect much on politics as such. I had suffered the terrible collapse of 1918 in heart and soul. It was very hard for me to adapt myself to a new republican form of government.

I could tell myself only this, that the Evangelical Church was slowly beginning to awaken to a sense of independent responsibility for the moral life of the nation.

But before the awakening was complete, something quite different was to overwhelm both people and church.

ℛETIRED

I HAD NEVER had anything in common with the National Socialists. Their loud-mouthed propaganda and the provocative behavior of the SA people disgusted me. With Hitler's telegram to the National Socialist murderers of Beuthen, the movement was finished for me.

It was from the papers that I learned of their seizure of power on January 30, 1933, and of the torchlight procession through the Brandenburg Gate. That is how it is in Berlin; one learns from the papers of revolutions made in the city.

The news was disturbing. But the church was not immediately challenged. We had to await events. And between the seizure of power and the elections to the Reichstag in March was time enough to reflect on what the future might hold.

There were some apparently heartening omens. The signs of moral decadence which had been evident all over Germany toward the end of the Weimar Republic suddenly vanished. We were living on the Fichteberg in Steglitz, in a green oasis in the stony desert of the big city. My children had for a long time been afraid to go up the hill alone in the dark. Now, with one sweep, the streets were apparently safe.

The "night of the long knives," which the National Socialists had announced, did not come about. Sporadic news that Jews had been ill-treated came to our ears, but much too vaguely for one to do anything about it. The situation in the Reichstag had been so hopelessly confused that some change simply had to take place. If Adolf Hitler was not what we would have wished, at least he was an energetic man who would be able to cope with the Communists. The National Socialists did not, after all, have an absolute majority. Even at the new elections they did not get more than 45 per cent of the votes. So they would not be able to rule alone. They would have to take other views into account. And, finally, Hindenburg was still President of the Reich. The fact that a man now filled the chief executive office who would not permit himself to be as ignominiously treated by the Western Powers as other German chancellors had been in the previous fifteen years gave grounds for hope.

As against all this there was the general anti-Christian position of the party. The many fine speeches about the "positive Christianity" to which it was committed could not, in my eyes, obscure what lay behind them. Others were more credulous. My old pulpit at Heilsbronnen was now occupied by Professor Fendt, who assured the congregation that he had it on the best authority that Adolf Hitler always carried a copy of the New Testament in his pocket and that he read Bible verses and stanzas from a hymnal every morning. This kind of thing was quite generally believed at the time. The longing for some positive change in the government of the German State created its own myth.

When the newly elected Reichstag was about to meet, the news reached us that Adolf Hitler had decided that the opening should be at Potsdam, in the old Garnisonkirche, so closely connected with Prussian history during the preceding two hundred years. Frederick the Great's tomb was there, and that of his father, the soldier king.

Potsdam belonged to my diocese. And even if the old Garnisonkirche depended directly upon the Supreme Ecclesiastical Council, I still felt that the responsibility was mine. I was determined not to permit an opening of parliament in the church, for I believed we would have to reckon with a turbulent opening session. But quite apart from that, a parliamentary session simply did not belong in a church as a matter of principle. We could not know that by the day of the opening the Communist deputies would all be under lock and key, and that hardly any party would dare offer open opposition to the new dictator.

My opposition induced a hard struggle. The National Socialists did not understand how anyone could oppose the express will of the Führer. The mayor of Potsdam, who did not want his city to miss the great event, kept entreating me to waive my objection. In the end we agreed on a compromise. First there was to be a service—an Evangelical service in the Nikolaikirche and a Catholic one in the small local church. Then there was to be a State ceremony in the old Garnisonkirche, with addresses by the President and the new Chancellor in an ecclesiastical framework, followed by a parade of the Wehrmacht. And on the following day parliament was to be opened at the Kroll opera house in Berlin.

On March 21, Potsdam was swarming with people. We had a hard time getting our cars through the crowd. I stood on the great terraced steps in front of the Nikolaikirche, together with Superintendent Görnandt and Pastor Lahr, to welcome the President of the Reich. Hitler and Goebbels did not come, but Göring was there with all the new Cabinet members who belonged to the Evangelical Church. Just before the service began, buses drove up with the National Socialist deputies. The men sprang out and stormed hurriedly up the steps. It was like an assault on the church by a hostile power.

Finally Hindenburg arrived, accompanied by his son. The cheers of the people obviously gratified him. When he greeted me he said in his deep voice: "Thank God that we have finally got this far!"

I preached the sermon. At the decisive point I said:

"We have learned from Dr. Martin Luther that the Church must not oppose the lawful public authority when that authority does what it is called upon to do—not even when it governs sternly and ruthlessly. We know the terrible words which Luther addressed to the nobility in the Peasants' War, calling upon them to act without mercy so that order might again be restored in Germany. But we also know that Luther adjured the Christian nobility with the same earnestness not to debase its God-given office by vindictiveness and arrogance, and that he urged justice and mercy as soon as order had been restored.

"This must be the twofold duty of the Evangelical Church at the present hour. If the State uses its office against those who undermine the foundations of public order, against those, especially, who seek with gibes and coarse language to destroy marriage, to make a laughingstock of religion, to besmirch the idea of laying down one's life for the fatherland—then let it use its office in God's name! But we would not be worthy to be called an Evangelical Church did we not add with the same candor as Luther that public office must not be confused with private arbitrary power. Once order has been restored, justice and love must reign once more, so that every man of good will may rejoice in his people. The two kingdoms between which Luther so carefully distinguished, the kingdom of secular power and the kingdom of divine grace, are one in the person of the Christian. This is our ardent desire, that a new future for Germany will be brought about by men who, in thankfulness for God's grace, sanctify their lives in discipline and love, and that the spirit of such men will permeate the whole people! Lord, let us again become what our fathers were: by God's grace a hallowed people!"

The National Socialists gave me dark looks. They never forgave me those words. Only Göring shook my hand as we escorted the President of the Reich out of the church. "That was the best sermon that I have ever heard," he said. I swallowed the question that was on the tip of my tongue: how many sermons had the Minister President heard in his life?

Then came the State ceremony in the neighboring Garnison-kirche. Hitler made a speech. I had never heard him speak before and was tense with expectation. The speech was disappointing. It contained nothing to make one's heart beat faster. Hindenburg answered with dignity, but without saying anything of consequence.

The State ceremony was over. I could dispense with the military parade.

As I drove home with my wife I said to her: "In six months we shall have a violent struggle between State and Church." I was wrong. It did not take six months; it took only six weeks!

With the opening of the Reichstag, the way was smoothed for the new Chancellor to assume dictatorial powers. Now the agitation of the German-Christians, as the National Socialist pastors had for some time been calling themselves, began to gather momentum. At first they had been only a handful. In the Prussian church elections in November, 1932, they had gained only one-third of the votes, despite the fact that the whole SA machinery had been mobilized in their behalf and most congregations had been completely helpless before their assault. Their leaders included men who had entered the ministry without any real vocation, and who now seized the opportunity to develop their potentialities in a different sphere. There were no outstanding personalities among them. Whatever they wrote in the press testified to their intellectual mediocrity. Nor did they have any genuinely religious aims. They lived on what the political movement tossed them, and their political enthusiasm blinded them to the brutality of an attitude with which they came into daily contact. As the Nazi party wanted power in the State, so they wanted power in the church. The church was to be the spiritual sword of the Führer.

Their numbers grew. Nothing succeeds like success, Stresemann used to say. That applied here, too. After the National Socialists came to power, more and more people, even within the church, discovered their National Socialist hearts, among them men of whom one would least have expected it. The first territorial bishop openly to become a National Socialist was a Balt, Dr. Bernewitz of Braunschweig. In the Prussian Supreme Ecclesiastical Council it was Vice-President Hundt. But while the German-Christians could not rally the majority of the pastors behind them, they grew steadily stronger as a group, relying for their support on the now almighty power of the State.

To the church leaders it seemed that this presaged the dawning of a new era in which the church would become a national institution, and that they should do something to meet it halfway. In particular, they felt, the organized church should join in the great drive toward unity which appeared to be sweeping through the entire German people. One party, one Führer, one people—and therefore, also, one church!

A committee met in the seclusion of Kloster Loccum to draft a new constitution for the German church as a whole. There was to be one national Reich church, the German Evangelical Church, instead of the Federation of Churches (Kirchenbund), and it was to be headed by a national Reich bishop and four ecclesiastical executives.

The church leaders were of one mind. But they were no longer in control of events. For the German-Christians, the first thing to be decided was the person of the Reich Bishop. Questions of practical execution or constitutionality did not interest them. All that concerned them was the person—the rest would take care of itself. In this, too, they were the docile pupils of Adolf Hitler. They already had their candidate for the post—Ludwig Müller, of Königsberg, an army district chaplain.

Müller had more stature than the German-Christians of Berlin. He was a distinguished looking man, with a strikingly small head. Like so many military chaplains of former times he had not learned the meaning of work. But he was accustomed to moving

140

in what are known as "influential circles." He had a nose for people. Basically, too, he was good natured. The trouble with him was
that he had no character, and absolutely no Christian or theological formation. His sermons were very straightforward and intended for simple soldiers, who listened to them not unwillingly.
He could touch on the most trivial points in his sermons; for instance, how a man comes to do a job in an apartment and when he
is asked whether he cannot work faster replies that he does not
like to do a sloppy job. From this he would draw an analogy to the
work of God, which is not sloppy either. His military chief, General Blomberg, once said that Müller's talks could just as well have
been given by a rabbi. That may well have been so—though the
memory of his pietistic beginning never vanished altogether. Un-
savory rumors were current about his relations with the opposite
sex.

All this, however, signified nothing in comparison with the single fact that he was the friend and delegate of Adolf Hitler. Hitler
had stayed at his home when he held his meetings in Königsberg.
Müller was the only Evangelical pastor who appeared to enjoy
Hitler's confidence. So Hitler made Müller his adviser on church
affairs. In that capacity Müller came to Berlin. He had as yet no
definite program; he intended to feel his way. He set up a small
office and appointed his brother-in-law, Admiral Meusel, as his
"chief of staff," a significant title. All expenses, at least in the beginning, were paid by the State or by the party.

The German-Christians insisted that no one but Müller could fill
the post of Reich Bishop, and they wanted this matter settled as
quickly as possible. After that they intended to fill all other important posts with their own men.

In the church, opinions were altogether different. Here all eyes
were directed toward a man who had never held office in any ecclesiastical administration but who enjoyed the love and confidence of the entire church, Friedrich von Bodelschwingh. His

ardent faith and personal holiness really made him the best man the Evangelical Church of Germany then possessed.

The church leaders would have liked to postpone the elections, but they finally had to give in to the pressure of the German-Christians. On May 26, 1933, the church leaders gathered in the Federation of Churches house in Berlin. I would not normally have attended the meeting; however, the Old Prussian Church had no theological vice-president at the time, since Dr. Burghart had resigned, and President Kapler requested me to assist him.

It was a memorable gathering.

To start with, Dr. Kapler announced that Ludwig Müller had asked to make a brief statement of his views on the position of the church. No one wished to deny the request of the "Führer's delegate," whereupon Ludwig Müller appeared—and made a campaign speech for himself!

He esteemed Bodelschwingh highly, he told us. But Bodelschwingh was not the right man for the times. He was a man for deaconnesses, not for SA men. And he did not enjoy the Führer's confidence, on which everything now depended. The only suitable candidate for the post of Reich Bishop was he, Ludwig Müller! "I wish my church," he concluded, "to develop in peace. If you elect Bodelschwingh, you will have strife; if you elect me, there will be peace!" With that he withdrew.

The gathering sat speechless. Such an address in one's own behalf was unheard of in the church. Since no one took the floor, I stood up and said that in the face of such a challenge there could be only one answer for men who had a Christian honor to defend —to elect Bodelschwingh unanimously.

But what was self-evident to me was by no means self-evident to the others. Only Dr. Marahrens, the Territorial Bishop of Hanover, supported me and remained steadfast as a rock. And with him, Dr. Kapler. The others weighed the pros and cons or decided openly in favor of Ludwig Müller. Finally a vote was taken. It resulted in a minority, but a substantial minority, for Ludwig Mül-

142

ler. Even the Southern German bishops voted for him, though not without immediately explaining that they were, of course, wholeheartedly for Bodelschwingh, but that the brunt of the now inevitable struggle would have to be borne by Northern Germany, and they did not think the Northern German churches capable of standing their ground in such a struggle.

The majority had decided in favor of Bodelschwingh. The decision was valid and unassailable.

The following evening Ludwig Müller announced on the radio that the ruthless struggle of the German-Christians against the Reich Bishop had begun.

The church leaders were optimistic. Friedrich von Bodelschwingh enjoyed a tremendous reputation throughout Germany. Expressions of joy and confidence poured in from all sides. Bodelschwingh immediately set to work with his customary energy and vision.

At this point a man emerged from behind the scenes, a man of a wholly different stamp from Ludwig Müller, a man who was the very embodiment of the spirit of the National Socialist State. His face, once seen, was not easily forgotten. He had an iron will and such relentless obstinacy that he could maintain, with apparent conviction, that five was an even number, and issue false reports without turning a hair. There was something almost impressive in his sheer malignity and in the energy and singleness of purpose with which he pursued his ends. His name was August Jaeger.

He was the son of a Hessian consistorial councilor. He himself had been attached to a provincial court in Wiesbaden and, after Hitler's seizure of power, had managed to insinuate himself into the Prussian Ministry of Culture. His purpose from the first was clear. He proposed to bring the Evangelical church in Prussia, and later the church throughout Germany, under his dictatorial sway by a twofold operation: he planned to assume the key government position in the administration of church affairs, and at the same time to succeed to Dr. Kapler's post as principal jurist within

143

the Supreme Ecclesiastical Council. With Bodelschwingh as Reich Bishop, this purpose could not be achieved. If there had to be a Reich Bishop at all, it must be Ludwig Müller, a man he could manage. Impatiently he awaited his hour.

He did not have long to wait. Dr. Kapler, that most deserving man, was weary of his office in the Supreme Ecclesiastical Council. He could no longer endure the daily, indeed hourly attacks of the German-Christians, and he resigned. The Supreme Ecclesiastical Council did not want to elect a new president in order to avoid anticipating any decision about a "Reich church." It appointed Superintendent-General Stoltenhoff as provisional president after he had declared that when the new constitution came into effect he wished to return to the Rhineland.

This was August Jaeger's opportunity. He persuaded the Minister of Culture that the Supreme Ecclesiastical Council had violated the agreement with the State which provided that the State must give its consent in the appointment of a new president. This was pure invention. But Rust, like most National Socialists, had not the remotest knowledge of ecclesiastical affairs. He believed what his party stalwarts told him. Trendelenburg, who had hitherto directed the government department for church affairs, was ignominiously ousted. On June 24, Jaeger had his appointment to the post of state commissioner for all the Evangelical churches of Prussia in his pocket. And he made his authority felt right away.

He began by dismissing Superintendent-General Schian of Breslau, then me, then all the others. And everywhere he entrusted German-Christians with the direction of the church.

We superintendents-general were powerless. I protested against my suspension, but it could be no more than a paper protest. As for the superintendents of my diocese, who at the last church rally in the Kurmark had assured me of their support, they went over, one by one, to the German-Christians. The same thing happened in the Consistory. The biblical saying that one should never put one's trust in man came more alive to me than ever before.

But out in the congregations the unrest grew by the day. Old Hindenburg wrote Hitler a letter forbidding such treatment of his church. And Privy Councilor Karnatz, who had succeeded to the direction of the Supreme Ecclesiastical Council, lodged a complaint with the political tribunal against the Prussian state.

This was a courageous act, and quite embarrassing to the National Socialists, for the administration of justice in Prussia had not yet been radically subverted. It was impossible to know what the political tribunal would do.

So Hitler gave in. The suspensions were rescinded. It was arranged that church elections should promptly take place throughout Germany—although the State did not have the least right to order church elections. The elections were to result in new institutions and new offices, as had been provided for at Loccum.

Peace had apparently been restored. But only apparently.

The church now had its first opportunity to experience in its own flesh Hitler's demonic ability to transform reverses into fresh victories.

The German-Christians had no intention of vacating the positions they had occupied. They felt themselves secure. The party and the State were behind them.

Then the elections took place. Had they been conducted fairly, the German-Christians would have had difficulty in getting a majority in the church institutions. But a totalitarian State does not know the meaning of fair elections. The whole party apparatus was placed at the service of the German-Christians. SA men streamed from the party offices to register as voters and then to vote. Votes were counted summarily, and under turbulent conditions. On the previous evening Hitler, the Catholic, had made a campaign speech for the German-Christians. Whereupon many of the German-Christian pastors declared: "The Führer has spoken; the elections need no longer take place; the German-Christian list has been elected!"

In this way the German-Christians obtained an average of 75 per cent of the votes throughout Germany.

Protests poured in that the elections had not been conducted in an orderly fashion. They were so numerous that they filled one room in the Ministry of the Interior to the ceiling. This did not prevent Secretary of State Stuckart from stating that not a single protest had been received.

And now everything developed as was to have been expected. In Old Prussia, the German-Christians, who now held a majority in all the synods, abolished the office of superintendent-general and replaced it by the episcopal office, although there was hardly a man among them who could have filled such a post. Ludwig Müller became first Territorial Bishop of Prussia and then Reich Bishop for all Germany. Bodelschwingh had resigned as soon as August Jaeger became church commissioner. All the key positions in the official church leadership were filled by German-Christians. Only in Bavaria had the National Socialists failed to win the elections. In Berlin, Dr. Karow, and in Breslau, Dr. Zaenker, were permitted to remain in office for a while; then they too had to resign.

Thus I found myself in retirement, at the age of fifty-three, together with nearly all my colleagues. For a few weeks I still reckoned with a possible appointment to a professorship in some university. But this dream, too, was soon shattered, and I had to face the somewhat bitter fact that under this government I would no longer be able to occupy any public function. Not even the simplest pastorate!

I decided, first, to make a break in order to bring the whole situation into perspective. On December 1, I left for San Remo, Italy, where I was to serve as chaplain to the visitors to the resort town. I remained there for five months. Those were instructive months. We were away, of course, from the fateful developments which were taking place at home. I had to tell myself that for the moment I could have done nothing to help. The German-Christians had attempted to prevent my departure for Italy. I assumed my functions at San Remo, dutifully spied upon by the Gestapo and somewhat uncomfortably placed among the Germans abroad, who took pains to proclaim to all and sundry the glory of the newly risen fatherland. One agreeable exception was the German Ambassador in Rome, Ulrich von Hassel, who visited me at San Remo; there was immediate understanding between us.

For the first time in my life in the ministry I had leisure, and also real quiet in that leisure. I employed the time to write a devotional book, *Heimkehr zum Wort* ("Return to the Word"). It was not intended as the usual kind of devotional book; it consisted of a continuous Bible reading divided into short sections, with a brief meditation and a short prayer for each day. The first edition sold in next to no time. Then the demand ceased, obviously as a result of the political situation.

Shortly after my departure from Berlin there took place an event which effectively laid the specter of the German-Christians, at least for those congregations which were loyal to the church.

On November 13, 1933, the German-Christians organized a big rally in the Sportpalast in Berlin. At this rally, the principal speaker thundered against the "cattle drover and pimp stories of the Old Testament." He repeated faithfully and literally the catalog of epithets spawned by Alfred Rosenberg in his *Myth of the Twentieth Century*. All "offspring of Jews" were to be excluded from pulpits and from posts in the ecclesiastical administration.

When I read these reports I immediately sought out some of my friends and said that this was the end of the German-Christians. I had not been mistaken. A wave of indignation swept through the great mass of pastors, superintendents, and consistorial councilors who had gone over to the stronger party. If this was the true face of the German-Christians, they felt, then they would have no more to do with them. Letters of resignation poured into the party offices. As quickly as the German-Christian movement had grown, it now declined.

But the National Socialist administration of the church remained. And under the sure protection of this administration, all those who had newly come to power in the church retained their positions.

I was back in Germany by July 1, 1934. Things had changed in every way. The National Socialist system had consolidated itself. The resistance of the old civil service, of the workers, and of the middle classes had visibly weakened. Old Hindenburg, raging over his own impotence, had withdrawn more and more. The members of the German National party who had entered the government in the beginning were being eased out. Adolf Hitler was the undisputed master of the situation.

To attempt anything against this ascendancy was absolutely hopeless—at least for anyone far removed from politics, with no taste for conspiracy, who always learned of events post factum. We were sitting one day on our balcony and heard the sound of uninterrupted shooting in the direction of the Lichterfelde cadet school. Only many days later did we realize that Röhm and all his followers had been executed that day in the barracks courtyard. On another occasion, when I had delivered a sermon, a foreign pastor came to see me in the sacristy after the service. He was staggered, he said, that a service should have been held in an Evangelical church without a word being said about the frightful events of the past days. I looked at him uncomprehendingly. Only then did I learn with consternation something of the "Night of Glass" (*Kristallnacht*) when all over Germany, Jewish synagogues had been burned down. Press and radio were in the hands of the party. They reported only what was ordered from above. That is how it was with everything and everybody.

My own duty could only be to continue, as before, to work with the church, and to leave to God how and when He would make that work fruitful for the community.

But here, too, I was at first a complete outsider. Before I left for Italy, a group of courageous pastors had banded together as a *Pfarrernotbund* (Pastors' Emergency Association) and declared

148

war on the German-Christian leadership of the church. Out of this Emergency Association gradually developed the Confessing church. I was not present at the first Confessing synod, at Barmen, which adopted the significant Theological Declaration. I was still at San Remo. On my return, I attended the second synod, at Dahlem, as a guest observer.

The synod flatly declared: "The men who have seized control of the church leadership in the Reich and in the states have separated themselves by their actions from the Christian Church."

There could scarcely have been a more radical decision. This was something like the language of the fourth-century councils. In my estimation, an Evangelical synod did not have the authority to hand down such verdicts. The synod then announced that it was endeavoring to set up a completely independent church organism. A Confessing pastor was to accept no instructions from the ecclesiastical authorities. Young students of theology should no longer take examinations set by the authorities or allow themselves to be ordained by the official bishops. Their only superior authority should be the Council of Brethren *(Bruderrat)*, which should gradually develop into a genuine administration. All funds—church collections, church taxes—should go to the Council of Brethren.

As I went home from the parish house in Dahlem with my old colleague, Dr. Vits, I said to him: "Fundamentally they are right, and their aims are right, but they have overshot the mark." How would a totalitarian State ever permit a church group to withhold church taxes—not voluntary contributions, after all, but church taxes—in order to finance an opposition to the church leadership desired by the State! It had only to send a commissioner and confiscate all accounts, and the dream would be over—which is, in fact, what happened. But in any case the Dahlem synod soon receded into the background of the consciousness of the Confessing church. Theologically and practically, the synod had gone too far. "And yet," as I said to my companion, "it is good that such a deci-

149

sion should have been taken. It shows the congregations that the struggle is in earnest and that everything is at stake; sooner or later that will bear its fruit." Not for a moment did I doubt that my own place could only be with this Confessing church.

Then Pastor Scharf came to see me. He was one of the few who had stood by me, and he transmitted to me the request of the Brandenburg Council of Brethren that I should join in its work. I agreed immediately and without reservation. I realized that such a collaboration would have its difficulties. So far I had always been one of the youngest in the circle of my colleagues, often the very youngest. Now I was suddenly to be the "old man" in a group consisting solely of young men. And among them were bound to be some who would regard the former superintendent-general with distrust as a representative of the "old church."

Yet only in such a group could I find my religious home.

But now another incident occurred.

A year or two earlier, a certain Pastor Falkenberg had asked me to help him. In the First World War he had served as an officer in the front line. Then, after disciplinary proceedings, he had been sent by his ecclesiastical superiors to South America to prove himself. Now he was anxious to return home again. Would I have a post for him in my diocese?

I was prepared to help him. There was a vacancy not far from Neuruppin. And so he became a pastor in my Kurmark. He was hardly settled when he was drawn into the party. He became a German-Christian. The city of Neuruppin was to be his springboard. He was elected to a pastorate there. He at once began to terrorize his congregation.

The local pastors appealed to me to come and enlighten the congregation on the subject of the church struggle. I did not want to refuse their request. The conference was not to take place in the church but in the biggest hall in the city, and it was to be followed by a discussion.

I arrived. I was told that the whole city was in an uproar and that there would be trouble.

A path was made for me with difficulty through the overcrowded hall. I began my talk with a calm survey of the previous two hundred years of church history. I said not a word about politics or the church struggle; that was to come later. But for the opposition—and despite the friendly greeting which I had received, it was quite obvious that there was an opposition—all this took too long. There was an interruption. Then a second and a third. The meeting began to get disorderly. The police officer who had been stationed there promptly broke up the gathering. Despite the excitement, the people left quietly.

There was a short sequel in the church. Then we went to the superintendent's house to discuss the events with the Council of the Confessing congregation.

It was here that a messenger from the office of the district president found me; he requested me to accompany him to that office for a discussion. I went with him and was received by Count Helldorf who was then Police President of Potsdam. Helldorf said that he had to arrest me. When I asked him why, he replied that if a disturbance arose, the responsibility lay not with those who had actually created the disturbance, but with the person whose appearance had occasioned it. Such reasoning was new to me. However, there was nothing to be done about it, and I was taken to the police prison in Potsdam.

The following morning my wife had an interview with Count Helldorf. Toward evening I was released. To what extent Helldorf's heart was in the affair, and what had happened behind the scenes, I never discovered. What we do know is that Count Helldorf was later put to death as an accomplice in the attempt on Hitler's life.

That might have been the end of the whole business. Who would want to dramatize such a thing? But it was not the end.

The Confessing congregation of Neuruppin approached me

again. Falkenberg, they told me, was basking in his victory and becoming more and more unbearable. In the meantime it had come out that it was he, together with his SA, who had organized the whole disturbance. Crouching behind his henchmen, so as not to be seen, he had kept crying out: "Traitor to the country! Traitor to the country!" Considering the strained political situation, the Confessing Christians pointed out, such a smear should not be allowed to adhere to the Confessing church. If Falkenberg did not formally retract the slur, I should take him to court.

I shrank from such a step. Christians should not go to court for reasons of personal affront. That is made abundantly clear in the New Testament. Could a superintendent-general, even if he were already in retirement, wrangle with another minister in the courts?

But my Neuruppin friends continued to insist. The issue was not my own person, they pointed out, but the Confessing church; its cause would be lost in Neuruppin if Falkenberg were allowed to rant and rage unchecked.

Finally I gave in.

My counsel, Dr. Gollert, has vividly described the course of the proceedings in a pamphlet which he wrote on his return to Germany after lengthy imprisonment in Russia. Only from this pamphlet did I find out—twenty-five years later—what unbelievable pressure the party had put on my counsel; a National Socialist, they told him—and Dr. Gollert was a party member—should not defend a man like me. Despite all threats and allurements, Gollert stood his ground. He was a brave man.

Falkenberg was convicted in two separate courts. The first time he was fined 1,000 marks, the second, 600. He had planned his defense in accordance with a well-known formula. In the first place, he argued, he had not said the words "traitor to the country." However, if he had, he had only told the truth, because the Superintendent-General really was a traitor, as was clearly shown by his book *Friede auf Erden* ("Peace on Earth"). In the first court it was chiefly the former contention that was at issue. But here the testimony of the witnesses who had sat near him at the meeting was so overwhelming and impressive that the statements of the other side could not prevail against them. In the second court, the issue revolved around my book. This time the opposition had prepared its case with care. High party dignitaries were quoted as saying that this book, which had broken a lance in favor of the pacifists, was a shameful literary concoction.

Would the court resist such attempts at intimidation? There were some critical moments. But the court did not allow itself to be influenced. However much the party and its press might rage, the conviction was upheld. Falkenberg was done for in Neuruppin.

As for me, I left Neuruppin both times with a heavy heart. I had now experienced personally what a totalitarian dictatorship was able to do to people in the space of a few years. Here was a pastor, whatever his past, but still a pastor, whose business it was to preach the Gospel. Now he was so hypnotized by the party that he no longer appeared to notice how many statements he was making which everyone in the crowded courtroom, friend and foe alike, knew to be untrue. Here were the National Socialist witnesses who had sat near the pastor at the meeting and who now swore, without moving a muscle, that he had never said an incriminatory word or given a signal to his SA men. Here was a big landowner of noble family and respected position, together with his wife, stoutly and unscrupulously joining in such assertions.

The presiding judge, who had long since realized that all these statements were false, tried in a friendly manner to get this land-owner-witness to admit that he was really giving a subjective opinion and not a statement of objective fact. The landowner suddenly realized that he was on the point of involving himself and his wife in a suit for perjury, and quickly took advantage of the loophole which the judge was offering him. Yet only a few years earlier, all these people had seemed to be decent, law-abiding citizens and Christians, incapable, surely, of such a thing as perjury.

The demonism of the dictatorial party had engulfed them. To do what the party demanded had become their sole guide to conduct All scruples had gone by the board.

We faced each other like people from two different worlds. A the end of the proceedings I was not even permitted to shake Pastor Falkenberg's hand, as I would gladly have done. His party friends with their wrathful looks surrounded him like a wall. Out side, a troop of SA, ordered there in the certain expectation of vic tory, were waiting to give Falkenberg an ovation. The ovation had to be dispensed with.

It was a bitter experience.

My collaboration in the Confessing church was at first very modest. I helped to build up the administration for the Branden burg province. But since I was the only theologian more or less conversant with administrative matters who could devote his full attention to the work—the others all had to look after their con gregations—the responsibility for these administrative matters in creasingly devolved upon me. As time went on, and emergencies developed, I was also drawn into the Berlin and Old Prussian Councils.

In addition, I wrote regular memoranda, appeals, and leaflet for the Confessing church which had to appear anonymously, but were widely distributed. For instance, there was a leaflet entitled *The State Church is There!* and another addressed *To the Au thorities and to the Evangelical Christian Body in Germany.* An open letter to Reich Minister Kerrl, to which reference will be made shortly, was distributed in millions of copies throughout Germany and abroad, this time over my signature.

The Gestapo suspected that I and none other was responsible for the anonymous publications, but they never found anything when they searched my place. They were not equipped to make textual comparisons, which would probably have provided them with a speedy answer. I was arrested a couple of times. Thing looked most serious after the Sunday services which I conducted at Dahlem after Niemöller's arrest. But I was released—with a prohibition to preach in my pocket.

The high point of this activity came in the spring of 1937. In order to gain the mastery in the vexatious church struggle, Hitler had appointed his old fellow fighter, Hans Kerrl, as Reich Minister for Church Affairs. As Minister of Justice at Peine, Kerrl had been a supporter of the church. Then he was borne up on the crest of the National Socialist wave. Now he found himself faced with a task for which he believed himself to be the right man, and on which, in true Nazi style, he embarked with the utmost confidence. The notion that in fact he understood nothing of church affairs did not so much as enter his head.

His plan was to eliminate the radicals of "right" and "left," to unite the neutrals with the moderate German-Christians and the moderates of the Confessing church, and thus restore peace and order temporarily. After that a great synod—a new Council of Nicea!—would decide on "dogmas" and settle all questions.

The plan was amateurish. Any church historian could have told the Reich Minister that not even the Emperor Constantine had succeeded in putting an end to the great church struggle of his day by means of a council. But Hans Kerrl was not one to accept instruction. He was fond of saying that he had read "very extensively." He felt superior to all theologians.

To start with, the "elimination of the radicals" was an impossibility. For—at least in the Confessing church—the whole strength of the movement lay in the radicals. It was hopeless to try to split the Confessing church from its leaders. As for the German-Christians, their radicals had the whole National Socialist party apparatus behind them. When Hans Kerrl eliminated some of these "radicals," there was a revolt of the territorial governors, and Hitler immediately took their part. In any case the whole purpose of this attempt at pacification was to keep control of the church in the hands of the National Socialist State. And it was precisely this

State-Church arrangement against which the entire Confessing church had taken its stand.

Nevertheless, there were some churchmen of rank and reputation who were prepared to lend themselves to Kerrl's endeavor. The former Westphalian Superintendent-General, Dr. Zoellner, a man of over seventy and one of the best men of the "old church," allowed himself to be persuaded to take part in a Reich church committee. This was an unqualified initial success for Kerrl. It even led to Ludwig Müller's being cold-shouldered. And this moved the Lutheran bishops who had retained their functions to view the situation favorably. And countless pastors and members of congregations did likewise.

I repeatedly explained to Dr. Zoellner that the scheme could lead nowhere. This troika of Confessing church, neutrals, and German-Christians might step out bravely, but the point would come when the horses realized that the driver was directing them with reins and whip where he wanted them to go, not where they wanted to go themselves. That driver was the National Socialist party. Zoellner did not like to hear this, but the day finally came when he himself realized that he could accomplish nothing against the influence of the party. In February, 1937, the Reich church committee resigned as a body.

Now Kerrl made his last attempt. He persuaded Hitler to issue a decree to the effect that elections to a general synod would be held, so that the "church people" might have a chance to settle the affairs of the church "in complete freedom." A sigh of relief went through the people. At last, "complete freedom"!

Immediately the Confessing church began to hold a large number of meetings. I myself traveled for weeks on end from city to city. Everywhere there was great excitement. Once, when I arrived at Kassel at 7 P.M., to speak at a meeting scheduled for 8 P.M., I was met at the station with the words: "You must come immediately to speak"—in this or that church—"three churches are

156

full already!" So I spoke five times in succession, ending at 11:30 P.M. In other cities it was much the same.

Everywhere I explained that elections in a National Socialist State, even church elections, would always be National Socialist elections, that is, a list would be presented, to which people would have to say "yes." Each time I said this a movement of consternation went through the whole congregation. No one had thought of such a thing.

In Kerrl's ministry hung a big wall map with little flags indicating whether the meetings all over the country had expressed themselves for or against the elections as planned. When the map showed clearly that there was opposition almost everywhere, the whole plan was dropped.

Shortly before this election campaign, Hans Kerrl had assembled the presidents of the territorial church committees to inform them officially that the Reich church committee no longer existed. At the same time he made a two-hour speech in which he developed his National Socialist brand of Christianity—a frightful mixture of race, blood, soil, and New Testament. This was what the church must preach from now on! He said that the Catholic Bishop, Count Galen, and the Evangelical Superintendent-General, Dr. Zoellner, had tried to teach him what a Christian was: a man who confessed that Jesus was the Son of God. That, according to Kerrl, was absurd and irrelevant.

For me this was a signal, just as the meeting at the Sportpalast on November 13, 1933, had been a signal. A Reich Minister had dared prescribe to the church what it was to preach, and by so doing had attacked the very foundations of all Christian faith. This required some clear speaking.

I wrote the open letter to Reich Minister Kerrl to which I have already referred. The letter was copied by countless hands, mimeographed and, where possible, printed. It was widely distributed

157

abroad, and innumerable newspapers in England, America, and other countries brought back the echo.

Kerrl raged. He instructed the office of the public prosecutor to institute legal proceedings against me. On August 6, 1937, I appeared in court.

The big chamber of the Moabit criminal court was packed. All representatives of the domestic and foreign press had been invited. They were to witness the conviction of an enemy of the State. All government ministries and party organizations were represented. The balconies were crowded with spectators, friend and foe.

The presidents of the church committees who had heard Kerrl's speech were called as witnesses. With one exception, they all confirmed that Herr Kerrl had in fact spoken as I had reported in my open letter. They could not remember the exact terms he had used, but they too had considered his words an attack on the foundations of the Christian faith. Then Herr Kerrl entered the courtroom with his staff, and everyone rose. He flatly denied ever having said anything of the sort, and contested my right to attribute such statements to him. His ministerial colleagues eagerly concurred. Then the State's attorney made his speech for the prosection, exactly according to pattern: the Führer had united the German people; then a group of pastors had started a church struggle for no good reason; my open letter constituted a high point in this agitation against the State. The State's attorney demanded that I should be sentenced to six months in prison.

I heard later that Kerrl had personally visited the State's attorney and told him that the trial must result in my permanent disappearance from public life.

My three defense counsels spoke. Then I rose to make a concluding statement. There was absolute silence in the courtroom. I said, very briefly, that I had wanted to be absolutely sure of my facts before writing the open letter. I had therefore checked with all the persons I could reach who had attended the meeting with Herr

Kerrl. And their unanimous reports had testified to so severe an attack on the Christian faith that it was the simple duty of an ordained minister of the church to raise a public protest. The issue, I said, was not my person, but the question whether the Christian church was still free to stand up for its faith in the National Socialist State.

During the recess I conferred with the lawyers. We reckoned with three months' imprisonment at the worst, a 300-mark fine at best.

When the session was resumed, I heard the voice of the presiding judge as through a mist; the court had acquitted me! The text of Herr Kerrl's words, said the judge, could no longer be ascertained; consequently the charge of libel and calumny could not be regarded as substantiated.

I accepted the good wishes of the court officers and of my friends, and returned home to my apartment at Lichterfelde as quickly as I could with my wife and eldest son.

Only much later did I learn of some of the developments of that evening. First, a directive went to the press from the Ministry of Propaganda that the Dibelius trial must not be reported. Then Hans Kerrl telephoned the Reich Minister of Justice, Gürtner, and taxed him furiously with this "miscarriage of justice." Gürtner could only reply that he had always counseled him against this suit and that he, Kerrl, must now bear the consequences. Kerrl then got Göring on the wire and demanded that I be sent to a concentration camp. But Göring, too, refused to come to his aid. Evidently spite had its part to play among party members too.

All the Prussian prosecutors-general were now summoned to Berlin, and told that a humiliation such as this suit had inflicted upon the National Socialist State must under no circumstance occur again. The Niemöller trial, which was to take place ten days later, was postponed for many months in order to give the prosecution an opportunity to prepare it more thoroughly.

The presiding judge, Wesenberg, suffered a nervous breakdown the following day. For weeks he had been under unbearable tension, caught between the demands of the party and his own sense of justice. He was dismissed from his post and died shortly after. He was a brave, upright man.

I cannot go into the whole history of the church struggle. I shall have to confine myself to that part of it which I experienced personally. And of that, too, I can mention only a few salient facts.

In 1938, Niemöller was convicted. Here, too, the Prussian judges refused to let justice be used as the instrument of politics. Niemöller was sentenced, but only to the long-obsolete penalty of confinement in a fortress. And this sentence was to be satisfied by his imprisonment on remand. But Hitler now intervened. Niemöller was sent to a concentration camp—to the indignation of the whole Christian world.

As the threat of war deepened, the position of the Confessing church grew extremely difficult.

February 22, 1936, was a black-letter day in the history of the Confessing church. The fourth Confessing synod had met at Bad Oeynhausen. So far, unity had prevailed. But no one believed it could permanently endure. Many had expected the rupture to take place in 1935. Now the time had come.

There had been a growing cleavage between the "intact" Lutheran churches and the "fragmented" churches, most of which had been "united" churches. It would take us too far afield to analyze the origins of this cleavage. The whole church struggle meant one thing to the "intact" Lutheran church governments which sought to assert their constitutional rights, and quite another to the Councils of Brethren of the "fragmented" churches, which sought, after the "old" church had so shamefully betrayed them, to create a new church structure based on faith and theological inference—but also on dubious legal foundations.

At first it looked as though the synod would not take place at all.

160

The Lutherans gathered in one hotel, the "united" in another. Negotiations were conducted through intermediaries. After much going back and forth, they finally got together. At the very outset, in his introductory report, Dr. Marahrens, the Territorial Bishop of Hanover, announced his resignation as president of the provisional church government. This provisional church government had consisted of men whose names were of no little importance within and outside the church. In addition to Marahrens there had been the president of the Westphalian church, Dr. Koch, for many years a German National representative in the Reichstag; Pastor Humburg of the Rhineland, a man highly respected in the youth movement and among the pietist groups; consistorial Councilor Breit, chief theological collaborator of the Bavarian territorial bishop, and Dr. Fiedler, representing Supreme Court Judge Flor, an outstanding man whose president had not permitted him to participate on a permanent basis in the direction of the Confessing church.

Now the Lutherans withdrew in order to create their own Lutheran council. In the face of this single fact all the carefully elaborated reports and theological explanations receded into the background. During the synod I conducted an improvised service of intercession for the removal of the schism. The prayer was not granted.

The Oeynhausen synod had no alternative but to elect a new provisional government, which was to be composed of three Berlin pastors: Müller of Dahlem, Dr. Bohm, and Superintendent Albertz, as well as Pastor Fricke in Hessen, Pastor Forck in Hamburg, and Judge Gunther in Berlin.

It was quite obvious that this new group would not be able to command the respect which the previous provisional leadership had enjoyed. To be sure, it was a unified body, and its members were able men. The endless tug of war which had gone on between the cautious Dr. Marahrens and the impetuous Dr. Humburg was at an end. Confessional differences no longer obstructed action. And the newly elected leaders did their duty prudently and fearlessly. But they were unknown outside the circle of the Confessing church. Essentially, they represented Berlin. It could not be expected that what they said should have much significance throughout the rest of Germany, whether inside or outside the church.

Niemöller had kept insisting that the salvation of the Evangelical church would be decided in the congregations and not in the church government. Fundamentally, his reasoning was correct, even if it tended to shortchange the concept of religious leadership. But what he had overlooked was the fact that, apart from a few splendid exceptions, the movement of the Confessing church had taken only very meager root in the congregations, particularly in the country districts of eastern Germany.

From the province of Saxony came the everlasting complaint: "We have Confessing pastors; we have no Confessing congregations!" In Brandenburg, a loyal peasant said to his pastor: "Make no mistake, Herr Pastor, if things get really bad, you will stand quite alone!" The many funtionaries who retained their loyalty to the church failed to understand why pastors should want to drive them into open disobedience to public authority. The Inner Mission, which depended on State subsidies for its institutions, did not co-operate. To the extent that people were politically opposed to Hitler, they were happy if the pastors were courageous; but that was all, as far as they were concerned.

The struggle of the Confessing church was a struggle of theologians, backed by a very small group of courageous laymen. That is how it was, and that is how it continued, more and more. The time simply had not come when such a hopeless struggle of the church against the State could be founded on the congregations. A great deal depended on having a church government of authority and weight. But since Oeynhausen, this was a thing of the past.

The "provisional leadership" and the "Lutheran council" re-

162

mained in contact. The separation was not complete, but neither was there unity.

In September, 1938, when war appeared imminent, the provisional church leadership issued a prayer to be used at the outbreak of war at special services. The author was Hans Asmussen.

This prayer liturgy was a detailed call to penance—to a very practical penance. It referred to the passion of Jesus Christ and to the fact that this selfsame Jesus had overcome death. It was not a prayer for victory—just as when war had actually broken out, the Confessing congregations never prayed for victory. This liturgy was a prayer for grace to resist hatred and revenge. It was a prayer for the people into whose countries the war would be carried.

This was something altogether different from anything an Evangelical church had ever said in time of imminent war. It was scriptural, and therefore it was right.

And yet something was lacking. What was lacking was a pastoral word for the soldiers who had to go to war, and for their families. What was lacking was the sense that the church, even in the appalling circumstance of an obviously unjust war, was at one with its people. National Socialism had eradicated this sense of oneness among the theologians in Germany—and with it the instinctive understanding of the effect such a prayer liturgy must have on people, especially if war did not break out. Anyone who had to send three sons to the war, as I did, must have realized this. Nevertheless, I naturally gave my support to this liturgy.

The inevitable happened. With a howl of indignation, the influential organ of the SS, the *Schwarze Korps,* fell upon the prayer. Indignation mounted, and a veritable hail of arrests, disciplinary actions, and salary stoppages descended upon the culprits. Hans Kerrl summoned the three leading Lutheran territorial bishops, Marahrens, Meiser, and Wurm. He placed these alternatives before them: either they must dissociate themselves definitely from the Councils of Brethren, or he would send them a finance commissioner who would for all practical purposes assume the direction of their churches, as had already happened in other churches. The three bishops fought hard for their position, but in the end they submitted. They announced that they disapproved of the prayer liturgy "on religious and patriotic grounds," that they "most strongly condemned the attitude expressed therein," and that they dissociated themselves from "the persons responsible for this publication."

That evening I sought out the three at their hotel in the Wilhelmstrasse. I was not one of those deemed "responsible" in their statement, and as a former superintendent-general I could speak with them more frankly and more fraternally than could my young friends. I shall never forget how they sat there together, all three the picture of guilty conscience. At this critical hour (there was no sense beating about the bush) they had betrayed their old comrades in the struggle. They apologized and referred to their responsibility for their own territorial churches, a consideration which I could certainly understand. But no apology could change the fact that they had denied their former friends. Old Dr. Wurm was tormented for years by this thought.

Our talk was not unproductive. Bishops Meiser and Wurm soon found the opportunity to disavow the statement they had signed. But meanwhile the bitter fact remained—the Confessing church with its Councils of Brethren now stood quite alone in its struggle.

Finally war broke out. One might have thought that the National Socialist State would now have something more engrossing to do than to fight the church. But that was not the case. Arrests continued. The church press was abolished. And at every opportunity we were told that, once the war was over, accounts would be settled with the church. Churches and parsonages were not envisioned in the over-all plans for the newly conquered territories. In the modern military formations, particularly in the air force, there were no chaplains. It became daily clearer which way the National Socialist State was heading.

Conscientious objectors were shot out of hand. With them the National Socialists had no problems!

Those who were loyal to the church went off to war facing these alternatives: if Germany won, the church would be finished; if Germany lost, there would be an unimaginable collapse. It was with this conflict in their hearts that the members of the Confessing church went off to war. These included my own sons. The spiritual burden was almost unbearable. I had once drafted a memorandum for the supreme command on the effect of the church struggle on the morale of the German people. That memorandum had been highly considered by the military, but in the National Socialist State it could have no practical consequences. Now the fears which I had voiced were proved justified.

At the beginning of the war, the church government then in office (there was no longer any superior ecclesiastical authority) had established an "ecclesiastical mutual trust council" consisting of Territorial Bishop Marahrens, the German-Christian Territorial Bishop Schultz of Mecklenburg, and Dr. Hymmen of Berlin. No one expected the council to have any significance. It sought merely to maintain contact with the State. From time to time it issued a decree which overflowed with devotion to the public authorities. It could not take any initiative; actually it did not want to.

In the first days of the war I went to see Dr. Hymmen, who governed the Old Prussian Church virtually singlehanded. He was Dr. Zoellner's son-in-law and as a church administrator in Munster had enjoyed a high reputation. I now suggested to him that he should issue a directive to the effect that all assistant pastors ordained by the Confessing church would be taken over by the official church. In this way, if they were drafted—and nearly all were drafted—their young wives and children would be provided for. I pointed out that no government office would dare now, at the beginning of war, to raise any objections to such a directive, and

165

a first step would have been taken toward a rapprochement between the church administration and the Confessing church.

Hymmen swung his head from side to side, as was his habit. There were serious objections, he said. He must consider the proposal very thoroughly. Briefly, he could not be persuaded to come to a decision.

We were sitting in the building of the Supreme Ecclesiastical Council, where for years I had been constantly in and out. Not everything that had been done here had been to my liking. Nevertheless, there had always been plenty of drive and no lack of readiness to take responsibility. It aroused my indignation to see woefulness personified seated at the desk in the president's office.

It was a consolation and an inner help to me in those bitter years to be charged with the direction of the Brandenburg branch of the Gustav Adolf Association. I was able to establish an office for the association quite close to home, where help was available and where I could do many things which it was not safe to do at home or in the office of the Confessing church. When Secretary of State Muhs, who was particularly hostile to me, threatened to suppress the whole Gustav Adolf Association if I remained at the head of one of its branches, I handed over the direction to my friend, Dr. Albert Dietrich. My work remained unchanged, though the Gestapo not infrequently paid us the honor of a visit.

This is not the place to enlarge upon what the Brandenburg branch was able to do in those years for the association as a whole. What may be mentioned is that we were able to make our small, practical contribution of resistance to the persecution of Jews. We employed three Jews: two brothers by the name of Herz, and one woman. In the end we were no longer able to protect the woman, and she was taken to Theresienstadt where she died. The two men we were able to protect to the end. When the front door-bell rang, they would slip to the back stairs so they could leave inconspicuously if it were the Gestapo. It was a game which involved all our necks, but we were thankful that we were successful.

It was not until 1942 that I learned from Kurt Gerstein, who has recently acquired a certain reputation in connection with Hochhuth's play, *The Proxy*, about the appalling extermination campaign undertaken against the Jews. Gerstein came to me late one night and told me about a gassing operation at Auschwitz which he had witnessed himself. I was shaken to the depths of my being. Because of the position in which we churchmen found ourselves at the time, I could do no more than transmit the news to the Swedish counselor of embassy in Berlin, with the urgent request that both the Stockholm government and the Swedish Archbishop at Uppsala be informed. It was absolutely impossible to do anything to help from within Germany itself. Nor was Kurt Gerstein able to do anything really effective. We were all surrounded by the Gestapo, who spied on every step we took and every letter we wrote. If anything could be done at all, it had to be done through the neutral states. The news was so monstrous that if it had been spread by America or England everyone would have regarded it as war propaganda.

We realized with great bitterness in those days how impossible it was to clear a passage of truth in a totalitarian State. And the scale on which the extermination campaign against the Jews was pursued remained unknown to us even after Gerstein's report. None of us, with the possible exception of Provost Gruber, ever even heard of Eichmann till long after the end of the war.

The territorial patrons helped us by permitting our illegal assistant pastors and their wives to live and work in their parsonages. The high military, too, men like General von Haase and Admiral Canaris, did not hesitate to receive me in their homes and offices. They made life easier for many of our young brethren. Dietrich Bonhoeffer was our unfailing intermediary in all these efforts.

But as for our prisoners, we were seldom able to help them. We had to look on while not a few took the road to prison or concentration camp, where some were brutally done to death.

Those were bitter years—for most of us, personally very bitter. I lost two sons, first the youngest, who had just finished school and labor service, and had decided to study theology, then the second, who had resisted all the allurements of the German-Christian church administration and developed into a very able pastor of a Pomeranian country parish; much could have been expected of him. It was very hard for us to bow again and again before the mighty hand of God.

Toward the end of the war I came into immediate danger again. We had gathered in Freiburg at Professor von Dietze's hospitable home to discuss the future of the Evangelical Church and of the fatherland as a whole after the collapse, which was no longer in doubt. Dr. Goerdeler took a leading part in the discussion. Then came the attempt on Hitler's life. In August, 1944, Goerdeler was arrested, and far-reaching confessions were extorted from him. Those with whom he had collaborated were arrested, one after the other. The names of our Freiburg circle also came to light. Professor Ritter, Professor von Dietze, Assessor Perels disappeared behind the iron gates. Dietrich Bonhoeffer was already in prison. Why the other participants in the discussions should have remained at liberty remains a miracle. The Gestapo knew our names, yet Territorial Bishop Wurm and I were not arrested. Gerhard Ritter in his biography of Goerdeler also expresses his astonishment at this.

The extent of the danger to which we, who survived the war, were exposed became clear to us only later. Each of us was exercised by the question: Why did the others have to die, and we to live on?

But a blessing that comes in times of great distress is that personal considerations are subordinated to concern for the whole. What would become of our country, no one could yet say. All we knew for certain was that a new chapter would open in the life of the church and that the church would be called upon to shoulder new responsibilities for its people. The inner strength of the

Evangelical Church in all those years had resided in the Confessing church. And this church had learned, even in circumstances which, humanly speaking, offered no hope at all, to look upon Him who told His disciples that He would be with them unto the end of the world.

ƁISHOP

THE RUSSIAN GUNS were still located near my apartment in Lichterfelde when we set about restoring the fabric of the Evangelical
Church in our German fatherland.

Our immediate concern was with Berlin.

Here, in Berlin, what was needed was not simply determination,
but also wisdom and prudence. A false step could have incalculable consequences. The Russians were in the process of establishing
their civil administration, the administration of a totalitarian State.
They would in due course come up against the church. If they
did not find a stable and unambiguous ecclesiastical organization,
if opposition forces within the church called upon them to intervene in church affairs—and in Berlin anything was possible—
then it could be expected with absolute certainty that they would
institute commissars for the church, as they had done throughout
the East. Instead of a National Socialist church administration, we
would have a Communist one. We would have it in Berlin, and
we would very soon have it in Dresden and Magdeburg.

This danger had to be countered. The Russians must find a
church where everything was clear, unexceptionable, uncontested.
All due legal forms must be observed. But this was possible only

171

if the new church structure was built up on the existing legal basis.

This was the last thing my young friends of the Confessing church desired. They had never known the meaning of an orderly and upright church administration. For them a consistory was the quintessence of indecision and ossification. It was "old church." And they wanted no part in anything savoring of "old church." Their spiritual home had been in the Councils of Brethren of the Confessing church, and there it remained. And their present plan was that such a Council of Brethren, with neither superior nor subordinates, should take the helm.

But for a church province of 4,000,000 Christians and 1,000 to 1,500 pastors, such a plan was altogether out of the question. The Confessing church had never known what it was to administer a whole ecclesiastical organism. It simply did not know what was involved—in the spiritual, juridical, economic, organizational, and other fields. But above all—and this was the crucial point—things would never have run smoothly had the Confessing church simply said: "Our Council of Brethren is taking over the direction of the church." Within three months dozens of pastors hostile to the Confessing church would have lodged a protest with the occupation authorities. I know what I am saying. In the Rhineland and Westphalia, where there was nothing to fear from the occupation authorities, such a course was all right. In Berlin, under the eyes of the Russian occupying power, it was impossible.

There was only one way for the church in Berlin to stand on more or less firm legal ground. The elections of 1933, which had produced the "brown" general synod, had been notoriously irregular. Consequently they had not been valid. This was a fact which no one dared contest any more. Hence the decisions of the synod were not valid. The superintendencies-general, which had then been abolished, still existed in fact. But who, of the old superintendents-general of Berlin and Brandenburg had survived? Two were dead. Another, Dr. Karow, was too old. Only I remained. According to our old constitution, which still stood, the presidency of the Consistory devolved upon me. I had therefore only to convoke the members again, with the exception of the German-Christians, of course, who had entered it under Hitler. Then we would be able to go ahead, step by step.

Actually there were enough consistorial councilors from former times, both theologians and jurists, some older, some younger, who had never bent their knee before Baal. They were duly assembled. Now the legitimate authority was constituted. Whatever members of our two Councils of Brethren, of Berlin and Brandenburg, were in the country joined, and the church government, *Kirchenleitung*, was established. For the body which we later called the church government, that is, the half synodal, half consistorial body whose purpose was not to administer but to lay down general policy, we did not immediately require a strict juridical form. Whatever had to be done according to strict legal form could be done by the Consistory. Everything else could be done freely, at least for the time being.

That, then, was the structure. Naturally it could be challenged. Legally, almost anything can be challenged. But it was solidly built, and it established itself.

For weeks I was haunted by the nightmare that some pastor might still approach the Russians and offer his services as a commissar. In 1918, Pastor Wessel—the father of Horst Wessel of unhappy memory—had done something of the kind. Would history repeat itself? Would the occupying power intervene after all?

What was most disturbing was that the German-Christians had no intention of giving up their game for lost. There was Herr Heinrich, President of the Consistory by the grace of Herr Kerrl. He refused to give up the official seal. He wanted to continue in office. There was Consistorial Councilor Fahland, Heinrich's right hand, who was just as anxious to continue. And the functionaries of the middle echelon regarded it as self-evident that everything would go on as before.

We breathed again when, after much vain negotiating, the

President of the Consistory announced that he now realized that his hour had struck and that he was resigning. Fahland followed suit. The other German-Christians did not remonstrate. Many were still in captivity. The clergy raised no objections. After four weeks, we could tell ourselves that we had succeeded.

For me it had been an experience in tightrope walking.

Now, as head of the organized church in Berlin and Brandenburg, I could pay my official visit to the new commandant in Berlin, Colonel-General Bersarin. He was the first Russian general I had met. He was quite different from what I had expected. A heavy-set, sturdy figure—that I had expected. But a man who respected the church—that surprised me. It surprised me almost as much as the Berlin school inspectors were surprised when told by the Russian general: "I want you above all to teach the children reverence for God."

Bersarin died very soon. Some of his men had found a brand-new motorcycle and brought it to him. He wanted to try it out on the spot, in the daredevil manner of Russians, and he had an accident which proved fatal. His death was a loss for Berlin.

The title "superintendent-general" would not do any more. None of the foreign authorities understood it. The Russians were always suspicious when they heard the word "general"—it sounded military! For them, at first, I was the "Metropolitan of Berlin." But that was no permanent solution. Some title had to be chosen which Russians, British, and Americans alike could understand. The church government decided that I should call myself "bishop."

That is the history of my "self-appointment as Bishop of all the Russias," as unfriendly critics termed it. I have never been ashamed of this episode. It developed out of its own inner necessity. There was no episcopal consecration. I could lay no claim to "apostolic succession" in the sense that Anglicans and Catholics use the word. My office remained what it had been since 1925.

Of course all this was merely provisional. It was understood that a new constitution would be drawn up which would finally settle

174

everything. But first one or two more questions had to be clarified, and the first was the question of Niemöller.

Niemöller had been pastor at Dahlem. Legally he still was. For seven years his congregation had prayed for him at daily services of intercession. Not many of the congregation were left, now, but those who were, waited for him.

Now Niemöller was at liberty again. No one blamed him for remaining in western Germany with his family in order to recover from seven years' captivity. But after that he would surely come! He was pastor of Dahlem, after all.

We all waited. But Niemöller did not come.

We could never really find out why he did not come. Apparently all kinds of misunderstandings were involved. We never sought to unravel them. After spending seven years in a concentration camp, a man has a right to expect his church to take on trust the decisions he makes concerning his life from thereon. He remained in Hesse, took over the direction of church foreign relations, and was eventually elected president of the Nassau-Hesse church.

Had he returned to his pastorate in Berlin, my life and the lives of many others would have turned out very differently. It was self-evident for me that the leadership of the organized church in Berlin belonged to none other than Niemöller. I made that clear often enough at the time. He had been the very embodiment of the church struggle. His sermons remained unforgotten. His defiant courage was alive in everyone's memory. The first place was his by right.

My task could only be to see to the provisional reconstruction. Once the new synod manned the offices—as I saw it—it would appoint Niemöller head of the church government in Berlin. The province of Brandenburg would be left to me for another year or two, and then—I would be seventy. And with that my public life would come to a close.

Things turned out differently. And I could accept them only as coming from God's hand.

I headed the Berlin-Brandenburg church province. When the synod finally convened, there was nothing much left for it to do but to confirm me in my episcopal office.

There were debates, nevertheless. The "old fighters" of the Confessing church were utterly opposed to having a bishop at all, and vented their long-standing rancor against the "bishops" of 1933 and the following years in passionate terms. Then there were the theologians who, with typical German thoroughness, insisted on first defining the intrinsic meaning of the Evangelical episcopal office. The systematic theologians, in their turn, presented profound arguments to show that a church structure based on Evangelical principles must never take the form of a pyramid—I could not understand why—and therefore there should be either two bishops or four or five.

Everywhere the fear was reflected that something like a Catholic episcopal office, or an episcopal dictatorship, might develop in our midst—as though experience had not long since proved that this was an impossibility. Alongside the bishop was the consistory, the church government, the synod. How could a dictatorship come about in such circumstances? Men with dictatorial leanings are to be found everywhere, of course, and not least in the Evangelical church. But after my long experience I can only say that they are more often to be found among the presidents of synods, the chaplains of deaconesses' institutions, and even among parish pastors than among bishops.

I was convinced that this office, once created, would develop, through its own specific gravity, into a genuine Evangelical episcopal office. Theological definitions do not always pierce through to reality.

At the second synod, which was to make the final decisions, it was apparent that my expectations had been well founded. The opposition was silent. The office of bishop had gained acceptance.

176

Now there was another problem to deal with, one of which the public took very little notice and which for all practical purposes failed to arouse interest even among the congregations loyal to the church, but which gave us, in the church goverment, considerable anxiety. What was to become of the Evangelical Church of the Old Prussian Union?

This church had once been the dominant church group in Germany. Now it lay bleeding from a thousand wounds. The other German territorial churches remained outwardly intact. Württemberg, Bavaria, Hanover, Schleswig-Holstein, Baden, Hesse-Nassau —all these were unimpaired. Only the Old Prussian Church had been truncated. It had lost half its territory: East Prussia, West Prussia, Posen, most of Silesia, most of Pomerania, Brandenburg beyond the Oder. Of course, people were still hopeful. One day there would be a peace treaty, and then this section or that would return to the fatherland and hence to the old church. But in the meantime it was lost.

Was it worth while to keep the remnants together—that is, the Rhineland and Westphalia, Saxony-Magdeburg and Berlin-Brandenburg, plus a couple of other small churches—as a single ecclesiastical unit?

We considered the matter carefully and at length. Finally the decision prevailed that we should hold on to the meager remnants of the Old Prussian Church. No one could know how things would develop. It is easy to destroy but hard to rebuild.

Not much was left of the governing body, the Supreme Ecclesiastical Council, which must in some way be involved in this work of reconstruction. By a miracle, the building on Jebensstrasse had remained standing. Slowly a handful of senior clerks and secretaries trickled back. But of the council itself only two members were still in Berlin, Dr. Tröger and Dr. Söhngen. They felt that if the council was to achieve anything, it must have a president who was not, as before, a jurist, but a theologian, a man whose name carried some weight, who had administrative experience—and who was available. So they approached me, and I agreed to serve.

177

I performed my duties as president of the Supreme Ecclesiastical Council along with my other functions. I performed them, so to speak, with my left hand, but I performed them gladly. There was still a breath of the atmosphere of former times in the work. Here no ordinances were issued of the kind that had to be revoked the following week. Here there was no theological jargon. Everything was carefully thought out and soberly executed.

Our first concern was with the East. What remained of Silesia and Pomerania could neither live nor die. It needed help, funds, and effectives. Wherever the administrative changes were not taking effect, we had to intervene. The proper legal means must be devised for dismissing any German-Christians who were still in office.

We had little connection with the Rhineland and Westphalia. We felt instinctively that a Berlin Supreme Ecclesiastical Council would not again be able to serve as the superior authority for those areas. What we did in Berlin could only be provisional. A future synod would have to make the final decisions. But that could wait. This, at least, was my view.

I was counting without my host.

We had assembled at Treysa. It was August, 1945. All our thoughts, discourses, negotiations, were directed towards the re-establishment of a united church in Germany. The negotiations were by no means as simple as one might have thought. But agreement was finally reached, and the Evangelical church in Germany was again a reality.

Then, on the last afternoon, a decision was suddenly delivered to me by a group of friends from the Confessing church. It was drawn up in due legal form and signed by the Councils of Brethren of the Rhineland and Westphalia, Berlin, and Görlitz. It was a draft constitution for the Evangelical Church of the Old Prussian Union, a constitution which simply destroyed that church as it had existed in the past. There was to be no unified administration, no unified management of church funds, no Supreme Ecclesiastical

Council. Each member church was to be independent. The only superior organ was to be a church government which should have as little authority as possible. The presidency should change hands annually. What we had built up again in Berlin in the space of four months was not so much as mentioned. It was a plan drawn up by the Rhineland and Westphalia. And the unwritten caption was: Away from Berlin!

The historic grievance of western Germany at having to be subject to a superior authority located in Berlin and composed in the main of eastern Germans—though men from the Rhineland and Westphalia were always being appointed to it—this historic grievance now found expression. The President of the Westphalian church, Dr. Koch, a man highly respected throughout Westphalia and by everyone in the Confessing church, had wearied in the latter years in his fight against the godless State. Now he was a man new born. Yes, for this, life was still worth living—to throw off Berlin and do away with the Supreme Ecclesiastical Council!

I was torn by contrary reactions. In the first place, I was tremendously disappointed that my own friends should have presented me with such an unreasonable demand. They had worked out a plan behind my back, and had put it before me for my signature at the exact moment when the synod was about to break up. It was really the most unkind proposal ever made to me. It showed me finally and unequivocally that these friends had never really regarded an old superintendent-general who did not profess allegiance to Karl Barth as one of themselves.

On the other hand, I had to admit that the contents of the draft did not really conflict with my own views. But I felt that not enough thought had gone into the program, which entirely disregarded the needs of eastern Germany. However, I certainly could not reject the draft out of hand.

Finally (and this for me was the crucial consideration), I was not prepared to disrupt the newly won ecclesiastical concord by conjuring up more strife on behalf of the largest of the participating churches. I was sufficiently familiar with constitutions to know that their bark was often worse than their bite. Obvious injustices and ill-considered provisions would be amended in due course. And so I signed.

This signified the beginning—in at least one sense—of some of the most thankless years of my life. The Rhineland and Westphalia pressed ceaselessly for the dissolution of the Supreme Ecclesiastical Council in Berlin, lock, stock, and barrel. They wanted me to dismiss all the old members, reduce salaries, and get rid of all that remained of the administration. Immediately, without delay!

I refused. Officials have a right to expect protection against arbitrary procedures. And such exceptional persons as those who remained of the old Supreme Ecclesiastical Council could expect their president to defend their rights. The German-Christians had to leave the administration—that was obvious. Officials who were already eligible for a pension could be retired, and this was done. But the others could be removed only in so far as the action was in conformity with existing regulations. In a Christian church loyalty must be given pride of place. And law must remain law!

Now the western churches tried using financial pressure. At first the Supreme Ecclesiastical Council still had sufficient funds to take care of the most urgent matters. But eventually those funds ran out. Now the Rhineland and Westphalia had to be reminded that it was their obligation to contribute to the needs of the Old Prussian Church. Both provinces declared that they would not pay a penny until the Supreme Ecclesiastical Council was abolished. Finally I had to state that I would lodge a complaint against the Rhineland and Westphalia with the court of arbitration of the German Evangelical Church. They wanted to avoid this, so they paid up. Only modest sums, to be sure, but at least the obligation was recognized.

Meanwhile the time had come for a new constitution for the Old Prussian Church to enter into force. This constitution, as agreed upon at two synods, was bad; indeed, of all the church constitutions I have seen emerge, it was the worst. The fault lay in the nature of the case. The Evangelicals wanted to be a real church, if only because the Lutherans set such store by being a real church—not only individual territorial churches, but also the United Lutheran Church of Germany. This, precisely, was to distinguish them from the Evangelical Church in Germany, which they did not regard as a real church. What was sauce for the goose was sauce for the gander. But the individual Evangelical churches did not want to concede to this "real church" the decisive right to expect of its member churches that they should sacrifice something of their ecclesiastical sovereignty for the advantage of the whole, and that a general synod should be able to make decisions which would be valid for all, whether they liked them or not. Without renunciation and subordination there can be no church. And a community for which no sacrifices are made can never be vigorous. Such sacrifices the individual churches were not prepared to make. In any case, the Rhineland and Westphalia were not prepared to make them for eastern Germany.

There were high-sounding words in the constitution about the vocation of the Old Prussian Church, and the concluding phrases lauded all its great achievements in the past, but one hundred years of church history were at an end! Nor was it a very brilliant end; of that there could be no doubt at all.

My own work for the Old Prussian Church was at an end too. I retired as President of the Supreme Ecclesiastical Council. And I did not personally occupy the seat which belonged to me as Bishop of Berlin in the new church government, but had one of the superintendents-general deputize for me on a permanent basis.

I always retained my personal attachment to my old and young friends who worked for the "Old Prussians." But I never again set foot on the premises of the Old Prussian Church which were in the same building as the offices of the Consistory.

An Evangelical bishop must preach, if he is not to fail both himself and what is best in his office. And he must be incorporated at a particular place in the great preaching office of his church. It is not enough that he should travel around, consecrate churches, and preach at festival services. The old church had established superintendencies-general without specific preaching obligations. That should not be repeated. The bishop must have a church—a "cathedral," as we call it now—in which he preaches regularly.

But where could we find a "cathedral" in Berlin? The Dom had been destroyed. Only in the crypt could services still be held. Had we still been living in National Socialist times, I would have asked to be permitted to preach in this crypt as a symbol that the church was living in the catacombs. But had we not just welcomed the hour of freedom regained? No one could predict how things would be under the Russians. It would have been unjust to act from the start as though we had to return to the catacombs.

Opposite the house into which I had moved, there stood the beautiful new Church of Jesus Christ which could be made serviceable again quickly. Niemöller had preached in this church. And in this church, following his imprisonment, I had conducted the services which earned me my third arrest. It was very tempting to make this the bishop's church. But Dahlem was the select residential suburb of Berlin, and the bishop's place is not primarily among the fine folk.

Only the Marienkirche, between the Dom and the Alexanderplatz, could fill the bill. It was the only big church in Berlin which had escaped serious damage from the air raids. It could seat 1,660 persons. Of course, considerable repairs were required on this church, too. And it is to Dr. Heinrich Grüber's lasting merit that he completed the work at a time when it was almost impossible to put large churches into shape again. He was provost of the Marienkirche. It was a respected office, on the strength of which he could operate at his discretion. He had been in a concentration camp where he had made contact with Communists. They all held him in high regard. They had a keen memory of the selfless kindness which he had shown many comrades at the hour of utmost danger. Now the Communists occupied positions of influence, and they were prepared to show their appreciation. Later, for many reasons, they ceased to do so. But for the present they did, and the Marienkirche profited by it.

At first I had to speak from a pulpit placed in front of the altar. In view of the length of the church, this put an almost inhuman strain on the vocal chords and oratorical powers of the preacher. Finally it was decided to move to the front the famous pulpit which Schlüter had built into one of the rear columns. It was a risky undertaking. Schlüter, genius that he was, had interrupted one of the supporting columns in order to set his pulpit in it. Would it be possible to pry it loose and build it into another column? The chief architect sweated blood in fear lest the whole church collapse. But it worked. Whatever other repairs were needed followed. The Marienkirche had become a worthy house of God.

I always felt that the service should constitute a unity, without gaps or lifeless patches, without organ voluntary or interlude during which the congregation simply waits for the end. There should be a joyous swing in the service, no lame songs with melodies that are either unknown or cannot be sung. Joy is the theme which should resound through the service. It should be a service "with shrill trumpets," as it is written.

Half an hour before the beginning of the service—the church was usually full by then—the organ and the choir played and sang in turn. This half-hour belonged to the church musicians. Promptly at 10:30, the service began.

I never succeeded in getting those "shrill trumpets." I was thinking of Bach's trumpets which would ring out with the organ and accompany the singing of the congregation. I was informed that very few brass players could play the shrill Bach trumpets, and that they were not available for regular services. I had to resign myself—though to this day I cannot understand why something should be impossible in our day which in Bach's time was possible

183

in Leipzig, Dresden, Berlin, and other cities. I had to be satisfied with the admirable brass quartet led by Deacon Hoffman, who subsequently became director of church music.

We also assembled a choir, first under Professor Reimann, then under Professor Grote.

As far as the sermons I preached there were concerned, I can say only that they dealt with current events. I hope I remained within the boundaries set for a preacher of the Gospel. For it was the Gospel I wanted to preach, and nothing more. That I have made sufficiently clear earlier in this book. These sermons were subsequently published in their entirety; everyone is therefore able to judge whether they were genuine Evanglical sermons. The daily papers, incidentally, took notice of them, sometimes including the East Berlin press, particularly when it felt called upon to work up indignation on behalf of eastern policies—a practice which became increasingly frequent. Once, when I said that the introduction of house commissars, whose official duty it was to check and spy on the occupants, was devilish, the city councilors formally decided that I had exceeded my authority. In reality I have never, perhaps, said a truer word. Minister-President Grotewohl said on one occasion that the generosity of the German Democratic Republic was never so clearly evidenced as in the fact that Bishop Dibelius was still permitted to preach on East Berlin territory.

There was one fear that haunted us constantly—that one day the Russians would cut off West Berlin completely and would thus make it impossible for the bishop, who resided in West Berlin, to conduct services in East Berlin. They tried it with the blockade. This failed thanks to the spirited American riposte, the air lift. Then they tried a different tactic. They cut the telephone circuits. They closed one intersection after another. When I once asked Herr Grotewohl: "Are you going to close everything?" he retorted in classic Communist style: "Herr Reuter [then mayor of West Berlin] has already closed a hundred intersections; who knows when he will close the last?"

The church authorities had prepared everything in view of such an eventuality. Parts of the administration had already been transferred to East Berlin. This had become unavoidable if for no other reason than the currency regulations which had been introduced at the time of the currency reforms of 1949. A kind of mobilization plan had been drawn up providing for the government of the church if West Berlin was blocked off.

This did not happen till August 13, 1961. But it had already become increasingly hard to reside in West Berlin and have one's pulpit in East Berlin.

The services in the Marienkirche were the spiritual backbone of my work. And what work it was!

The Berlin-Brandenburg church province in 1945 was in a sorry plight. The big and beautiful Berlin churches, as I said before, were all more or less in ruins. In Potsdam, the Nikolaikirche, the Garnisonkirche, the Heilig-Geist-Kirche, which had lent such indescribable beauty to the town, were mere rubble. At Prenzlau, my father's home town, no serviceable church was left. The picture was much the same in the other towns of the province. And where the churches were still standing the windows were broken, the roofs were damaged, the towers unsafe. It was worst of all in winter. There could be no heating. The congregations—small, scared little groups—would gather in whatever rooms were to be had. In many parishes services were no longer held at all, for the war had taken its dreadful toll of pastors too. There was no more religious instruction. Where the Lord's Supper could be celebrated, water had to be used. The shops were empty. People lived on rations distributed by the occupation authority. Pastors received the next to lowest quota.

From this state of total collapse, such as West Germany never experienced, there could be only a gradual and slow recovery. Reconstruction could not be undertaken at will. In the Communist-controlled East, every brick belonged to the State. Every pane of glass had to be wheedled out of the Russian commandant, and later from the Communist civil administration, which was still worse.

Everything was "earmarked." The church, too, received its quota of building materials. But it was ridiculously low. As is inevitable in any planned economy, every roof tile involved a mountain of written forms, and precisely what one needed was never available at the crucial moment. Finally, the State had sole control of manpower supplies, and the Communist State does not lightly make its manpower available for church reconstruction. No one who has not gone through it himself can imagine what it is like to complete a building project in a Communist totalitarian State if the State regards the project as superfluous and indeed undesirable.

Actually all such building problems were supposed to be dealt with by the parishes. The Consistory was supposed to have as little to do with them as possible. Decentralization was the guiding principle of all my administrative work. But in this instance the parishes were helpless. If the central office in Berlin did not take advantage of a favorable opportunity, if Provost Grüber did not clap an old concentration camp pal on the shoulder and say "Come on, do this for me," then no headway could be made at all.

The churches of West Germany and especially of America would gladly have helped, but that would have given the lie to Communist dogma. Just as in Russia, so now in East Germany a regime was built up on dogma. That dogma included the principle that in the Communist State everyone was well off, every need was provided for, there was enough of everything, and everyone lived in comfort and freedom with the exception of the enemies of the State. In the capitalist countries, conversely, everything was bad—currency, goods, the standard of living. The East could assist the West at any time, but never the other way round. Help from the West must therefore be made altogether impossible.

This was one of the fundamental principles of the regime. A small minority believed in it, or at least affected to. The great majority did not. The stream of refugees which poured ceaselessly from East to West despite all counter measures was sufficiently eloquent testimony to the fact. But what voice has the majority in a totalitarian State? The small minority which holds the power lays down the law. What the majority thinks about it is of no consequence.

At first it was still possible to have prefabricated churches and all kinds of building materials imported from the West or from Sweden. But this became increasingly hard. Every doctrine, after all, becomes more inflexible as time goes on. In the early years, western currency could still be exchanged for eastern currency and transferred to the East—at the rate of 10 marks to one, later four to one. But eventually this became impossible. The Communist State insisted on parity—or rather, on a rate of 80 pfennigs to one West German mark, which was ridiculous.

Ten years after the entry of the Russians, the impoverished East was left to fend for itself. Of the necessary reconstruction, not one-fourth had yet been completed. It had not been possible to touch any of the big projects, such as the Marienkirche in Prenzlau or the Oberkirche in Cottbus. And where the Communists, in the manner of totalitarian States, put up big new settlements, they refused point-blank to make provision for a church. We were familiar with this from National Socialist times.

As soon as the city synod had been set up again in Berlin, the modest sums which could be put by each year were invested first of all in the reconstruction of the eastern sector. This was the right thing to do. A good deal was done in East Berlin before conditions became increasingly difficult. When that happened, more efforts were directed to West Berlin. But it was impossible, from the current receipts of the Berlin churches, to restore in a year or two the splendid churches that had been built up over fifty years with the greater fortunes of those earlier times. It must not be forgotten how seriously West Berlin, cut off as it was on all sides, lagged in the general economic development. When the production index for West Germany had long exceeded the 150 mark, West Berlin's still stood at only 75. Yet, goodness knows, people worked hard in West Berlin. The great Kaiser-Wilhelm-Gedächtniskirche remained a bizarre ruin for ten years, till the city of Berlin undertook a vigorous renovation of the district around the zoo station within the framework of its general plan of reconstruction. The city would have preferred to tear down what remained of the church, but the Berliners, even the non-churchgoers, did not want to do without their Gedächtniskirche. Slowly a plan came into being which represented a compromise, though an unsatisfactory one.

There were also the mushrooming settlements areas for which church facilities had to be provided.

The important thing in all this was not the buildings, but the people. Within the preceding decades, countless people had lost the most priceless thing in life, the thing which is really distinctive in man—the ability to listen to the voice of conscience, of faith, of inner freedom. They had lost it as a result, first, of the rapid development of technology, then of National Socialism, and finally of war.

The propaganda of materialism began to belabor them from the East, not blatantly as in the Weimar period, but with a quiet, relentless, and comprehensive indoctrination which no one could escape. The constitution of the German Democratic Republic provided indeed that "every citizen enjoys full freedom of religion and of conscience" and that "private or civil rights and duties will neither depend upon nor be restricted by the practice of religion." However, after Walter Ulbricht assumed dictatorial powers in 1958, it was openly declared that the German Democratic Republic was an atheistic State, and that no one who was not an atheist could be either a teacher or a functionary of the State, or could perform any public function. The Christian in the German Democratic Republic thus became a second-class citizen.

188

What could be done? Were we witnessing the fulfillment of Luther's prophecy about the rain shower which falls once and never returns? Was the Christian faith in Germany, which once had been the strength of a whole people, finally to be regarded as obsolete?

For there could be no mistake about it; with us, in eastern Germany, there was none of that native attachment to the church which characterized Catholic Poland, or which was to be found in Scotland a century ago. Our parishioners had never really learned to appreciate their church. They were all inclined to remain Christian "at heart," but to betray nothing of it on the outside. Only a very few were prepared to jeopardize their worldly fortunes for the sake of their religion and their church.

In all those years we were very conscious of the gravity of the problems confronting us.

A bishop must guard against illusions, yet he must not give way to pessimism. He must believe and work. In those years I learned to measure the greatness of the prophet who was told with ruthless frankness that his work would be in vain, and who could cry, nevertheless: "Here am I; send me!" My own motto in those days was taken from the Book of Revelation (13:10): "Here is a call for the endurance and faith of the saints."

We had to do something about the youth.

Religious instruction had almost completely ceased. Prior to 1948, when the Communists broke up the city council and assembly, we had had a unified Berlin. Greater Berlin was unified also in this sense, that religious instruction was everywhere regarded as the concern of the church; the school should no longer impart it. This was an expression of the long-standing antagonism of the teachers' associations to the church, backed up by the completely secularized attitude of the big city. In the background stood the Russians. People did not want to be Communists (with the exception of the few who had now achieved positions of influence) but in their hostility to religion they were of one mind with the Communists: No more religious instruction! Let the church see how it could manage!

Of course there were exceptions, at least in the teaching body. But among the school inspectors at first there was hardly one.

Now, when religious instruction in the schools was no longer compulsory, we could take stock. It became apparent that nine-tenths of all teachers in Berlin had taught religion unwillingly. What blessing could have been attached to such teaching? What blessing could have been attached to the whole huge public school system if every concern with the highest and ultimate things, every sympathetic introduction to the history of the Christian faith, every movement of reverence for God, every persuasive instruction on the imperatives of the Christian conscience, was regarded as a burdensome interruption of school life?

The church had to face the fact, however bitter it was. It could do only one thing—take religious instruction into its own hands.

But in order to do this, the church needed a tremendous number of teachers of religion. For it was quite impossible for the pastors and their few assistants to cope with the task single-handed. In Berlin alone there were approximately 250,000 children to be taught. Even if they could all be assembled in classes, there would still be some 15,000 hours of teaching per week. And Berlin had 600 pastors.

It is to the lasting credit of Dr. Lokies that he took on the tremendous task of conjuring up a new category of church workers, the catechists, and of training and organizing them. In only a few years all was ready, and the church was giving religious instruction with its own forces, men and women teachers who for the most part were miserably paid but joyfully and genuinely devoted to their work.

These catechists deserve a word of high appreciation and sincere thanks. Naturally they varied in their teaching abilities. There were even some who, faced with a class of children to whom

190

respect for authority and reverence for the sacred had become altogether alien, failed in their effort to make real the world of the eternal. And yet, if the heroes of the great church struggle (if Christians may speak of heroes at all) were the young theology students and assistant pastors of the Confessing church, the unsung heroes of this new period under Communist domination were the catechists. They were surrounded by downright hostility and opposition (most of the school principals did whatever they could to make things difficult for them); they had little or no support from the parents; they lived in uncertainty and poverty—yet their sole concern was to prepare the Lord Christ a dwelling place in the hearts of the young. Their work will never be forgotten.

My own contribution to this development consisted of only two things. In the first place, I kept the ecclesiastical bureaucracy from interfering in this newly emerging educational apparatus. My principle was that education could flourish only in an atmosphere of freedom. Of course, a department of education gradually develops a bureaucracy of its own. That is inevitable in all administrative work of any magnitude. But in this case it was a kind of family bureaucracy. Decisions were made not by consistorial councilors or superintendents, but by people who had risen out of the ranks of the catechists themselves. The organized church stood by ready to help, not to rule.

The other thing I could do was to help facilitate arrangements for attaching this religious instruction in some way to the school. It would have been impossible to get the children together independently of the school—in the afternoon, for example. Some understanding with the school was essential. And it was finally agreed, after lengthy negotiations, that the church might give its religious instruction in connection with the regular school program, and on the school premises. In practice, however, the Communist-inclined school principals put every kind of obstacle in our way. Religious instruction might not be given in the morning, when the children were still fresh, but in the afternoon, when their powers of retention were weaker; there should be outdoor recreation periods before and after the religious instruction; and more chicanery of the same order. In the East, the Communist school principals had the right to supervise the church's religious instruction, even when it was not given in the school building. Nevertheless, a more or less tolerable situation was finally established.

Only in West Berlin could a fairly satisfactory relationship be established between church and school administration, thanks to the sympathetic support of Senator Tiburtius.

It was not enough for the Communists that they had got rid of religious instruction in the schools. A campaign was started against church-run kindergartens and day nurseries, church-run boarding schools, church-run training centers for nurses, teachers, and so on. Christianity must be driven out of the hearts of the rising generation. The climax of this systematic campaign was the attack on the Youth Congregation *(Junge Gemeinde)*.

This is what happened. When the Russians came, they began by banning all associations. There was to be no organization that was not directly subject to the authority of the State. But the church youth, in city and country alike, were all organized in youth associations. The church rightly regarded it as its duty to continue to concern itself with the youth it had confirmed. And the obvious way to do so was through the association. The German must have his associations!

But this was just what was no longer to be allowed. So instead, youth congregations began to form; that is, young people loyal to the church would come to services and Bible classes at the parsonage, the church house, the church. All this without membership, without dues, simply as members of the congregation. The Russians looked upon this with suspicion. To them it was unthinkable that a dozen healthy boys should gather in their pastor's office to study the Bible. There had to be something behind it—a resistance organization, or something of the kind. "On the table you have a Bible, and under the table you have a staff map with which you are preparing an attack on Russian soldiers!" Meetings were often disturbed and arrests were made. On the whole, however, the Youth Congregation managed to establish itself.

Its great foe was the high school, which most of our confirmed youth attended and which was now to be developed as a training center for materialism. Every teacher was under obligation to turn his class into a Communist "collective." But the members of the youth congregations would not allow themselves to be drawn into such "collectives."

Then the Free German Youth was formed to which every boy and girl in the Russian occupation zone was to belong "voluntarily."

When this organization was established, we had lengthy negotiations with General Tulpanov, who headed the Russian civil administration of Germany. He was a man of squat build, mongoloid features and crafty eyes, always polite, both as a host and as a negotiator, but purposeful and dangerous. He pressed us not to take a hostile view of the Free German Youth. It was only to be the over-all organization; within it each group was to have full freedom of action, even the Evangelical youth. We could only reply that that was how the Hitler Youth had started, that he could not expect us to have much confidence in a new totalitarian youth organization, that he could not ask us to betray our Evangelical youth a second time, and that the memory of Ludwig Müller was still very much alive among us. Tulpanov did not like the reference to the Hitler Youth; Communists resent nothing so much as being confronted with the similarities between all totalitarian States. We undertook, finally, to let some representatives of the Youth Congregation join the executive of the Free German Youth, and for the rest, to wait upon events.

We did not have long to wait. The Free German Youth became patently more Marxist and materialistic, first in its action, then in its regulations. The representatives of the Youth Congregation resigned. The open struggle had begun. In 1961 it had gone so far that the Free German Youth, complete with steel helmets and arms, could have been brought into action in a civil war against West Berlin.

From the start, the young people of the eastern zone took little part in the activities of the Free German Youth. But the Communist leaders placed every obstacle in the way of the activities of the Evangelical youth. One device employed was that when a district meeting of the Youth Congregation was announced for a certain Sunday, on the previous evening all the cars hired for the outing would be called in for inspection, found defective, and declared incapable of operation. Then, if some 2,000 young members of the Evangelical Church managed to assemble after all, the Free German Youth would organize a counter-demonstration to which it would bring youngsters from far and wide—and it would still not be able to assemble more than 200 or 300 of them.

Finally they decided to use the big stick. Hearings were organized in all the high schools. The pattern was always the same. The whole school was assembled. The teaching staff had to be present too. The school inspector was there, representatives of the Free German Youth, representatives of the State security agency, sometimes even uniformed police. And then the boys and girls who belonged to the Youth Congregation were called forward. Each was individually interrogated, threatened, and harassed. Each must sign a declaration to the effect that he, or she, was now convinced that the Youth Congregation was an illegal organization, hostile to the State, and that he would no longer belong to it.

There they stood, the sixteen- and seventeen-year-olds, denounced, threatened, abused, heckled. None of the teachers was permitted to come to their aid. The school principal led the chorus of accusation and harassment. It was the most shameful action in the history of German education.

194

Some signed. A large number remained firm and were expelled from school.

Of course the church did not leave its brave young confessors to fend for themselves. Some were placed in boarding schools which had been hastily established in West Berlin. Others were helped to continue their studies in various parts of western Germany.

Just as the persecution of young Christians had reached its apogee, there was a sudden reversal of policy.

We Evangelical bishops had requested an audience with Minister-President Grotewohl in order to present our various grievances. We had little hope that our request would be granted, and still less that it would lead to any practical result.

Suddenly we received an invitation to appear on June 10, 1953. We duly arrived. I made a short introductory statement, after which each bishop in turn briefly set forth one of our complaints. When we had finished, Grotewohl said: "Gentlemen, all your wishes will be acceded to." The persecution of the Youth Congregation would stop, the young people who had been expelled might return to their schools, the institutions which had been confiscated would be returned, the State would again pay the prescribed subsidies, with some reductions, and recent arrests would be re-examined. He said all this in the presence of the Communist Minister of Education, Wandel, the Minister of Internal Security, Zaisser, and Minister-President Nuschke. There could be no doubt about it; the promise was meant seriously. This was a total reversal of Communist church policy.

Behind all this, of course, were instructions from Moscow. For reasons which to this day are not apparent, the Russians wanted a pause in the cold war—and therefore a pause also in the church struggle. The Russians were obviously not indifferent to the measures that were being taken in regard to the church. But this did not mean that they were concerned that the charges made against the Youth Congregation were malicious and untrue. Truth

195

and falsehood are not recognized categories in the thinking of a totalitarian State.

For the Youth Congregation there was now a breathing space too. Few of those expelled returned to their old schools. Most of them were unwilling to become students again in schools where they had been so disgracefully treated. But no new disciplinary measures were taken for the time being.

Yet no one could pretend to himself that the work of the Youth Congregation had not suffered severely. The organization never again flourished as it had before. It was not the youngsters who had grown fearful, but the parents. Terror always has its effect. It was no different in the persecutions of the early Christians.

On June 17, 1953, the uprising of the workers in Berlin and throughout the Russian zone of occupation took place. It was quickly put down by the Russian military. But it immediately gave the radical elements, led by Walter Ulbricht, the upper hand. And this had its effect on the church too. At first the promises that had been given were kept; then the relations between the Communist State and the Christian church gradually returned to the state of cold war.

Let no one think, however, that the leadership of the Evangelical church had hardened its heart against the Communist system from the outset, and regarded everything that came from the East as, *a priori*, the work of the devil. Precisely the contrary was true. We were determined to avoid a repetition of the days when the Socialist movement came up against a church which did not know how to deal with it. If the Communists had now come upon us, was this not also a dispensation of Providence, intended for our instruction?

We opened wide our hearts and minds, and kept pondering how we could honorably change our thinking. Had we concerned ourselves enough with the workers? Should we not re-examine our ideas about private property in the light of the teachings of the

New Testament? Had we not attached more importance to the family than was consonant with the Gospel? Had we not interpreted the concept of freedom in much too bourgeois a sense? Ought we not to think out our whole philosophy of life anew, down to the last detail, in the light of the Gospel, and had not God sent us the Russians for that very purpose?

I pondered these questions over and over again. I had the West and the East before my eyes daily. The West was a familiar world, to be sure, which was slowly finding its way back to its accustomed grooves. But the general picture it presented was anything but gratifying: a youth whose motto was "Count me out!"; a universal straining for money and pleasure; a work force without ideals; marriages falling apart; moral ties weakening. A sign of the times was the enormous circulation of illustrated magazines with which the bourgeois world encouraged its own progressive decline into stupidity. Did not the East have something better, healthier, more really genuine to offer than this western world?

My long inner conflict led me to the conclusion that however one may judge the traditional and present-day outlook of the West, the Christian can never identify himself with the Communist philosophy. The influence of the Gospel has made itself felt, directly or indirectly, over the past two thousand years, in matters of property, of family, of freedom. And the Christian must always be in a position to link up with that influence in matters concerning the renewal of the life of the nation. Radical Marxism, however, is materialistic through and through. Socialism, as we see from the contemporary world, is possible without subscribing to the philosophy of Karl Marx. Communism is not; in any event, not at this time. It remains to be seen whether things will one day change in this respect. At the present time, the world in which the Christian is at home can nowhere find a door through which it may enter the Communist world. The wall of materialism is hermetically sealed. Those who subscribe to Communism have no alternative but to offer unconditional obedience to "big brother,"

197

an obedience extending to every aspect of life, external and internal. For "big brother" there exists only one thing—power. To all this the Christian can only say "No!"

Even the argument that Communism, at least for Russia, was a liberation—the oft-cited "liberating storm" or, in Christian terms, the judgment of God, preparing the way for His grace—could not stand. It was while studying the Russian Revolution that I first realized that bloody revolutions, too, must be judged by Christian standards. I do not ignore the stimulating effects of the great revolutions of history. Their "achievements" must not be underestimated, however certain it may be that these achievements would for the most part have been produced without revolutions— although later, perhaps very much later. But the Christian can think only in terms of human souls. However incomprehensible it may sound in terms of modern theory, the accelerated industrialization of all Russia and China cannot, for the Christian, make up for the death cry of the people who paid the price of that industrialization.

After long reflection, I learned, as a man of seventy, to say "No" to Communism and to everything it thinks and does—the "everlasting 'No'" of Thomas Carlyle's *Sartor Resartus*. I learned it not on political grounds but for the sake of the Christian religion. For the sake of that religion, there could be no weighing in the balance of reason what was good in the Communist social order and what was less good. The only thing to do was to penetrate to the roots and to recognize the spirit permeating everything. That spirit was one of radical secularization of human existence and, as a logical corollary, the eradication of every link with anything supernatural, in particular with the Christian faith. This spirit was no accidental adjunct which could be disregarded in a judgment of the movement as a whole; it was vitally present in everything that took place in the Communist world. I have never been able to understand how a professor of theology like my friend Hromadka in Prague could sponsor the proposition that the church should regard the atheism of the East as nonexistent.

For this reason, and for this reason alone, the Christian church had to say "No," clearly and unambiguously. For on this point it had a responsibility.

I have never been obstinate, either in affirming or in negating. But in contrast to those, in the West as in the East, who are inclined to minimize grave situations, there had to be a clear "No." It must be left to God whether that "No" should, in the future, be regarded as obsolete.

In my official capacity, I had daily dealings with the representatives of Communism. The first encounters were with the Russian generals. They varied considerably one from the other, but the peasant type predominated. But one also found a man like Marshal Sokolowsky, who for some time was in command in Berlin. He was an elegant, highly cultivated man, who knew his Goethe as well as his Bible and Karl Marx's *Das Kapital*. He complained to me that Germans showed little reverence for their national monuments. He had been horrified, upon entering Weimar, at the miserable condition of Goethe's house, and had at once given orders for its careful restoration. In a conversation about agrarian reform, he stated emphatically that there was no question at all of simply reproducing the Russian system in Germany; the German peasant, he said, must live in a German atmosphere and in a German tradition. I was told that Sokolowsky (that is not his original name) was the son of an ambassador in Tsarist times. But the deeper one penetrated among the politicians, the more compelled one was to turn away; their Communist training had effaced all humanity from their thinking and feeling.

Then there were the Germans who were playing the Russian Communist game. At their head was Minister-President Grotewohl. None of us denied him a certain respect as a man. He could be practical, and when he agreed to anything, the agreement was kept, at least for a time. Provost Grüber maintained relations with the rest of the Cabinet; I personally had little occasion to meet them. The most controversial figure among them was Otto Nuschke, whom Grüber always defended very warmly. He represented the Christian Democratic Union of eastern Germany, occasionally attended church-sponsored events, and even came to my house. What he disclosed as his confidential opinion cannot be reported here. But at decisive moments—for instance, when we were having a discussion with the whole Cabinet, along with the representatives of the Catholic church—he had to "do his duty," as they say in the East. Only under that condition was he tolerated in the Cabinet. Hardly any of us ever spoke to Walter Ulbricht.

The centralization of authority progressed from year to year. At first there were still individual governments and minister-presidents in the various territories and provinces. We had a good many skirmishes with Rudi Jahn, the Minister-President of Brandenburg, who wanted to force us to move our church government to Potsdam so that we should be completely under Communist influence, but we usually emerged victorious. At last the separate governments were dissolved and replaced by a larger number of district offices. These were afraid to make any decisions at all; everything was decided in Berlin. It was not worth dealing with them, except in matters of exclusively local interest. And even then, one had to bear in mind constantly that one was dealing with Communists who were simply not permitted to recognize any obligation to tell us the truth or to keep their promises.

The conflict was never-ending. There were constant arrests; activities and publications were banned; students and school children subjected to discriminatory meaures. It never stopped.

Our most serious concern in this permanent cold war was whether we would be able to preserve the clergy from the influence of Communist ideology. The Communists used the same tactics that the National Socialists had tried. But it was clear that all the conditions were lacking for a movement like that of the German-Christians—at least at first. The clergy had had their taste of a totalitarian State, and had learned that the only way to withstand its oppressive might was for Christians to stick to-

200

gether, firmly and uncompromisingly. The National Socialists had begun by asserting that they were going to establish a "positive Christianity," and had impressed many with this slogan. With the Communists, there could be no question of this. Here it was clear from the start that a flat contradiction existed between Communism and Christianity. The attempt to win over any considerable number of Evangelical pastors to the Communist regime was doomed to failure.

It was tried nevertheless. A bridge was to be constructed by setting up pseudoneutral organizations and trying to rally the Evangelical clergy behind them. Now there would be a National Front, now an Alliance of the Friends of Peace, and so forth. The minister-presidents personally sought out the pastors and sent their official cars to take them to the meetings. It was a complete fiasco. The pastors did not come.

Another tack was tried. Members of the clergy were approached who had been National Socialists, or who had infringed some regulation of the new State. They were told that all would be forgiven and forgotten if they would undertake to act as government spies: they should furnish reports on statements by bishops and superintendents-general, on discussions in the consistory and at pastoral conventions.

When I first learned of this, I went to Tulpanov and told him that if this kind of thing did not stop immediately I would go to each of the congregations concerned and announce from the pulpit: "Beware of your pastor; he is in the service of the political police!" This had its effect. Six weeks later Tulpanov asked me with a smile whether any other such cases had come to my ears. I could only answer truthfully that none had.

But (this at least was my experience) directives such as Tulpanov must have given are effective in a totalitarian State only for a few months. Then the old ways, which after all are related to the very essence of the totalitarian State, set in once more.

We demanded of every pastor that he should reply to such suggestions with a categorical "No," and assured him that if he did so nothing would happen to him. And such was indeed the case, with very few exceptions. As soon as the agents of the secret police came up against a courageous attitude, they withdrew—although there were cases where such strength of character was put to the test, even to the point of physical torture.

But such an attitude required courage. And not all are brave. There were cases where the nerves of a pastor or of his wife broke down, or where the family's misfortunes were already so great that no further burdens could be assumed. Then nothing remained but to transfer the pastor, sometimes to West Berlin or western Germany. Mostly a transfer within the zone was sufficient.

It was an occasion of constant thankfulness on our part that the clergy as a whole endured bravely. The clergy were the only academically trained body which held out in the East. They were assailed and harassed at every turn, economically inferior to the skilled worker, prevented from giving their children a decent education. Despite all this, they held out.

There was a tiny group of so-called "progressive" pastors in Brandenburg. Some of them were pastors who had been subjected to disciplinary proceedings. Some were quickly rejected again by the Communists because they had shown themselves to be psychologically unbalanced. And there were also a few incorrigible opportunists.

In the other territorial churches the number of progressive pastors was somewhat greater, but they did not acquire much influence there either, at least not in the first fifteen years of Communist domination.

Only during my last years in office did the picture change. The number of so-called progressive pastors remained small. But by the same token there was an increase in the number of those who wanted to avoid conflict with the Communist masters. It had now become obvious to everyone that there would be no speedy reunification of Germany. A pastor had to accommodate himself to facts. Of course he wanted to resist when God's commandments clearly required it, but such occasions were not frequent. And for the rest one would just have to put up with things—even with an atheistic school for one's children. After all, so the argument ran, every regime has its positive sides, even a totalitarian regime. And, perhaps, if one zealously co-operated in everything that appeared justified in the light of common sense, for instance, in "peace" propaganda, in "voluntary" harvesting, and so on, then all this might be rewarded. Life would become easier for oneself— and for the church. This, and nothing else, was the authentic Christian outlook on life. The important thing was to avoid ever-lasting conflict, everlasting opposition. One must show love. One must "love Communism to death," as Professor Heinrich Vogel dramatically declared at one of our synods.

The only problem with this approach is that the New Testament says something different—quite different.

A new church struggle had come upon us. But this time the word "struggle" had to be put in quotes. Opponents within our own ranks maintained that we represented a "crusading ideology." But this was merely arguing in slogans. Who among us called for a crusade? We did not even have an organized underground move-ment, as we had had in Nazi times, to confront the Communists. We could protest from time to time against arbitrary measures and the use of force—vainly, of course. For all our protests landed in the wastebasket. We could tell our congregations and our Com-munist opponents what was contrary to our Christian faith in the ordinances and proclamations issued by the State. I did so re-peatedly, for my part, both orally and in writing. When Minister-President Grotewohl declared in a long, official speech that the party determined what was good and bad, I stated in a widely circulated open letter that a Christian could not be at home in such a State.

We did these things. For the rest, we preached the Gospel. Was that a crusading ideology?

The signs of progressive weariness accumulated. In the steady stream of refugees, there were fewer and fewer who said that they had left the eastern zone because they did not want to expose their children to a systematically anti-Christian education. Most had left for quite different reasons. When it was decided, at the all-German synod, to establish an Evangelical ministry to the armed forces, the great majority of eastern members agreed because this was a question of elementary responsibility for the church as a whole which no Christian could shirk. But at the next synod, a member from Brandenburg declared: "We went too far. We simply cannot stand up to the tremendous pressure of Communist propaganda any more. We have to withdraw our co-responsibility for this pastoral action."

Who would reproach our brothers from the East on this account?

This raised the very serious problem for the church government of whether a pastor should leave his congregation and flee to the West. Who would think ill of a pastor who, carrying out his ministry year in, year out, under the pressure of a totalitarian State hostile to the church, was finally overcome by the longing to be free again? Free from being everlastingly spied on, free from the malevolence of party officials who could prevent every vacation trip, every visit to relatives, every participation in important church activities, free from book censorship, free from postal censorship, free from the fear of being arrested on some pretext or other, free from the oppressive compulsion of having to deliver his own children to a materialistic system of education, and without any hope that they would one day be able to engage in a satisfactory profession! Yes, who would blame him for yearning to be free?

Then there were the pastors' wives. For years they had had to share house and kitchen with unfriendly compulsory tenants. They had to perform, unaided, the kind of work in house and garden which overtaxed their strength. Doctors were no longer readily available. In addition they had constant worries about husband and children. More and more frequently the cry of distress arose from the parsonages: "We cannot go on this way any more!"

The world heard the cry. The church government heard it. But we heard it with other ears than the public at large. For had we not gone through all this before? Had not most of us who now held positions of responsibility in the church experienced personally what it meant to be spied upon day and night, arrested, held, sometimes for years, in concentration camps, subjected to endless interrogations by night, ill-treated or—if it did not get as far as actual torture—crushed in body and soul? Had we not seen our children treated as second-class human beings at school, at labor service and everywhere else because they wanted to remain Christians? Many of us would never forget the scene in the schoolyard: Hoisting of the flag. Roll call. Class 9 present: 21 students and 1 saboteur! The saboteur, of course, was the pastor's son. Should not we, the older ones, say to our younger brothers in the ministry: "What we endured, can you not endure too—for the sake of Jesus Christ and His church?"

But the difference was that in Nazi times we all shared a common fate; there was no escape—not for anyone. Now, however, there was the West at the door. There, people lived in freedom. There, one could perform his office as pastor in freedom. Freedom was palpably near. Could not a pastor whose ministry had become intolerable in the East continue to discharge his duties in the West?

What would not the church government have given to have been able to open wide the door to the West! But it was not possible; it really was not possible. A church government is primarily responsible for life in the congregations. And what was the situation, now, in the East German congregations?

The number of pastors had dwindled. The rising generation of pastors was a very meager one. One reason was that Hebrew, Greek, and Latin were hardly taught any more in the schools of the East. We established the category of non-academically trained preachers. But this could not meet the need. At first young pastors still came over from the West, eager to serve, prepared to help. Some would have come, too, later on, but by then the door was closed. No pastor from the West was permitted by the authorities to take over a ministry in the East. Here and there lay members of congregations—church elders and others—would conduct services where there was no longer a pastor. We encouraged this as far as we could. But still only very few were ever prepared to expose themselves to the dangers involved in such a public stand. The number of orphaned congregations grew with every year that passed despite all our efforts.

But what should the parishioners say if the pastor deserted them? They themselves had to carry on. Perhaps because they were too old to make a new beginning on the other side. Perhaps because they could not uproot themselves. Perhaps because they were afraid. For in the totalitarian States the medieval law again prevailed that a man, with his physical and mental powers, belonged to the State and must not leave his country without special permission. There were severe penalties for "fleeing the Republic," and people feared them. They preferred to stay. But the pastor—one day he was gone and had left them to bear their burdens alone! Yet had he not sworn before God's altar that he would be a true shepherd of his flock? Had he not read out from the pulpit that the church urgently requested its members to stay and not to flee? And now he was gone!

No, it really was not possible to allow every pastor who so desired to leave the East in order to serve a parish in the West. The church government tried to help all who were in any particular need; it tried to help them both spiritually and materially. And if one did flee because he believed himself to be in danger of his life, then it did not cast in his teeth what is written in the tenth chapter of the Gospel of St. John about the hireling, nor did it remind him of what the Lord Christ commanded those to bear who desired to follow Him. To be of firm heart comes from within; it cannot be commanded. So we would set mercy above justice, and no pastor who had discharged his ministry honorably needed to fear for his future within the church.

But limits had to be drawn. Each case of flight by a pastor was brought before a disciplinary committee which had to decide, independently of the ecclesiastical authority, whether any guilt attached to the action or not. Every request by a pastor to be permitted to leave in honor was submitted to a committee of pastors for their opinion, for it should not be said that the church was being governed in authoritarian fashion. It was agreed with the church governments of the West that no pastor from the East should be installed in a western pastorate if he had not previously been released by his native church.

Public opinion in western Germany had very little understanding for all this. There the position was: Poor pastor! He has had to suffer so much, and in gratitude his own church bars his way to freedom! Very, very occasionally a pastor would seek to justify, in the press, an escape undertaken on his own responsibility. If possible he cited Scripture into the bargain, or he sued his church government for not allowing him sufficient funds.

The church government had to remain firm. Let me repeat: Only a very small percentage of the clergy was unfaithful, or tempted to be unfaithful. But for the bishop and for everyone else concerned, it was a heavy and bitter burden to conduct all the pastoral discussions and often endless negotiations which each individual "case" required, and in the end to have to say "no" when the voice of the heart would so gladly have said "yes."

The conflicts which the political situation had gradually aroused within the church finally found dramatic expression in the debate about the "powers that be" *(Obrigkeit)*.

The occasion for the debate could hardly have been more insignificant. In honor of the sixtieth birthday of Territorial Bishop Lilje, I had written a short monograph—which was printed privately—in which I raised the question of whether, in the German translation of Romans 13, some word other than "powers that be" should be used. I said that "powers that be," as Luther had understood the term, no longer existed either in the West or in the East, and that the term used in the Greek text had a different meaning.

This private monograph had become quite widely known. And now the storm broke. It swept the public throughout Germany, in church and political circles alike. What aroused all this agitation, of course, was not the question of how best to translate a passage, but what I had said in that connection about modern State power, particularly about totalitarian systems.

Countless articles were written on the subject. It was discussed in every kind of committee. And finally it was the principal item of discussion at two tempestuous synods.

As is usual in public discussions, particularly those involving political issues, virtually nothing was contributed to the subject itself. Most people seized on points which were purely superficial. Opinions were decided beforehand. People did not want to listen to arguments and reflect on them but simply to express their own convictions.

There was little apparent concern with the tremendously grave question of how a Christian should conduct himself in relation to a totalitarian State—not so much outwardly, as in his personal judgment. Karl Barth had written that even the totalitarian regime was a regime for which the Christian must be thankful, and that there would never be any lack of opportunity for loyal co-operation. This satisfied many. It could not satisfy me. I could only note with sorrow that what St. John says on the subject in Revelation, and what Luther wrote about it in words of tremendous power, had ceased to be of consequence in present-day theology.

I was largely to blame for all this excitement. In the small private edition—only five hundred copies had been printed; several thousand reprints were subsequently made without my permission being requested!—I had expressed myself very freely, on the assumption that what had become obvious to me must have become obvious to others. For the rest, I had said that the practical consequences of a man's basic attitude to the "powers that be" would have to be discussed some other time. My easily aroused opponents could not even know, as yet, what my practical conclusions really were.

Here again it was evident that in the Evangelical Church, passions were aroused only in connection with political issues. The fact that, at that very time, something resembling a movement had emerged among the theologians opposing infant baptism, thus arrogantly dismissing a practice dating back nearly two thousand years—that, apparently, worried no one. But when politics was involved, passions awoke. Then even theologians of my own church government saw fit to attack their bishop publicly—while that bishop remained the target of an uninterrupted Communist campaign of lies.

In these circumstances, all that really happened at the two synods to which I have referred was that a particular theological movement vented its spleen, after which a conciliatory formula was sought, consonant with the spirit and dignity of an Evangelical synod. A formula of this kind was found each time. Only a very small minority fought it to the bitter end.

Inevitably, the Communist authorities put their oar in, too. It was officially declared that my services in the Marienkirche in East Berlin were at an end. The declaration was repeated several times. But when my next sermon was due, I proceeded as usual to my pulpit in the Marienkirche, escorted by the entire church government. Nothing happened. Nothing happened on subsequent Sundays either. The Prosecutor-General of East Berlin instituted a preliminary inquiry into the case. But the inquiry was not carried out.

A few words should be added here about the propaganda which was directed against me.

As long as the administration of the eastern zone was in Russian hands, the propaganda remained within bounds. Only gradually did a change occur. No totalitarian State can manage without official propaganda. That we had learned under Josef Goebbels, and we expected nothing else of the new totalitarian regime which had come upon us. In proportion as the Russians handed over control to the German Communists, the propaganda became more shamelessly totalitarian in method.

One of the primary principles of totalitarian propaganda is that attacks should not be dissipated. One target must be selected, a target which for some reason appears important. On this target all attacks must be concentrated. The attacks must be uninterrupted, and they must be identical. Hundreds and thousands of times the same thing must be said, till it is indelibly imprinted in the memory and then, perhaps, passes into the heart and mind.

This was the method used in the propaganda against the church. And the target on which the attacks were concentrated was myself.

The first theme was that I had been a National Socialist and had blessed Hitler's arms. But it was not altogether easy to get the congregations of my diocese to believe this, for everyone knew how I had fared under National Socialist rule. So, what words were powerless to achieve, pictures would have to substantiate. But despite all searching, no picture could be found of me with Hitler or with any other high Nazi official. Failing this, there was the picture of March 21, 1933, where I, together with the clergy of the Nikolaikirche in Potsdam, was seen greeting Hindenburg in front of the church. What the picture showed was an elementary act of courtesy which is performed as a matter of course all over the world when the head of State takes part in a solemn service. This picture could hardly be interpreted as evidence of National Socialist leanings.

Finally another picture was unearthed, taken during the official ceremonies in the Garnisonkirche at Potsdam at which Hitler and Hindenburg had made their addresses. This picture showed a gowned clergyman sitting in the chancel behind Hitler. It was

210

asserted that I was the clergyman—although it was plain at a glance that I was not present. It was pure fakery.

Two years after the Evanston conference, it was suddenly alleged that I had said, at the conference, that the atomic bomb was really not so bad after all; it simply sent 100,000 people to heaven more speedily than usual! It was impossible to find anyone who had actually heard such a statement with his own ears. On the other hand, those who had been at Evanston stated one after the other that they had never heard me say any such thing. Nevertheless, the statement was reiterated in all schools, at all Communist meetings, in all the newspapers, for years on end. I kept receiving letters from pastors saying that there was talk of it in the congregations, and was there any truth in it? In the streets of East Berlin, along the Autobahn and in many other places, huge bill boards showed the "Atom-Bishop," with appropriate captions. When one of our leading clergy had it out with the Secretary of State for Church Affairs, saying that the authorities knew perfectly well that the story was pure invention, he was told: "If it is against Bishop Dibelius, then any stick will do!"

In 1960—to mention just one more item from the abundance of propaganda charges leveled against me—a film was shown in the eastern sector which took up the "Schnorr case" of 1927. The case, to which I referred earlier in this book, was so presented as to suggest that I, together with a reactionary high bailiff by the name of Friese, had tried by every possible means to protect a murderer, Pastor Schnorr, whose sinister past was known to me. My motive was supposed to have been a political one. The film was so riddled with outrages that the Consistory considered whether it should not sue the narrator, Kaul, who was and is the Communists' star lawyer and resides in West Berlin. I could not agree. I never replied to all this propaganda—apart from answering questions addressed to me personally by letter. It is written: "Blessed are you when men revile you and persecute you and utter all kinds of evil against you falsely on my account. Rejoice and be glad. . . ."

211

This propaganda, as far as I could see, did not hurt my church, and that was all that mattered. Evangelical Christians know what to think of totalitarian propaganda.

I was very much distressed when—like the Catholic Bishop of Berlin—I was suddenly refused the pass I needed as a West Berliner for every trip inside my province. Without the pass I was confined to Berlin. Nevertheless, so long as the special status of Berlin was retained, not a week passed without my having personal contact with pastors and members of the congregations of the province. But being passless was a serious privation and an impediment to the exercise of my duties.

I consoled myself with the knowledge that the functions which I was no longer in a position to discharge were being outstandingly discharged by the two Superintendents-General of the East, Dr. Jacob and Dr. Braun.

Abroad, and to a large extent, too, in my native Germany, all this has earned me the reputation of being a sincere and intrepid fighter against Bolshevism. Nothing could be less true. I have never had the temperament of a fighter, and I have always found it hard to say "No." I learned to say it only when I found myself faced with the responsibility of seeing to it that men were not denied free access to the Gospel of Jesus Christ, and that that Gospel was not falsified.

I had once learned from Karl Barth—and I have always been grateful to him for the lesson—that between German idealism, from Kant right up to the present day, and the message of the Christian Gospel, there was a deeper cleavage than I had realized in my youth. Now I saw myself faced not only with the militant atheism of the Communists, but also with certain theological positions having their source in the same Karl Barth, positions which I believed myself obliged to oppose. For instance, there was the position of some of my old friends favoring "solidarity between Christians and unbelievers." Here I could only say that this was in contradiction to the clear statements of the New Testament, and must therefore have disastrous consequences for the church of Jesus Christ. In such circumstances I learned to say "No."

This does not mean that I have adopted a friend or foe attitude, as it is called nowadays. I have always regarded it as a test of the character of a Christian if he can rejoice when he is wrong. And I have been able to sustain personal friendships even with persons who passionately opposed my theological views.

It will not, I hope, be taken amiss if I refer to a little episode in a life incomparably greater than mine. Bismarck, an old man at the time of this story, was standing in the parsonage at Schönhausen. On the wall hung a portrait of him after Lenbach's painting—the cuirassier's helmet, shining eyes, a lordly bearing. He studied the portrait and said: "That is supposed to be a likeness of me? I am not like that." And he pointed to a picture hanging on the other wall—Peter sinking, reaching out for the saving hand of Jesus. "That is I," he said.

Yes, Peter sinking—that is what I have been all my life!

COUNCIL PRESIDENT

ON AUGUST 27, 1945, we gathered at Treysa to discuss the future of the Evangelical Church in Germany.

Things looked bad in Germany at the time. In the Evangelical Church too. Order and leadership had been restored in the separate territorial churches, if only on a provisional basis, and perhaps only superficially. But the All-German Church—that entity known in Weimar times as the German Evangelical Federation of Churches (*Deutsche Evangelische Kirchenbund*), and in 1933 (for the benefit of the National Socialists) known as the German Evangelical Church, and which all too soon, under August Jaeger, developed into a dubious institution in which the distinction between right and wrong had become blurred—this church for all practical purposes was a thing of the past. August Jaeger was dead. Ludwig Müller died during those same months—a natural death. Hardly any of the former members of the church office of foreign relations or the ecclesiastical chancery remained. And if any did remain, they could not even be considered for service in a renewed church.

Something new had to be created, and this new thing must in some way still be the old. For no one doubted that essentially the

215

German church as a whole still existed. Its organs were dead, its representatives were dead. But the church lived on. In the times of worst confusion, the various church governments and Councils of Brethren had known themselves to be members of a single body. The church as a whole had survived its ordinances and legal paraphernalia. When we met at Treysa, we knew that the German church existed. All that was needed was to give it a form and the right leadership.

The form, of course, could not be established overnight. It takes time to develop a new church constitution. Only one thing was decided immediately: from now on the church was to be known as the Evangelical Church in Germany (*Evangelische Kirche in Deutschland*) instead of the German Evangelical Church (*Deutsche Evangelische Kirche*). It was imperative to make clear that its essence was not *German*. Its essence was the church of Jesus Christ; Germany was the territory in which that church existed. This we had learned from Söderblom, and the Nazi times had impressed it upon us once again.

The most urgent provisional administrative offices were quickly established, so that the church's work could start again. Everything else would be provided for in the new constitution.

As for the persons who were to fill the principal offices—that was simple. There was Dr. Wurm, the seventy-six-year-old Territorial Bishop of Württemberg. All those last years he had courageously striven for a unification of the churches. He had constantly mediated between the Councils of Brethren and the so-called "intact" churches. Everyone trusted him. He was the obvious choice for president of the new council which was to be constituted. No one else was even considered.

Friedrich von Bodelschwingh, the former "provisional Reich Bishop," might have been considered. But Bodelschwingh was not willing to be drawn once more into the arena of ecclesiastical administration. He was present at Treysa, animated and active as ever. His warmheartedness and his piety made him an ideal inter-

216

mediary at crucial moments. But he did not want to accept a post in church government again.

And alongside Dr. Wurm, of course, we must have Niemöller. For the sensation at Treysa had been that Niemöller was with us again. Most of the rest of us had seen each other in the years since 1937. We had corresponded—cautiously, as one has to in a totalitarian State, but still we had kept in touch. With Niemöller no one had been able to speak or to correspond. Now he was with us again! Nervous, excited—but present! The love and attachment of his friends surrounded him once more, warmly, fraternally. And even those who had some reservations about him were caught up in the general enthusiasm.

Niemöller must be the junior partner alongside the aged Bishop Wurm; on that point there was only one opinion.

Then (here too there was unanimity) the Bishop of Berlin must have his place on the governing body as representative of the eastern territories.

These three should actually have sufficed. But the Lutherans announced that they wished Dr. Meiser, the Territorial Bishop of Bavaria, to have a place on the council too. It was already being rumored that a closer alliance was in the making among the Lutherans, although no one knew exactly which way the wind was blowing. The request could hardly have been refused. When the Reformed churches demanded to be represented also, they too were included. Finally there were twelve churches making up the council.

Events were to show that this was not a bad number at all.

Finally we had to decide on the direction of the office of foreign relations and of the ecclesiastical chancery. Foreign relations could only go to Niemöller. His name was symbolic of German resistance to the Nazi regime. He alone could represent our church in a world still bitterly hostile to everything German.

Hans Asmussen was selected to direct the ecclesiastical chancery. I had opposed the choice. How could so original a theologian, whose thoughtful but always opinionated work exerted a far-reaching influence on students of theology, be asked to head a small chancery? But Niemöller insisted on it. He himself was going to take a vacation abroad for a month or two, and he would have no peace if he did not know that a man with whom he was linked by close ties of friendship occupied the key position at home. This carried the day. The most important thing for all of us was that Niemöller should be at peace again, both inwardly and outwardly. We were prepared to take the risk.

The attempt miscarried. In a very short while the friendship between Niemöller and Asmussen turned into bitter antagonism. Asmussen followed his own line. He became more and more resolutely Lutheran and sought to establish friendly contact with the Catholics. This—and other things—brought him into sharp opposition to Niemöller. Everything was affected by this conflict. The only solution was for one of the two to withdraw, and in the nature of things that one could only be Asmussen. It fell to me to find a way for Asmussen to withdraw with honor. We owed him a great debt of gratitude for his vigorous action.

An inner conflict had been apparent, even at Treysa, which underlay our joy at being together again. It was the same conflict which had led to the split within the Confessing church in 1936 at Oeynhausen.

On the one hand, there were those who had belonged to the Councils of Brethren. As long as the struggle lasted, the Councils of Brethren had embraced all who opposed the German-Christians, among them many liberals, church politicians of the Weimar period, strict Lutherans. Many of these, once the struggle was over, found their spiritual homes elsewhere again. What remained of the members of the Councils of Brethren were now, with few exceptions, the group who derived their theology from Karl Barth and who thus evidenced a "Reformed" coloration, even if basically they felt themselves to be Lutheran. The Theological Declaration of Barmen meant more to them than the confessions of the sixteenth century. For the most part, they retained little of the patriotic sentiment of earlier generations. They had emerged in National Socialist times in opposition to everything in Germany that savored of government and officialdom. At the same time they wanted to make the influence of the church felt in public and political life—in the spirit of Karl Barth, of course. Their leader was Niemöller.

Numerically, this group was not strong. But they had assumed the leadership in many of the territorial churches, and particularly in the Reformed and United churches. They were a vital and active group with great self-confidence, and they took it as a matter of course that their views should prevail, regardless of the views of others. They had borne the heaviest burden in the church struggle. Now, they were convinced, the government of the whole church properly devolved upon them.

As a rule, these former members of the Councils of Brethren objected to the whole idea of bishops. They echoed the petulant remarks which Niemöller had made about bishops as such at the height of the church struggle. The subsequent course of the church struggle was not calculated to prove those bitter remarks wrong. In West Germany one could practically sense the atmosphere prevailing in a church if it was headed by a bishop or by a church president.

The members of this group cared little for territorial church frontiers. They were a unitary movement and they wanted to remain so. They wanted a unitary Evangelical church for the whole of Germany. Not, of course, under the dictatorship of a Reich Bishop, as had been attempted by the German-Christians, but under council leadership. The "council" of the Evangelical Church in Germany (the word was taken from the vocabulary of the Confessing church) was to be something like a Council of Brethren. It was to direct the EKiD (Evangelical Church in Germany) fraternally, as an authentic church.

That was one element. Then there were the former "intact"

churches. During the church struggle they had also had their Councils of Brethren, but they had never had any real experience of church administration by council. These were in the main the big Lutheran churches—Bavaria, Hanover, Hamburg in the West; Saxony, Thuringia, and Mecklenburg in the East. Now they all had their bishops. They felt bound together by their structure and by their creed. They had not been caught up in the early nineteenth-century unity movement, but had remained unalterably true to their Lutheran confession. For them, the Barmen Theological Declaration, which their own leaders had signed, was not as important as it was for others. There was a conservative tendency in these churches. The clerical collar of the pastors, the crosses of the deans, the sung liturgy, respect for the episcopal office—all these were not uniform among them, but they gave these churches a character which distinguished them outwardly from the rest.

At this very time they were on the point of forming an administrative unity too. It was a blow to the ranks of the United churches to learn that the Lutherans were setting up their own United Lutheran Church. At first the news was met with general incredulity. Bishop Meiser had made the preparations in absolute secrecy. And when doubt was no longer possible, it was still hoped for a time that not all the Lutheran churches would join in forming this bloc within the EKiD. The hope was vain.

What happened, finally, was this. With the exception of Württemberg and Oldenburg, all the Lutheran churches of eastern and western Germany joined the new United Lutheran Church as active members. They brought with them 40 per cent of all evangelical pastors and congregations in Germany. Württemberg and Oldenburg became permanent guests. Later the little Pomeranian church joined in, again not as a member of the United Lutheran Church, but as a member of the Lutheran World Federation.

Dr. Meiser had hoped that after the second great German collapse, the United churches would finally break up. He hoped that the Lutheran elements in the United churches—and that meant the tremendous majority of the congregations—would now call themselves Lutheran again and ally themselves with the Lutheran churches. Thus a Lutheran Church of Germany would emerge, embracing 80 per cent of all Evangelical congregations. This big Lutheran church would then set up a common administration with the remaining small Reformed and United congregations; but it alone would be the actual representative of German Protestantism.

This ambition was not realized. And because it was not realized, the United Lutheran Church did in fact become something like a bloc within the Evangelical church in Germany, a bloc which from the very start could jeopardize the recently established unity—the more so since it claimed for itself the title of a real church. Its dogma was that the constitutive element of a church was its creed —in my opinion an untenable, but thoroughly German, dogma. Since the EKiD, so the Lutheran argument ran, had no clear creed, but embraced the Reformed as well as the Lutherans, it was a church alliance, not a real church.

This whole mode of thought was alien to the United churches. In their view, it betrayed an erroneous interpretation of the Lutheran confessions. The reality of church life, they maintained, could not be compassed by the theological codifications of the sixteenth century. And if the Lutherans declared that they were bound in conscience (and that known truth brooked no compromise), the United people could only reply that, in Germany at least, a person was not a Lutheran because he had recognized the truth of Lutheran teaching but because he had been born in the Lutheran church; one could not thus throw the question of truth in the face of an Evangelical who, because he had been born in a United church, thought differently about these questions.

But these were and are problems for theologians. They do not interest the congregations. That is something a church always has to bear in mind. And theologians should not imagine that theology is the only important thing in the church.

There was yet another reason why the United churches found

these discussions difficult to conduct. The modern Lutheran dogma, if carried to its logical conclusion, meant that not only the EKiD, but also the United churches of Prussia, Baden and elsewhere were not really churches at all. Such a conclusion must be completely unacceptable to those churches.

To the credit of the Lutherans it must be said that they did not take the step which, from their theological principles, would have been quite logical, namely, to withdraw from the EKiD again and confine themselves to their Lutheran church. They were content to draw more closely together and to establish the greatest possible unity in liturgical and other internal church matters. This they did on the basis of very comprehensive theological study. For the rest, they co-operated loyally within the EKiD, although in many questions which the United churches accepted as a matter of course, the Lutherans raised all kinds of difficulties: this and that could be dealt with only by a church founded on a definite creed, and therefore not by the EKiD.

Thus a burden of inner discord lay upon the EKiD right from the start. And this burden was intensified by personal differences.

The United Lutheran Church had elected Dr. Meiser as its "leading bishop." He was the Lutherans' spokesman. He was not a great theologian, or an enthralling preacher, but he was a thoroughly solid, responsible, and careful paterfamilias of his church. He was temperamentally a functionary—a high functionary. When a cause which he considered right was to be championed, he could be relied upon to do it well. The confidence he enjoyed in his territorial church had been impressively evidenced when he was placed under house arrest on the orders of August Jaeger; his Bavarian congregations had demonstrated their loyalty by repeated ovations in front of his house. This grateful trust remained, far beyond the frontiers of the Lutheran church, till his retirement in 1955.

His antagonist—that is the only word to use—was Dr. Niemöller.

This hostility had existed from the very beginning of the church struggle. When they found themselves face to face again at Treysa, after years of separation, the conflict flared up immediately.

Niemöller, in contrast to Meiser, was anything but a functionary, however remarkable his gift for administration. He did not like to weigh the pros and cons; he preferred to take risks. Even as an elderly man there was a quality of youthfulness about him— and this instinctively won him the hearts of the young. He was not careful in his speech, but spoke out, usually aggressively, exactly as he thought. In so doing he often hit the nail on the head—but he did not make himself popular!

There is one incident which I shall never forget. It took place during the Nazi period, shortly before Niemöller's arrest. Niemöller had spoken to someone on the telephone about Bodelschwingh, whom he happened to be annoyed with at the time. He had expressed himself in no uncertain terms, as was his way. The conversation was tapped by the Gestapo and reported to Reich Minister Kerrl. Kerrl was jubilant. "If I publicize this speech, Niemöller will be done for in the church! The Evangelical Church will not tolerate anyone speaking like that about Bodelschwingh."

This was reported to me. I went to Niemöller and told him the story. Hardly had I finished than Niemöller jumped up and grabbed the telephone. I tried to pull him back. "What are you going to do?" "I am phoning Kerrl to demand that the conversation be published within three days. The world must see the methods the State police are using against the church!"

That was typical of Niemöller. Any other pastor would have been troubled, he would have considered how to extricate himself from so dangerous a situation. Niemöller immediately turned the tables and passed to the attack!

He still feared no one, and not for a moment did he bow before those whom the world esteemed. He antagonized everyone—Federal Chancellor Adenauer, the American general who had liberated him and his fellow captives from Dachau, scholars, journal-

223

ists, bishops. Whenever he felt that someone was trying to restrain him, he took the offensive. In attack and contradiction he was really at his best.

He could also lose his temper. His outbursts of anger were feared by friend and foe alike. The insulting letters which he wrote to everyone were famous throughout Germany.

Those who loved him forgave all that. Prophetic natures cannot be judged in the same way as the rest. And those less close to him often felt sympathy in spite of themselves when they saw him in the grip of a tension of which he was the principal victim, and from which he could free himself only with great difficulty.

The fuel which fed the opposition to Niemöller within the council, especially during the early years, was Niemöller's statements on politics. We all agreed that political differences must not divide us. After Dr. Heinemann founded his own political party, he was no longer elected President of the Synod—an Evangelical synodical president must not at the same time be the leader of a political party—but he remained on the council. And the other council members worked with him in the friendliest fashion, even after certain political developments had put this friendship to the test. Nor did we ever take it amiss when Niemöller took a different stand from ours on political questions. But we were entitled to expect that a church president, who was a member of the council of the EKiD, would use some moderation in his language. The remark, for instance, that Konrad Adenauer's State had been "conceived in the Vatican and born in Washington" was really hard to swallow, quite apart from the fact that it was particularly painful and offensive to Catholic ears.

Much in Niemöller's development is reminiscent of Adolf Stoecker. And just as Stoecker had a following which stuck to him through thick and thin, so Niemöller had his faithful who did not, perhaps, approve of everything he did, but who still supported him unreservedly at critical moments. Stoecker's name, despite everything, is still alive in the history of his church, while the names of most of his opponents have passed into oblivion; in the same way, Niemöller's name will still be spoken long after all our names are forgotten.

As long as Niemöller remained on the council of the EKiD, there could be no close, fraternal association among us. Nevertheless, we tried to keep him on it. For the whole purpose of the council was that the great church conflicts should be aired and resolved within the council. It was by his own choice that Niemöller resigned on November 3, 1955.

No one ever doubted the inner strength of his Christian faith. It was not so much what he said in his sermons that made so deep an impression, but the instinctive awareness that here was someone who was speaking from the unity of inner conviction. My personal respect for him, which I have never lost, was renewed again and again in times of crisis as I thought of Luther's splendid phrase: *"Pecca fortiter et crede fortius."* Which means, in plain language: "Sin, but hold on to your faith the more firmly."

The years immediately following 1945 were taken up with the work of reconstruction and the elaboration of the new constitution. This new constitution—fundamental law (*Grundordnung*), as it was now called—was adopted at Eisenach in 1948.

Two days of preliminary discussion preceded the actual opening of the synod. There was a feeling of uncertainty and a desire to collect oneself.

The question whether one could speak of an Evangelical *church* in Germany at all touched off heated debate. An equally thorny point was that of fellowship in the Lord's Supper. The United churches took it for granted than any Evangelical Christian in Germany could partake of Holy Communion in any Evangelical church. For the Lutherans it was not so obvious. In practice, however, most of them took the same view. But there were strict Lutheran circles who tolerated no members of Reformed churches at the celebration of the Lord's Supper, and who themselves, when they were in the territory of a United church, kept away from any Holy Communion service. These circles had to be taken into account too. For the Lutherans, this was a question of their very existence.

It almost appeared as though the synod of Eisenach would end like that of Oeynhausen, where the fighting comradeship of the Confessing church had broken up. On the following Sunday, I preached the sermon in the great Church of St. George; the text was Ezekiel 37. Afterwards Bishop Meiser shook my hand; the sermon, he said, had dissipated the tension. Later on, he often reminded me of it. I do not know whether the others felt the same. However that may be, the atmosphere on Monday was different. There was a quick flow of discussion. A preamble was agreed upon which provided that the Evangelical Church in Germany was an alliance of churches determined by creeds, but that this alliance was also to constitute a Confessing church. On the question of the Lord's Supper, it was stated simply and soberly that full agreement did not exist.

In neither case was this a solution. These were formal compromises—the compromise regarding the Lord's Supper I had suggested myself. But they helped remove the roadblocks which were threatening access to the newly constituted church. The important thing at that particular point was that the major obstacles had been cleared away. The rest would work out; it had to work out.

Half a year later, in January, 1949, the first regular synod of the new Evangelical Church in Germany took place at Bethel. Now the council had to be elected, and the president and vice-president designated by the synod. This last was the crucial item.

Bishop Wurm had meanwhile reached the age of eighty and was relinquishing all his offices. The gratitude of the entire Evangelical Church in Germany accompanied him in his retirement.

His deputy from the start had been Niemöller, and nothing was more natural than that the deputy should now be appointed to the presidency of the council. Niemöller himself expected it, and his friends took it for granted. But now it became evident that in those four years since Treysa, much bitterness had accumulated against Niemöller. Most of the Lutherans opposed him. Even among his old associates in the church struggle were many who felt it impossible to have a man of his temperament at the head of the whole German church.

The members of the synod who represented the churches in the eastern zone wanted the supreme direction of the church to be in Berlin; this, they felt, would help the hard-pressed churches of the East. After hours of unpleasant debate, I was elected president by a vote of 110 to 26.

Since I belonged to a United church, the vice-president had to come from a Lutheran church; that was the general opinion. Among the Lutherans, Dr. Lilje was the obvious choice.

This meant, however, that Niemöller, who had hitherto held the vice-presidency, would be left out of the inner circle of government. And that again was undesirable. The synod was prepared to revoke the constitution it had just adopted in order to provide for a triumvirate: Lilje, Niemöller, and myself. It was not a good idea, but it would undoubtedly have been adopted had it been put to the vote. It was not. Niemöller refused to insinuate himself into the top leadership in such a way. After a long debate —it was still more unpleasant than the first—Dr. Lilje was elected vice-president. One hundred and one votes were cast in his favor, with thirty-one abstentions. Niemöller received two votes.

Six years later, at the synod of Espelkamp, elections had to take place again. I was approaching my seventy-fifth birthday, and was entitled to think of giving up all my functions and retiring—though between 1933 and 1945 I had already anticipated twelve years of retirement. I was asked to accept the nomination for another six-year term. I agreed.

The reason I agreed was that only a short time previously I had

227

been elected one of the six presidents of the World Council of Churches. It would have created an awkward situation had I resigned immediately thereafter from the presidency of the council of the Evangelical Church in Germany. For my election to the presidency of the World Council of Churches had been in no small measure determined by my status as president of the council of the EKiD. So I stood for re-election, and was duly re-elected.

Dr. Lilje remained vice-president.

Thus for twelve years I held the presidency of the council of the Evangelical Church in Germany. What were my duties, and how did I seek to perform them?

My duties were far more narrowly circumscribed than an outsider might imagine. The inner life of the church, which is the whole reason of its existence, has to be lived in the individual territorial churches, not in the EKiD. Fundamentally, it has to be lived in the individual congregations.

It is altogether erroneous to suppose that individuals, or even directive organs, can exert a decisive influence on the inner life of their church. That inner life follows its own laws. To speak in Christian terms, it is directed and determined by the Holy Spirit. The individual is carried on the wave; he cannot direct it. Not even Karl Barth could do that. Not even Martin Niemöller. How should the president of the council have been able to? Outsiders have no conception of the constant self-restraint exercised by responsible church leaders as they observe the ups and downs that take place in the life of the church about which they can do nothing decisive one way or another. One can do his duty, his very modest duty. Everything big one has to leave to the providence of God.

In any case, the whole organization of the Evangelical Church in Germany was not such as to give the president of the council any opportunity for acting in the capacity of an archbishop. Everything was scattered. The ecclesiastical chancery, the principal organ of the council, was located in Hanover, the office of foreign relations in Frankfurt, the office for social relief in Stuttgart, and the plenipotentiary to the federal government had his office in Bonn. In Berlin I had a fairly small staff of collaborators, most of whom worked for the EKiD on a part-time basis. The council itself met on an average of once every two months for a day or two, and was always glad if it managed to complete its heavy agenda in one fashion or another. There was rarely time to discuss important questions. Moreover, many were swayed by the deep anxiety that a "dictatorship of a Reich Bishop" might once more develop within the Evangelical Church.

The president of the council was confined within very narrow limits indeed!

Primarily the president of the council was the bishop of his diocese. There lay his specific task. In relation to the EKiD he was to preside over the council—nothing more. He was not to direct the council, much less the Evangelical Church.

I had to concentrate my efforts in the first place on keeping the council together, and consequently the EKiD itself. That was a very elementary, very thankless, but very necessary task—the most necessary of all. It was also a difficult task, not merely on account of the conflicts to which I have already referred, but also for quite different reasons.

In former times, the Evangelical Church was held together by strong external buttresses—concern for the congregations abroad and, above all, concern for the unity of the Reich. A Reich Ministry for Internal Affairs, located in Berlin, handled important legal and financial questions affecting all the Evangelical territorial churches in Germany. It was therefore vital for all these churches to have a central office in Berlin to represent their interests. Moreover, the church governments were all penetrated to the core by strong national sentiment. All this held them together.

Now the situation was altogether different. The overseas congregations still existed, but they had suffered gravely in two wars simply because they were German congregations. They wanted a looser relation to the mother church. They no longer wanted to be outposts of a German national church. They wanted greater independence. And many of them gladly accepted the help which the Lutheran World Federation gave them. Politically this was harmless. And the new confessional consciousness prompted some overseas pastors to look to the United Lutheran Church more than to the Evangelical Church in Germany.

As for the unity of the Reich, it no longer existed. The congregations of eastern Germany had to deal with the totalitarian German Democratic Republic, the territorial churches of the West with their state governments and, in particular cases, with the federal government in Bonn.

At the same time, the individual churches had awakened to a new sense of independence. The western provincial churches of the Old Prussian Union, that is, in the Rhineland and Westphalia—but chiefly the Rhineland—wanted to make their own church policy, both external and internal. They wanted to establish independent ecumenical relations—with Moscow, with Warsaw, with Prague, and so on. They could afford to do so. They were very well off financially. The existence of the EKiD was not a matter of life or death for them.

As to national sentiment, the returns, to use bureaucratic jargon, were for the most part nil.

In a word, there was no longer any compelling force holding the churches together. Their association in the EKiD was purely voluntary. And this voluntariness had to be daily renewed if the the new form of unity was to be preserved. A primary agent in the preservation of unity was the ecclesiastical chancery, that is, the administrative organ which a living church is least interested in. Personally, I had found the manner in which Asmussen directed the chancery not unattractive.

As I noted earlier, Asmussen was full of initiative and ideas. He was always making new suggestions. And before the council could even take them up, he would have publicized them in addresses and newspaper articles. But the council was not prepared to receive a constant stream of directives from the head of its chancery, or to have him prescribe its agenda. It simply could not absorb the challenges which Asmussen was constantly throwing at its feet. If the reconstruction of the church was to be consolidated, an altogether different technique would have to be adopted.

We managed to have Dr. Brunotte appointed to succeed Asmussen. He was equally outstanding as a theologian and as an administrator, with the deliberation and dependability characteristic of the Lower Saxons. Thus he brought with him all the qualities required at that juncture. Since he was at the same time the administrative head of the United Lutheran Church, he constituted the best guarantee that the Lutheran Church would not grow away from the EKiD. My friends of the United and Reformed churches were violently opposed to the nomination. They accused me of handing over the entire EKiD to bureaucracy and confessional Lutheranism. The nomination was nevertheless confirmed, and the decision proved itself abundantly justified. The action of the chancery was no longer marked by the spontaneity which had characterized it in Asmussen's day. On the other hand, method was established in the administration, and this was really essential in view of the ever-increasing duties that confronted the church. Nor was there any dearth of able collaborators.

Among these—to mention at least one—Edo Osterloh, the theologian, occupied a very special place. But when he was invited to join the federal government in Bonn, I had to counsel him, albeit reluctantly, to accept. We could not provide him with a post within the church government corresponding to his abilities. And in any case the church could only be thankful if men issuing from its ranks held posts in the central government. Osterloh did not disappoint our expectations either as a ministerial counselor in Bonn or, subsequently, as Minister of Culture in Schleswig-Holstein.

What still remained to be settled was the representation of the council at the seat of government. For without permanent contact with the State an "official" church cannot survive—even when there could no longer be any question of a State church. We remained, like the Catholic church, what the English call an "established church," that is, a church with its legally ordained place in the State. This necessitated constant negotiations—about religious instruction, about church institutions, church taxes, and so on. Such negotiations could not all be handled in writing.

The chancery could be transferred neither to Bonn nor to Berlin. At both these centers we had to create a kind of nunciature, to use a Catholic term. In Berlin this was not so important. I was there as president of the council. During the early years I was able to discuss a number of questions with Minister-President Grotewohl and other members of his government. I had my small staff of collaborators who remained in touch with the government authorities. And then there was Provost Grüber, who could always be counted upon to lend his good offices. Eventually the government of the German Democratic Republic broke off official relations, first with me, then with Provost Grüber—in his case without prejudice to a certain personal affection—and finally with all who approached it as representatives of the EKiD. Nothing all-German was to be recognized; division was and remained the watchword. But by then so much headway had already been made that an all-German chancery office located in Berlin could handle internal ecclesiastical affairs independently, no longer with an eye upon the State.

In Bonn the position was altogether difficult. Here a thousand possibilities were offered. We were able to place the work in the very best hands. Superintendent Kunst of Herford, who took it on, was singularly successful in gaining the confidence of the most varied political and ecclesiastical authorities. From the federal President to the cleaning woman, from the Chancellor to Carlo Schmid, from Niemöller to Meiser—everywhere Superintendent Kunst established friendship, sometimes a pastoral relationship, without surrendering his own viewpoint.

He had his connections with the world of industry, and received willing assistance from businessmen—for instance, for his favorite charity, the remarkable settlement of Espelkamp in Westphalia. He was responsive to all real church needs which were brought to his attention, and knew what to do when everyone else was at a loss. It was he, together with that unforgettable friend of ours, Hermann Ehlers, who introduced the Evangelical morning devotions in the Bundestag which the deputies themselves conduct. At the same time, he carried on large-scale financial transactions on behalf of his church with remarkable business acumen.

But his heart belonged above all to the German East. History will be able to appreciate what he did for the oppressed congregations east of the Elbe. The time has not yet come to speak of it.

Everyone knew that this man did not think of himself, but few knew of his greatest personal sacrifice. After the premature death of Dr. Herntrich, Kunst was offered the territorial bishopric of Hamburg. He was the ideal man for the post. Every fiber of his being drew him to it. But he believed that what he was doing for the church in eastern Germany could not as yet be placed in other hands, and so he declined. It was the decision of a man who knows what it means to serve.

The administration was built up. Thanks to its quiet, purposeful work, the EKiD was gradually welded more firmly together. Once, only once, one of the smallest of the member churches was angered at a decision and refused to collaborate within the EKiD. It very soon came back to the fold. No member church could cut itself off from the church as a whole without injury to its own responsible action. That was what we had achieved.

But of course administration as such could not be the all-important consideration. The question was whether the work had any effect on the inner life of the church.

One of the first things the council tackled was the revision of Luther's translation of the Bible.

The revision had long been due. The last careful revision of

Luther's text had been undertaken in 1894. The half century which had elapsed had not only produced new insights into the Hebrew and Greek originals but had also witnessed changes in the German language. Many expressions which were understood without difficulty in 1894 had, in the meantime, disappeared from the language. From every quarter came the lament that people no longer understood Luther's Bible. Above all, youth no longer understood it. And how could the church reawaken to a sense of the importance of the Scriptures if its youthful membership no longer understood the text in its existing translation?

A new German version was needed. And the new version would have to take account of the accepted findings of Biblical scholarship, to replace incomprehensible constructions by comprehensible ones, and still retain as far as possible the power of Martin Luther's prose. For Luther's Bible is of tremendous significance in the history of the Evangelical Church and of the whole German people. There is no parallel to it anywhere else in the world.

It was a much more complex problem than might be imagined. Martin Luther had set down his translation of the New Testament in the lonely Wartburg at one stretch, and completed it within a few weeks. He had written it in his own inimitable style. To revise such a text, and at the same time retain its literary power, had to be the work of one individual—an individual himself possessing a powerful style, who would not let himself be deterred by the liberties and audacities which Luther had permitted himself again and again. Committees do not have a style. If a translation, or even the revision of a translation, is entrusted to a committee, then every sentence is put to the vote. And in votes it is the mediocre and the conventional that triumphs. Every proposal containing a trace of originality is defeated. At least, that is how it is in Germany. Germans have not learned to produce anything fresh and alive in a team.

But the council of the EKiD was itself a team, and it was unthinkable that it should commission an individual to revise the

234

text and then check the revision. So a committee was formed, in the first place for the New Testament. This committee quickly came to grief. Disagreements arose both on details and on matters of principle, and each side insisted unyieldingly on its own viewpoint. There was nothing for it but to dissolve the committee.

A new committee was formed. This time I myself assumed the chairmanship. I felt that there could be no nobler task for the president of the council than to help his church achieve a new translation of the Bible. The work began. In just two years we were ready.

It was an exacting task. Often it meant searching for two days in a row, from morning to night, for expressions which would do justice to the text, weighing the proposals of others and discussing them at length before finally coming to a decision. The hardest part about it was to have to bow to the decisions of the majority even if one felt that its decision was absolutely wrong. One had to be a good loser if one did not want to lose one's own good temper in the process. I tried to be a good loser, although sometimes it was really hard. And the others tried too!

What we finally produced was anything but a masterpiece. The 1894 revision had not been a masterpiece either. But the territorial churches and the Bible societies accepted our work. There was no question of the revision arousing any passionate public interest, such as was aroused in England, for instance, by the new version published in 1961.

Another committee was formed for the revision of the Old Testament. Its task would obviously be both easier and more difficult than that of the committee on the New Testament. In any case, it would be much more comprehensive. I would gladly have presided over this committee too, but my other functions had grown so extensive in the meantime that I had to give up the idea.

All of us on the council were agreed that the church must never again allow itself to be taken in tow by a political party, whatever its hue. On the other hand, the church cannot simply ignore political problems. Least of all could it have done so at a time when a defeated nation was trying to build up a new political life for itself. In eastern Germany everything was political anyway. For totalitarian systems, everything that exists under the sun is political. So in eastern Germany the church was faced with the choice of retiring into a ghetto—which was what the rulers wanted, but which a genuine church can never do—or of taking a courageous stand on political questions. It chose the latter alternative. But it did not enter into the service of any one party, either in the East or in the West.

This is not the place for a discussion in depth of the extent to which a church should involve itself in politics. It is one of the most complex problems facing the churches in the modern world. All I intend to do here is to illustrate, by means of one or two examples, the kind of decisions which the council of the EKiD came to during the time I occupied the presidency.

There were three questions, in particular, on which it felt the church had to take a stand. The first was the question of the division and reunification of the German fatherland.

Our friends from churches abroad often used to ask us whether we should not accept the division of Germany with humility as the judgment of God on the events of National Socialist times. One could be a Christian too, they said, if one's native land was split up, and fraternal Christian fellowship should not be prejudiced by new political boundaries. Was it not true that our patriotic sentiments were in fact stronger than our Christian conscience, and would we not finally have to learn to distinguish carefully between patriotism and Christian faith?

We did not answer such remonstrances with political arguments of any kind. We did not say that it was inhuman to require unconditional surrender of a nation and then to impose on it an arrangement under cover of which one of the occupying powers constantly created new situations of fact, with the result that,

236

sixteen years after the end of the war, a people of nearly 70 million still did not know what was to become of it, and did not even have a voice in deciding upon its political structure. That we did not say. We simply pointed out that Germany's present position, and in particular the frontiers which had been arbitrarily drawn across German territory, had created so much human suffering and so much moral distress that it was a matter of plain Christian duty to do whatever was humanly possible to remove the causes of that distress. That, we said, was not sentimentality; it was a Christian duty.

We also said that, under the present conditions, 16 million Germans were being forcibly held under a regime which was systematically thrusting the Christian religion to the wall. Our duty was to do whatever we could to win back for our German brothers and sisters, and especially for their children, the freedom to live their faith in earnest. But this freedom would never be achieved so long as a Communist dictatorship cordoned them off from their fellow Christians in the West. This, too, was a matter of elementary Christian duty.

Naturally the church can only pray for reunification—as it does without ceasing. The church has to proclaim the Christian's duty to approach his brothers and sisters on the other side of the iron curtain in a spirit of loving self-sacrifice, not in the spirit of hatred which Communist propaganda tirelessly preaches. And above all, the church must be there! By its vital presence, it creates a firm bond between the two halves of the fatherland.

As a result of the consistent Communist policy of division, the German people lost their unitary features. Not that in the East the majority became Communist or in the West that they adopted an American way of thinking. Far from it. But they began to be strangers to one another. The worker in the East, goaded daily by the party slave drivers, unable to change his place of work at will and forbidden to look beyond the frontiers of his territory unless considered politically "safe"—this worker gradually began to feel

237

differently, think differently, work differently from the worker in the West. The businessman in the West, who had to calculate and to take risks on his own, but who could also reap a profit, had an altogether different outlook from that of his counterpart in the East, whose business was owned by the government and who had to sell, with more or less indifference, the goods allotted to him.

The training of youth, of soldiers, was different. Universities were completely different in character. The same was true of doctors, judges, journalists. Not only conditions but also human beings changed under the grip of the totalitarian State. It is difficult to conceive of any country where the effects of barbarous dictatorship over the souls of men could have been sensed more keenly than in Germany, which despite all its diversity had nevertheless retained its essential unity for hundreds of years.

There was only one force which was called upon to resist forcible change—although it, too, was not altogether immune to such change. That force was the church, the church in all its ramifications. The Evangelical pastor in Düsseldorf was bound by the same ordination oath as the pastor in Chemnitz. The deaconess in Pomerania performed her duties in the same way as the deaconess in Württemberg. The congregation in the Thuringian forest listened to the same Gospel as the congregation on the North Sea coast. Despite the multiplicity of opinions, here was a unity, founded on the Gospel, founded on the one Bible as translated by Luther. To preserve this unity was an obvious duty. On that score there was no disagreement.

The difficulties began in relation to points of detail. For instance, avowed Evangelicals were far from unanimous in their approval of Konrad Adenauer's policy of linking West Germany as firmly as possible to the western powers, in order to secure an impregnable bastion against the Communist East. In the first place, many Evangelicals felt that this policy had a Catholic origin; secondly, it was a policy which often enough, and especially in the early years, appeared to lack that passion for reunification which

238

the Protestant East expected. The greatest disappointment came in the spring of 1952. Stalin's note, offering reunification provided West Germany undertook to keep out of all military alliances, had made an impression. The Communist functionaries in Berlin ran around visibly disturbed. Their wives, I was told, had already begun to pack their bags. They all knew that their day would be over if reunification took place.

Was it not the church's duty to lend its support at such an hour? Its support for peace and freedom? The council, it was urged, should take a courageous stand. Most of such voices came from West Germany. In the East, where people knew Communism better, there was considerable skepticism about anything proposed by that side. I refused to reconvene the council and get it to take a decision which could be made public. To my mind, the church does not have the right to interfere in matters within the sphere of responsibility of the political authorities, not even at such a critical moment. It had to suffice that a member of the council traveled to Bonn on his own initiative to report on the feeling in church circles in Germany, and that others should similarly bring the position of many Evangelicals to the attention of the authorities.

Adenauer rejected the offer. Whether his refusal was politically wise, a later generation can decide. What happened immediately thereafter was in any case not calculated to convince those who disagreed with him that the federal Chancellor had acted unwisely.

Rearmament, arising out of Adenauer's alliance with the West, posed an altogether different problem. It will ever remain memorable that the western powers, after destroying Germany's military potential down to the last pillbox, suddenly arrived at the conclusion that Europe could be defended against the forward march of Communism only if Germany contributed half a million soldiers. Germany must therefore rearm as quickly as possible!

239

The problem had its political and military aspects; it also raised a question of principle.

From the point of view of principle, the question was whether, after a few years of complete demilitarization, Germany should or should not return once more to its old military tradition. It was a question bearing on the inner structure of the life of the nation. Here the church could not remain on the side lines.

The National Socialist period had sufficiently shown us what "soldierly bearing" can signify if it comes to govern the national life of a people. Such an experience should not and must not recur. The church of Jesus Christ, by its very nature, must be a force for peace on this strife-ridden planet. Here one can make no distinction between "inner" and "outer" peace. The message of Jesus Christ breathes peace both within and without. This the church had to make absolutely clear, so that everyone might understand. The foolish talk about the church blessing arms—even the German Christians never did that—must finally come to a stop.

This does not mean that the church has to turn pacifist. It is altogether erroneous to identify soldierliness with aggression and the will to power. The modern soldier's first and principal purpose is to defend his country, if necessary at the cost of his life, in case of aggression. This the church realized, the Evangelical and the Catholic alike. It never preached a radical pacifism.

But what the church has to do is to take full account of those who say that, on grounds of their Christian conscience, they are not willing to bear arms. In such cases, the church has to insist that the Christian conscience—even a conscience which the church believes to be in error—must not be violated.

This I had stated as far back as 1927 in my book, *Friede auf Erden*. Now, in April, 1950, the all-German synod at Weissensee declared it to be the unanimous opinion of the Evangelical Church in Germany.

But there were many in our ranks for whom this did not go far enough. They demanded that the government recognize the right

240

of every citizen to refuse armed service in a given situation. They argued that there was a political as well as a Christian conscience, and that it must be protected, No one should be forced to take part in a war which he did not consider just.

Behind this argument were the bitter experiences of the Nazi period. The council of the EKiD took even this demand into account and transmitted a pertinent memorandum to Bonn. I did not oppose it, but neither did I agree to it. And the government did not act on it either. It would have relinquished the very status of government had it agreed that at every crisis it must first find out whether its armed forces were inwardly prepared to defend their country.

At the church rally at Essen, the council issued a statement which included the sentence: "We cannot support German rearmament, either for the West or for the East." It was the only statement of this kind which the council had adopted by a majority, instead of unanimously, and made public. We stood by that statement. We never supported the mustering of military forces. But most of us realized that the day would come when such a mustering would in fact take place. Even if a neutral belt were established from Scandinavia to Switzerland—the dream of many at the time—soldiers would have had to be stationed everywhere, in Sweden, Denmark, Switzerland. But we did not want to be implicated in any precipitate remilitarization. The church should not provide the martial music for new troop levies. Moreover—this too must be added—the national sense of honor had not yet really recovered from the collapse; hence people saw no shame in having foreign military in their country five or ten years after the end of the war, and entrusting the defense of the country to them.

Despite all opposition, remilitarization became a fact—openly in the West, covertly in the East. Some of our friends in the West were reluctant to believe that the East had built up its army in the meantime. But it had. Now the West followed suit.

241

Whereupon, as in duty bound, we set up a military chaplaincy in West Germany; it was not possible to do so in the German Democratic Republic. The undertaking was beset with difficulties. The pacifists worked off their extremism by attacking anything approaching the idea of a "military pastor." They were not troubled by the thought that, if they carried the day, the Catholic soldiers would have their chaplains, but the Evangelicals not. Some territorial churches favored leaving this pastoral duty to their civilian pastors, although in practice this was not feasible. As always happens in such cases, the loudest voices were among the radicals, particularly in the Rhineland and Hesse. At times it looked as though a majority in the Evangelical Church had joined the pacifists, and were prepared to leave the defense of their country to God and the Americans. In fact, of course, there was no such majority.

The agreement between the federal government and the council of the EKiD concerning the ministry to the armed forces was initialed by the federal Chancellor and myself, and adopted both by the synod of the EKiD and by the Bundestag.

From a religious point of view, the agreement was altogether satisfactory. It gave the churches and the individual chaplains every conceivable guarantee that their ministry to the soldiers would be conducted in Christian freedom and independence. The great danger inherent in any military pastorate—that senior officers might exert a decisive influence—was eliminated, to the extent that such a danger can ever be eliminated. Nowhere in the world does the church enjoy greater independence in its ministry to the forces.

The merit for negotiating the agreement goes to Dr. Kunst, our plenipotentiary in Bonn. He was subsequently elected first Evangelical bishop to the armed forces.

We had proposed a similar agrement to the German Democratic Republic to cover eastern Germany. But the Communist government rejected it in disobliging terms, even though the conclusion of such an agreement might have resulted in the EKiD recognizing the German Democratic Republic as a State. But the atheistic principles of the Communist regime were of greater importance than any such consideration.

One thought worried us all at the time; that the introduction of universal military service in western Germany would prevent any reunification of Germany for a long time to come. The Russians asserted this time and again. We took it for granted that as soon as universal military service was introduced in the West, it would be announced in the German Democratic Republic.

For the Christian population of eastern Germany this represented a new and terrible threat. Any eastern army was compulsorily committed to an anti-Christian ideology. We could see for ourselves that the soldiers of the "voluntary" *Volksarmee* (people's army) were forbidden to own a Bible or a hymnal. Participation in religious services was out of the question. Officers were obliged to leave the church. Anyone who married in a church had to reckon with expulsion from the service. The militarism of the East was a declaration of war on the church in every sphere of life.

I put these anxieties before Chancellor Adenauer at the urgent request of the Brandenburg church government. The all-German synod which met in Berlin in June 1956 did likewise. Adenauer and his Christian Democratic Union did not allow themselves to be deflected from their course. The Russians, they maintained, had no intention of introducing universal military service in the eastern zone. On the contrary, they were reducing the numbers of their own forces.

Adenauer's political insight was proved right. Whether it will have been right in the long run, only the future can decide. The eastern zone, at all events, continued to arm for a civil war, neither more nor less than before. Universal military service was not introduced there. We all knew why! But the youth were pressured into "voluntarily" joining the "people's army." And we had to experience the shame of seeing huge contingents of German girls and women receive training in the use of weapons.

243

All these questions came to a head with the introduction of nuclear weapons. That the church should declare itself, over and over again, against such weapons of mass extermination was obvious. So it was really the most inept of the eastern German propaganda lines to describe me, the president of the council, as the "Atom-Bishop."

Among the multitude of functions which devolved upon me as president of the council, some mention is necessary of the relief agency (*Hilfswerk*) which I directed.

This agency had been created by Dr. Eugen Gerstenmaier, a man of vision and energy. He realized that even amid the thunders of war, some churches abroad, particularly in America, were preparing to assist the devastated countries. They had in mind not only the countries which had fought and suffered on the side of the Allies—France, Belgium, Holland, Norway, and others—but also Germany. The Christian community of the world, or at least the major part of it, this time steered clear of the hate psychosis which swept the ranks of the victorious powers and which would have liked to turn the whole of Germany into a grazing land for sheep. Christians were prepared to help the defeated foe to his feet again, in spite of everything!

Gerstenmaier also realized that, as soon as such relief work was set in motion, the Americans would require a German agency which enjoyed their confidence and to which they could entrust the detailed distribution of relief. When the time came, therefore, he brought the relief agency of the Evangelical Church into being, thereby creating an agency which, he hoped, would be more than a center for the distribution of foreign funds. Perhaps—perhaps—it might become the starting point for a new stewardship movement within Germany itself.

There was no dearth of collaborators. Diplomats, commissaries, businessmen were available. The collapse had thrown thousands of men out of their careers. Gerstenmaier could pick and choose.

244

And as he had a sure eye for people, he very quickly set up a first-class staff of assistants.

Millions upon millions of marks now passed through his hands. He quickly saw that, given the languishing German economy, it would be best to import not money but raw materials, and have them processed in Germany, or else to put the incoming funds to work in industry and thereby to double their value—sometimes even to enhance it tenfold.

The Americans, with whose funds the relief agency was principally financed, trusted the agency. This was of overriding importance, particularly in the early period. Setbacks are inevitable in any industrial undertaking. And differences with the customs authorities can easily arise. But when the situation became critical and some church circles were already beginning to cry: "Another Dewaheim affair is in the making!" the American plenipotentiary, Dr. Michelfelder, set all apprehensions at rest. The name of Dr. Gerstenmaier was enough for him. And each time his quiet confidence was proved justified.

The relief agency thus became a helper in a thousand needs. There is hardly a religious institution, hardly an Evangelical congregation in Germany, which in those most bitter days did not receive some form of support from the agency.

New projects were undertaken too. Evangelical building societies were formed. Ventures were made in book publishing and film making. The relief agency did magnificient work, and it did it with drive and enthusiasm. It really looked as though the whole benevolent action of the church, which in the last century or more had had to confine itself increasingly to charitable institutions, might now be placed on a new footing.

But then the tide changed; it was inevitable.

The funds placed at the discretion of the relief agency gradually diminished. The German church, thus far merely the recipient of benefits, now had to begin to assume some of the costs of distribution and transportation. It had to assume responsibility for the

245

newly initiated undertakings, for assistance to emigrants and many other projects. It could do so only with the aid of the territorial churches and their church taxes. The individual congregations were not yet in a position to contribute twice or four times as much as they were already giving for purposes of Christian charity. Nor was this the moment to launch a campaign urging greater self-sacrifice. Where was there a congregation which was not in dire need itself?

So the Evangelical Church in Germany had to assume the financial burden. It must add close to a million marks to its annual budget. The proposal went through all the official channels and budgetary committees—with the shameful result that only about half the necessary funds were appropriated. The other half was to be taken annually from the capital which Gerstenmaier and his friends had accumulated by careful management and which was to have served for the financing of great new projects.

This spelt the death warrant of the relief agency as originally conceived.

From now on, the financial branch of the church bureaucracy had the final say in the agency—with the best intentions, naturally. Budgetary committee, audit, staff—everything that goes with bureaucratic financial administration—now made its appearance. The relief agency was forbidden to engage in industrial undertakings. Big decisions could no longer be made, big projects could no longer be launched.

The staff of assistants disbanded. When Gerstenmaier invited his first collaborators to celebrate the tenth anniversary of their undertaking, only a handful were still with the agency. Most of them had become secretaries of State, directors of ministries, captains of industry and so on. Only later was it realized what outstanding people had run the relief agency. Gerstenmaier himself went into politics. His successor, Dr. Krimm, was a very able man. But his gifts lay more in the direction of careful and scientific planning than of the organization of individual works of charity.

And he, too, resigned at the last moment to join the theological faculty at Heidelberg.

In the end, the only solution was to merge the agency with the traditional Inner Mission. But the problem of awakening a new sense of lay responsibility, in a spirit of *diakonia* (service), among the Evangelical congregations and of injecting into the secular welfare State a new and generous impulse from the Gospel, remained unresolved. It is to be seen whether the work of charity arising out of the merging of the Inner Mission and the relief agency will resolve the problem. There will certainly be no lack of sincere endeavor. The great "Bread for the World" project is a promising start.

It is appropriate to say something here about the church rally (*Kirchentag*), which constituted a unique counterpart to the quiet, almost silent action which the Evangelical Church in Germany undertook to carry out through its council. The moving spirit of this church rally was Dr. von Thadden who threw himself into the work almost immediately after his release from Russian captivity.

The rally became immensely popular. Up to 500,000 persons took part in the proceedings which took place every year, for a time, and then every other year. These hundreds of thousands were no mere mob. They assembled for just under a week and were divided up into sections, each with its special activities. And even when all the sections came together in a single, vast crowd, Heinrich Giesen, the Secretary-General, welded them into a single, joyful family or, better, a joyful congregation, addressing them as he did with originality, imagination, and warmth.

It was understood that the members of the council of the EKiD should take part in these all-German church rallies, and that the president of the council should be among the preachers and should recite the concluding prayer at the final assembly. The church rally was intended as a lay movement. Nevertheless, it could not

247

dispense altogether with the clergy whose names were familiar to the congregations.

The attraction of the rally—and at the same time its limitation—was that everything about it was entirely voluntary and without commitment. One could listen, one could discuss, but one did not have to undertake to do anything. This atmosphere of freedom is appropriate to the Evangelical Church. It is not the most important thing, but it must sometimes find public expression. It found that expression, most impressively, in the church rally.

Only once could the church rally take place in the eastern zone. The rally in Leipzig was the largest, numerically, that has ever been held. The divisive policy of the Communists made a repetition impossible. In 1961, when the Communist government offered Leipzig as the site for a second rally, the invitation was accompanied by conditions which made it impossible to accept. In any case, what business has a government to prescribe the site of a church rally? The Saxon church government refused to invite the rally to Leipzig. It had its reasons. Should the church rally bow to a government fiat?

It was decided to hold the rally in Berlin again. The German Democratic Republic made every conceivable difficulty. It refused all assistance in the matter of traffic. It sent back 30,000 to 40,000 inhabitants of the eastern zone who wanted to travel to Berlin. Nevertheless about the same number got through. It was a magnificent all-German church rally!

The *Kirchentag* continues. And the simple and dignified manner in which Dr. von Thadden has directed it will never be forgotten in Evangelical Germany.

PRESIDENT OF THE WORLD COUNCIL OF CHURCHES

UNQUESTIONABLY the true originator of the ecumenical movement was the great Swedish Archbishop, Nathan Söderblom.

To be sure, the idea was being dreamed of by many in those years between 1919 and 1925.

Even before the First World War, small groups had sought to bring the Christian churches of the world closer together. In Germany, Dr. Siegmund-Schultze was the pioneer in this field. A world organization to foster friendship among the churches had been formed. Preparations were going forward in Switzerland for a big, if possible world-wide, conference. Then came the war, and put a stop to everything.

Only a few well-meaning persons, professors, pastors, and others, had been behind these endeavors. They could accomplish nothing in the face of the momentum of political events. And the churches as a whole had been little touched by ecumenical ideas— least of all in Germany.

But after the war the atmosphere changed radically. People were ashamed of what had taken place. At all events, people in the church were ashamed. For four years a bloody war had been fought in precisely those continents where the Christian church had taken firm root. For four years, hatred between people had had its day. And the churches on either side had allowed themselves to be driven by those demonic forces—some certainly not without an earnest attempt to preserve a Christian attitude even in the hour of bloody warfare, others giving free rein to their passions, self-righteous, fanatical, but all in some way drawn into the political passions of the day. Rarely was an attempt made to throw a bridge of love and peace across the chasm, in conformity with the spirit of Jesus Christ. Could things—should things—continue thus?

And then there was something else. During this long war, the world had begun to grow smaller. There had been fighting in Africa as in Europe. Asian soldiers had been sent into the front lines on European battlefields. No one with the most elementary sense of missionary responsibility could fail to realize what this meant for the future of the Christian church in the world. The area of missionary responsibility was now no longer restricted to a number of more or less inaccessible territories. Everything had grown close. If the Christian church was not to declare itself bankrupt before the non-Christian world, then a new venture in Christian evangelization must be attempted. But this meant that the Christian mission must no longer appear before the world in its old divisions. The non-Christian world would certainly not be won by missionaries who refused to sit together at one table and who branded each other as heretics. Unity—the unity of the church of Jesus Christ—must be the watchword.

This was what the Christian churches sensed. Yes, the ecumenical idea was in the air.

In the English-speaking countries, especially in the United States, plans were afoot to convene a great Christian conference for the purpose of examining the theological foundations of the disunion of the churches. This was to be a first step in the direction of unity. It was to be a conference on Faith and Order.

It was true, of course, that the churches could never arrive at genuine unity if they did not first agree on the fundamentals of their belief. On the other hand, discussions on these questions could only be conducted by theologians and churchmen who, while enjoying high repute and respect on their own account, had no authority whatsoever to make any decision on behalf of their churches. Decades, perhaps centuries, of work would be needed before the churches themselves revised their faith or their order in the light of new theological perceptions.

But those who felt an urge to action did not want to set their sights so far. The problem, for them, required speedy but also prudent action. Their idea was to try to assemble responsible men from all the churches of the world and persuade them to reach out their hands to one another in the name of their churches, with a view to embarking on joint practical work, without prejudice to their theology.

This was Söderblom's great hour.

His plan might at first sight have appeared fantastic. It was to call a conference of the official representatives of all the churches of the world, most of whom knew of each other only by hearsay. But how could this be done? How could all these people who felt themselves worlds apart from one another be assembled in a common enterprise? How could such a conference be organized and financed?

Only Söderblom could have triumphed over all these difficulties. He sent his envoys to the Balkans, to the Middle East, and to Africa. He had long been in regular contact with the countries of Europe and America. Sweden had prospered during the war. Financially certain things were now feasible in Sweden which would not have been feasible in former days—even if the bankruptcy of the principal financial backer on the very eve of the conference caused the Archbishop no little embarrassment. His ecclesiastical position and the respect he enjoyed in the theological world gave everything he did the necessary cachet. He had worked long enough in different countries to speak fluent English, French, and German, in addition to his native Swedish. He had influential friends everywhere. But the most important thing about him was his bold, vital, genuinely religious personality which drew into his following even those who opposed his ideas.

In August, 1925, the World Conference on Life and Work met in Stockholm. Faith and Order had to yield; only two years later could those questions be tackled.

And to be sure, they really were there, all of them! The committee of the German Evangelical Church was present, reinforced by a number of other leading figures of the church world. The Swiss, the French, the Dutch were represented by their principal ecclesiastical dignitaries. Neither of the two English archibshops attended, but Bishop Woods of Worcester was present, formally accredited by his church. The Free Churches and the Scots were represented, of course, as well as the different American churches. And above all, the Orthodox came. Not the Russians, because Russia was already under Communist rule, but the Patriarch of Alexandria, who under diplomatic protocol enjoyed the rights of a sovereign and on solemn occasions walked at the side of the King of Sweden; and also the Arab Patriarch of Jerusalem, and archbishops and metropolitans from Bukovina, Serbia, Greece, and elsewhere. The Scandinavians, of course, were all represented. Sweden, which possessed at the time a remarkable array of prominent personalities, and included them all within its state church system, had them walk in together at the public meetings as though they were all practicing Lutheran Christians—Sven Hedin, Selma Lagerlöf, Hjalmar Hammarskjöld,· and others.

Only the Roman Catholic Church was absent. Whether Söderblom ever seriously hoped that the Vatican would find some way of taking part, directly or indirectly, is doubtful. He did invite it. But he had to be satisfied with the presence of two silent Catholic observers. It could hardly have been otherwise.

· Hjalmar Hammarskjöld, father of the late Dag Hammarskjöld, was Prime Minister of Sweden from 1914 to 1917.

The discussions themselves did not always proceed very smoothly. Between the Germans and their neighbors, particularly the French, there loomed the memory not only of the war but especially of the dictated peace of Versailles, into which Clemenceau had poured the fullness of his hatred of Germany. When a Frenchman spoke and the gathering applauded, no German hands contributed to the applause. And when Pastor Gounelle addressed the Germans with rhetorical flourish in the words from *Antigone*: "I am there not to hate but to love!" the response was icy silence. Professor Julius Richter remarked that the way the Danes had settled the minority question in northern Schleswig after Germany had been forced to cede the region was exemplary. The following day he had to leave the conference. The other Germans had intimated to him that such a statement about an "enemy" State was undignified and intolerable.

No, the time was not yet ripe for genuine Christian understanding.

But we did not throw in the sponge. A first world conference of this kind could only be a beginning. One could not expect the impossible of it. It was necessary to go on working together, seriously, practically. A continuation committee which would simply keep the ball rolling was not enough. We had to be more ambitious.

At one of the final meetings of the conference, the Swedish bishop, Billing, had submitted a proposal (which of course had been kept in reserve since the beginning) for the establishment in Geneva of a "Christian-Social Institute." This institute was to be maintained jointly by the churches; its purpose was to develop a joint Christian approach to the social problems of the time. The proposal was adopted. The institute came into being. Dr. Schönfeld, a German, was appointed director.

Thus something had been accomplished which could not be so easily undone this time. The ecumenical idea began to emerge from the nebula of problems and to take firm shape.

I had taken part in that world conference at Stockholm, though by no means in any leading capacity. The German delegation was led by the German Evangelical Church committee and its chairman, Dr. Kapler. I was not a member of that church committee. The fact that I had long concerned myself with the life of other churches and had written a book on religious life in Scotland had aroused not the slightest interest in my church. At forty-five, I was still considered a very young man by my venerable colleagues.

But in the meantime I had been to the United States as the representative of the Berlin Supreme Ecclesiastical Council, and I knew English, which at that time was still unusual in ecclesiastical circles. As Superintendent-General of the Kurmark, I held the highest spiritual office in our church. Consequently I was taken along.

I came to know Söderblom. Our acquaintance deepened when I took part in the other world conference, on Faith and Order, which was held two years later at Lausanne. The conference was under the direction of Charles Brent, the Episcopal Bishop of western New York. Söderblom headed the much-discussed committee 4. I sat next to him and worked with him on the committee report, which went far beyond the actual subject of discussion in Lausanne. The report proposed the creation of something like a permanent international council of churches, which would voice the reaction of the Christian conscience to the changing problems facing the nations.

That had been Söderblom's idea from the start. I took part in these plans enthusiastically. We had to have more than just a Christian-Social Institute. We had to have an organ which would voice the common will of the churches and which would be in a position to act. That is what took place later in the World Council of Churches as it is presently constituted. But in 1927, at Lausanne, the plan ran into bitter opposition on the part of a group of Anglo-Catholics assembled around Canon Douglas. What was behind this opposition was not quite clear. But I could not avoid the impression that the purpose of it was to prevent the Archbishop of Sweden, who had already organized and directed one world conference, from again being raised to pre-eminence at a second conference which was pursuing an altogether different line. In the conference on Faith and Order the direction should remain in British-American hands.

The report of the Söderblom committee was not "adopted" like all the other committee reports, but only "received." That meant, in the polite language of such conferences, that it was rejected. The previous evening, when it was already apparent which way the wind was blowing, Söderblom had left. Nevertheless, he was still to emerge the victor.

At Lausanne, I was elected to the continuation committee so that I was now permanently attached to one of the two branches of ecumenical work. The committee itself acquired importance from the fact that William Temple, who was later to become Archbishop of Canterbury, assumed the chairmanship. He was a man of great vision, statesmanship, and readiness for bold action. For the Church of England he was what Söderblom had been for the Church of Sweden.

I had not much to contribute to the theological discussions in which this continuation committee indulged. Here the professors were in their element, especially the systematic theologians. But systematic theology was not my specialty, nor was I particularly interested in it.

I still remember my embarrassment when William Temple asked me, in the corridor of the University of Lausanne, what was the teaching of the Lutheran Church in Germany on atonement. A professor of systematic theology might, perhaps, have been able to tell him in a couple of sentences from a printed manual, though it would still have been doubtful whether another German professor of systematic theology would have recognized those sentences as correct and binding. But I did not know what I should describe point blank as the "teaching of my church." I had learned to think historically and, in all theological questions, to go back to the words of Holy Scripture. That alone was Lutheran for me. So I proceeded to tell him what I understood of St. Paul's various statements and metaphors concerning the Cross of Christ and the justification of the sinner. Temple listened to me attentively, but he was not satisfied. He had expected me to present him with a concise exposition of an accepted Lutheran doctrine. I could not do that, nor, had I been able to, would I have wanted to. In my view the whole task of Faith and Order was not to play off doctrinal systems against each other, but together to place ourselves in the light of the New Testament.

Although I was not an expert in systematic theology, I was still an ecclesiastic. That was why I had been elected to the group. For if any benefit is to accrue to the church from theological discussions, they have to be attended by persons who are concerned not only with scholarship but also with the church.

William Temple had written several books on theology, but with his whole being he was an ecclesiastic. His thinking towered over the traditional approach of his church. Nothing in our conversations impressed me more deeply than what he once told me in connection with the international conference on missions in Jerusalem, which he had attended in 1928. The scales had fallen from his eyes, he said, and he had realized that no European nation had the right to rule over other peoples as colonial powers. I often thought of those words as the colonial system collapsed before our eyes.

It became increasingly difficult to take part in ecumenical work after the National Socialists came to power. Anyone who cultivated independent relations with persons abroad was, a priori, suspected of engaging in treason. That is how it is in all totalitarian States; they all have a guilty conscience, and they can hold on to their power only so long as their dogma is not confronted with reality in the world at large.

Nevertheless, during the first years it was still possible. Once the church struggle had broken out, our ecumenical friends abroad recognized only the Confessing church as the legitimate representative of German Christianity. Sometimes they had to take the others' claims into account when legally there was no way to circumvent them. But they did so unwillingly and always came back again to the Confessing church. The only exception was Dr. Headlam, the Bishop of Gloucester, who had been influenced by Professor Wobbermin in Berlin and obstinately clung to the view that Hitler only wanted to unite the Evangelical Church in a single entity, and that the Confessing church was trying to prevent this.

The position for us was untenable. I remember a session of the continuation committee on Faith and Order in Switzerland. Most of the Germans who were long-standing members of the committee belonged to the Confessing church, and we stuck together. But there was also present Dr. Zoellner, whom the church committee had appointed as an "observer" in 1927. He had just placed himself at the disposal of Reich Minister Kerrl for his last attempt at pacification. Now he thought that he should represent the German church on the continuation committee. He had brought his people along. We sat at different tables. We were polite to each other, but we avoided conversation—except when I embarked on a lengthy discussion with Zoellner in an attempt to convince him that his work of mediation under Kerrl was doomed to failure, a prediction in which he partially concurred. A situation where there were two German camps before the eyes of the other churches of the world was intolerable.

It had been even worse the previous year, when Dr. Heckel, who directed the ecclesiastical foreign relations office in Berlin, undertook to represent the Evangelical churches on Life and Work. I was not present myself, but the events were subsequently described to me over and over again by many different persons.

The meeting took place on the island of Fanö. Heckel was leading a German delegation whose members were not all absolutely "safe." From time to time, August Jaeger, the National Socialist "guardian of the law," who was then in the prime flush of his sins, would telephone from Berlin and threaten Heckel. He would tell Heckel that he knew everything, even about the private conversations which Heckel had conducted with foreigners, and he demanded an unequivocal National Socialist stand. As the committee was sitting in a room overlooking the beach, a small airplane hove in sight and landed on the sand. Consistorial Councilor Birnbaum of Berlin, a German-Christian, stepped out and made straight for the meeting, with which he had absolutely nothing to do. He had come to supervise Heckel and his friends on behalf of Ludwig Müller. The chairman, the Bishop of Chichester, with quiet, British courtesy, let him have his way. The result was that Dr. Heckel declared on behalf of the German delegation that the developments affecting the church in Germany in no way signified any violation of the church by the State; what was happening was "a concentration of church leadership and measures of church order." Now, he concluded, there were more opportunities for proclaiming the Gospel than before. Everyone knew that this was not true.

It is well-nigh impossible for a churchman condemned to living under a totalitarian regime to travel in a foreign country and to take part in ecumenical proceedings where he is expected to report frankly and honestly on conditions at home. The deposed Hungarian bishop, Ordasz, did so in exemplary fashion—but in other circumstances—at the Conference of the Lutheran World Federation, which took place at Minneapolis in 1957. No one who was there will ever forget it. But such cases are very rare. However, as I have said, one should not be too hasty in reproaching others.

These were matters we had to ponder when the two world conferences proposed to hold their second big meetings in Oxford and Edinburgh just before the Second World War. Should we of the Confessing church attend them or not?

The decision was taken out of our hands. Two officials of the Gestapo turned up at the homes of those of us who might have taken part, and demanded our passports. From now on there could be no more foreign travel.

What remained were occasional personal contacts with individuals whom we had met through our ecumenical work. Those contacts, too, became increasingly rare, particularly after the outbreak of war. The secret intermediaries were Dr. Schönfeld in Geneva and Dietrich Bonhoeffer in Berlin. We could only follow events from afar.

At last the Second World War, with its unspeakable suffering, was over. We had convened at Stuttgart as the provisional council of the Evangelical Church. Suddenly there appeared—I had known nothing of any such plan—a number of friends from the ecumenical movement: the Bishop of Chichester, the newly elected Secretary-General of the World Council of Churches, Dr. Visser 't Hooft, and others. They wanted to greet us and to discuss with us how to effect the re-entry of the German churches into the ecumenical community. A declaration had to be published. I drafted the text myself. But it was Martin Niemöller who added the decisive passage: "With great pain we say: Through us, infinite suffering has been brought upon many peoples and countries. What we have often declared before our congregations, that we now declare in the name of the whole church: For long years we struggled in the name of Jesus Christ against the spirit which found its frightful expression in the National Socialist regime of force; nevertheless, we accuse ourselves of not having confessed more courageously, prayed more faithfully, believed more joyfully and loved more ardently. Now a new beginning must be made in our churches."

That was the confession of guilt at Stuttgart.

It was not easy for me to agree to Niemöller's text. I had been the only one in the group to experience personally the arrival of the Russians. The others were all of the West. But for us in the East the terrible things which we had witnessed and experienced

259

were still in our bones. Not to say a word of these, and to confine ourselves to the guilt of the Germans, was not easy.

But we did not want to speak to the world, after all, except as a Christian church to other Christian churches. And the Christian does not weigh the guilt of the various sides against each other, but confesses before God what his own guilt is. And that guilt was truly great enough. The church also had the priestly duty to make such confession on behalf of its people, even though it had opposed the developments as far as it could, and had suffered for that opposition.

That such a confession of guilt should evoke criticism among the German public had to be accepted. The churches abroad understood it in the spirit in which it was intended. The doors sprang open. The ecumenical community was restored. And the stream of assistance which now poured over Europe, and not least over Germany, showed that this community was no empty word.

A new phase began with the Amsterdam world conference in 1948.

The idea had meantime gained ground—perforce without much assistance from the German side—that the two branches of ecumenical work should be united, and that a World Council of Churches be formed, as Söderblom had envisaged. The founding took place in Amsterdam.

Every six years a big world conference was to convene. In the meantime, a central committee of some ninety members would lay down general policies and for this purpose would meet every year. From that central committee, again, a small executive committee was to be formed, which, together with the six presidents of the world council, would formulate and supervise the detailed projects. The actual organization of business would rest with the Secretary-General in Geneva, whose collaborators were to be chosen from the different churches of the world.

This structure was judiciously conceived, even though, inevitably, subsequent developments necessitated various modifications and extensions. The draft was adopted without difficulty.

There were three reasons why things had gone so smoothly. In the first place, it had become clear to everyone during the previous sixteen years that the ecumenical movement could no longer continue to move along two separate tracks. Life and Work needed to be permanently fructified by theological work. And the theological discussions on Faith and Order needed a powerful impetus from the practical life of the church if they were not to lose themselves in theory.

We had the men to whom this new organization could be entrusted: Dr. Bell, the Bishop of Chichester (after the death of Söderblom, he had become the soul of the movement), Archbishop Fisher of Canterbury, Bishop Berggrav of Oslo, the Orthodox Metropolitan Germanos of London, and Pastor Boegner of France. They enjoyed the confidence of the churches throughout the world. They were elected presidents. Dr. Visser 't Hooft, who had been elected Secretary-General, had already given proof of his exceptional ability as an organizer in the World Student Christian Federation, and his far-seeing and determined action earned him the confidence even of those who were theologically or politically in disagreement with him. Thus the leading posts were admirably filled.

Those sixteen years of preparatory ecumenical work had not been in vain. There was hardly a trace of the political tensions which had so seriously hampered any meeting of minds in 1925, at least not among the representatives of the churches. That the mood in Holland, where the conference was taking place, should still have been very hostile to everything German, so that it was better to speak English rather than German in the street, was not surprising. And that continental European Protestantism should not be represented on the presidium of the new world council by a German, but that Dr. Berggrav of Norway should have been elected instead, was understandable to any intelligent person. For the rest, we were completely open with one another, whatever church we came from. And it was no coincidence that I, a German, should have been chosen to say the concluding words at the great and solemn final meeting.

Six Germans were elected to the central committee, among them myself. On the executive committee there was only one German, and he, of course, was Martin Niemöller. We could only rejoice that we could have him in the place of honor in the ecumenical movement.

Naturally we did not stop at organizational work. A theme had been enunciated: "The disorder of the world and God's plan of salvation." This theme had been divided into subsections, and the churches had been urged long before the conference to concern themselves with the problems arising out of them, and to submit written contributions. This the churches had done. The Germans had worked most eagerly on them. After being cut off for so long we had been seized by a real hunger to take part in world-wide church discussions again, and to bring out something of what we had learned in the years of church struggle. These German contributions filled five volumes. Like the rest, they went into the great melting pot of committee debate. Small trace of the original was to be found in the final drafts.

But the resolutions of the general conference (the same is true of all international conferences) were of relatively small importance. Agreed, printed, distributed, and soon forgotten—that is the fate of such decisions. If a thousand men from all the countries on God's earth have to agree, how can their decisions amount to more than an andante for the *Well-tempered Clavier*, exciting no one and interesting very few?

This does not mean that such work is useless. If the churches are to grow together, they must not, at such gatherings, talk about the weather. They must raise fundamental questions and discuss them. Only thus does it become apparent how they think and what are their goals of Christian testimony. Only thus do people get to know and understand one another. The fruits of such work can ripen only gradually.

Six years later we met in Evanston, Illinois.

Here everything was still more generous, more enthusiastic, more American than at Amsterdam. For we were in America, and we had another six years of ecumenical development behind us. The meeting was overshadowed by the great political anxieties of the postwar period. The question of the atomic weapon exercised all minds. There was general concern about the aggressive imperialism of the Russians. And the churches realized that all this placed a new responsibility upon them. The committee on international affairs had gained in importance. It had not yet been able to accomplish much, but it had followed the political developments very closely, and on more than one occasion had voiced the views of the churches very emphatically at the United Nations. Its reports were listened to with the greatest attention. The great hall in the immediate neighborhood of the university city, where the plenary meetings were held, could seat 10,000 persons and was often filled to capacity. The conference exerted great attraction throughout the world. In Germany, the council of the Evangelical Church had at first said that because of lack of funds, it could occupy only twenty-four of the thirty-six seats assigned to the Germans. But in response to pressure put upon it from all sides, it revised this decision and took all the places. Then various agencies offered to place funds at our disposal for still more delegates. In the end there were over eighty of us from Germany, as members, guests, correspondents, and so on. It was much the same in a number of other churches.

At Evanston, too, the decisive thing was the organizational development. It had become evident that a World Council of Churches could no longer be directed only from Geneva. An American branch agency had to be established. The number of committees which were to meet in the different countries must be increased. Attention was directed more than ever before to the so-called young churches of Asia and Africa, and to the national committees in America and Europe. But at the same time the finance committee of the council had to announce that it would henceforward be impossible to place the costs of the whole organization, which was constantly expanding, upon the American churches; so far they had financed practically everything. Now the other churches must try seriously to contribute to the costs. In particular, they would in future have to pay for the trips of their committee members themselves. For many churches, including the German churches, this was quite a tall order. But it was a step in the right direction. If the World Council of Churches was not to become an American institution, the other churches must also make their sacrifices.

The other organizational development of general significance was the serious discussion of merging the International Missionary Council with the World Council of Churches. This reflected the extraordinary transformation in church relations in the world. The Christian congregations of Asia and Africa no longer wanted to be, and no longer should be, offshoots of the churches of Europe and America. The national consciousness of the peoples of those continents had increased immeasurably since the Second World War. In some Asian countries, in China particularly, the Christian congregations had been harassed as outposts of the western powers; members of the congregations, but especially missionaries, had been arrested, tortured, expelled. A Christianity imported from the West met with a wall in the East. There remained no other way than to recognize the "young churches" of those countries as independent churches and to let the mother churches give them the support which they would long continue to need through the World Council of Churches. From now on they must enjoy equality of status with the other churches. Such a readjustment of international church work could of course be effected only very carefully and with great discretion. For conditions were not everywhere equally favorable. But unanimity was achieved on principles. The execution of the decision would take longer.

For me personally, Evanston signified a change for which I had not been prepared. I had written to Dr. Visser 't Hooft to say that it was time for me, at the age of seventy-four, to make room for a younger man, and I had asked not to be re-elected to the central committee. Visser 't Hooft would not hear of it, but I stuck to my intention. Evanston was to mark my exit from ecumenical action. I no longer concerned myself with the proposals made to the so-called nominating committee for the manning of the various offices and committees.

Then I suddenly heard, to my astonishment, that it had been decided as a matter of principle not to re-elect the presidents of the World Council of Churches, but to nominate new candidates every six years, and that I was to be one of the six to be elected this time. I was very reluctant. At the same time I had to tell myself that it was right for the Evangelical Church in Germany to return to the position which it had occupied at the outset of the ecumenical movement, and that the president of the council of the EKiD was the obvious person to represent it. Even before I had finished thinking it over, the proposal had been formally presented in plenary.

It is common practice at large conferences for candidacies submitted by the nominating committee to be accepted in plenary without discussion. That is what had always been done at world church conferences before. This time, however, there was an objection from the German side. The committee declared the following day that it stood by its proposal, whereupon the assembly adopted it without further opposition.

That is how—if in somewhat embarrassing circumstances—I became one of the six presidents of the World Council of Churches. The others were two Americans, Dr. Sherrill, the presiding Episcopal Bishop, and Archbishop Michael, head of the Orthodox Church in America; the Methodist Bishop Barbieri of Latin America; Juana Mar Thoma, Bishop of the Thomas Christians of India, and Dr. Baillie, principal of the leading Scottish college in Edinburgh.

The function of these presidents was essentially decorative and representative. The Archbishop of Canterbury, Dr. Fisher, put it this way when he spoke on behalf of the retiring presidents: "Our job was to do nothing, and that job, I think, we performed satisfactorily." Of course, that was only half the truth, and was only intended as that. But it was true in the sense that everything really important was done by the Secretary-General in Geneva and by the chairman of the executive committee. The presidents learn next to nothing about details. But they have to take part in the meetings of the executive committee and the central committee, which normally means considerable journeys twice a year, to America, Australia, or some European country. As a rule they are also expected to speak on such occasions. And above all they are expected effectively to promote the ecumenical idea in the part of the world to which they belong.

I tried to carry out these expectations.

Emumenical work will acquire increasing importance as time goes by. Even today no church anywhere in the world can remain vital if it shrinks back into its own shell. We are connected with one another on a world-wide scale, whether we like it or not. And particularly the church. The age of technology changes not only conditions but also people. Man loses his soul to the material world. And just when it seems that countries with a longer industrial history have reached a point where man is master of technology, technology opens up new dimensions which again absorb all his mental and physical forces. The problems resulting for the human element in man are everywhere the same. And with them the problems which confront every church.

The old Lutheran principle that the church of Jesus Christ has no other task than to preach the Gospel is certainly true. But in a secular age, in which everything is calculated to make an unreality of the Gospel, the church will also have to try to create modes of living which will permit the Christian, young and old, to live his faith.

The political materialism which is advancing from the East stakes everything on preventing the emergence of such modes of living. If it cannot simply eliminate the churches, at least it will place difficulties in the way of religious education, church services, and normal Christian congregational activity, suppress them, wherever possible, and wipe out the heritage of Christian thinking in the life of the peoples. In forty years of antireligious propaganda, the Communists succeeded in reducing the number of practising Orthodox Christians in Russia from 90 per cent to about 3 per cent of the population. In other countries where the Communists dictate the way of life the situation is similar.

All these churches should be assisted so that they do not wither away under the strain. By outward means one can do little for them, and only occasionally. But one can let them take part, if only in a very limited measure, in the spiritual life of the whole Christian community by sending them theological books which reflect the way Christians elsewhere deal with the problems of the times. Sometimes visits can be exchanged. Such visits pose their own problems. Often one meets only those who have learned to toe the line and who no longer realize what mortal danger the totalitarian State represents for the outward and inner life of the Christian. But sometimes one does meet others too. And something remains from each such visit—on both sides. Christians in the so-called free world badly need to know about others who are persecuted for their faith.

Of course each individual church can do its part in this field. But it is of decisive importance to have a central agency whose responsibility it will be that the oppressed churches are not for a moment forgotten. And we can already say that this has borne fruit for more than one of these oppressed churches.

267

The same kind of action is required on behalf of the small churches which build up their lives in countries of non-Christian religion, or which struggle for a modicum of freedom in countries with an overwhelming Roman Catholic majority. For these churches it is of vital importance that they should be associated in the life of the Christian world, and find their way out of the confinement of their daily anxieties in the larger community.

But the main thing is, and remains, that through the ecumenical movement, the churches of the whole world draw closer together, and not merely outwardly. Only today, when the population of the whole world lies open before our eyes, are we in a position to realize how small is the percentage of avowed Christians in relation to the world population. Only now do we see the task clearly before us, to permeate the world with the message of Jesus Christ. That is why it is essential that the individual churches do not remain fixed in their old traditions, but that they develop those traditions jointly, from within. This is the standing task of the Faith and Order movement. We are at the threshhold of a new era of church history—the decisive era, judging by the signs of the times.

The church must entreat her heavenly Lord for the strength it will need for this task. A World Council of Churches will never be the holy mountain from which streams of living water flow down upon the whole world. Nor will it so easily become for the non-Roman Catholic churches what the Vatican is to the Catholic world, even when the period of construction is over and the organizational tasks recede behind the spiritual ones. The strength of Christianity arises out of the life of the congregations. A genuinely religious confirmation class is of greater importance than an all-day session of an ecumenical conference.

Nevertheless, in the century of the printed word, of the word transmitted by a thousand technical media, the religious life is also fed by what peoples all over the world think, say, and write. The way Americans organize their church life, the impulse Karl Barth gives to theological thinking, the example Albert Schweitzer gives in the solitude of Central Africa—all this shines out to the whole world. And if it is to have any lasting effect on the Christian church, then there must be a central agency which absorbs it, not in order to use it as propaganda but in order to pass it on by spiritual and organizational means.

Then there is the work of assistance to the "less developed nations" which the ecumenical movement had set in motion long before the big countries of the free world, disturbed by the advance of Communism, realized their responsibility for those areas of the world. What the churches can do in this field, however impressive the figures might be, will always remain trifling in relation to the tremendous possibilities available to the political States. But it will have no political strings attached. There will be heart in the work. And that will give it its great, enduring significance.

The important thing is not that individual churches unite together. Such unions are accomplished almost every year. The international Christian community is gratified to note that the multiplicity of individual churches is gradually giving way to larger unions of churches. But it is also aware that such unions do not always come about because the churches concerned really want to unite. The impetus to union is often given by external circumstances, although the present ecumenical atmosphere certainly facilitates union. What is really important is that the churches realize that they have a common Lord and a common task in the secular world.

In the six years of my presidency I was able to do only one thing for the World Council of Churches which was perhaps of some significance: I organized a European church conference.

What happened was this. A group of Germans interested in ecumenical affairs had conceived the idea of arranging such a conference, specifically with the aim of bringing the churches of the eastern satellite States into closer contact with the West. The aim was a good one. The trouble was that in good German fashion they fancied that, together with a group of friends in church politics, they could organize a conference of this kind on their own.

I looked on uneasily. The constitution of the World Council of Churches required that such conferences be the responsibility of the official representatives of the participating churches. This was a legacy from Söderblom, and we had to abide by it.

We discussed the problem repeatedly in the council of the Evangelical Church in Germany, and the council requested the Westphalian Church President Wilm, who directed the project together with Dr. Emmen of Holland, to give it up.

Now the Secretary-General of the World Council of Churches, Dr. Visser 't Hooft, brought up the question for discussion at the meeting of the central committee at Yale—it was not clear whether he was for or against the project. Dr. Lilje arose and explained briefly why the Lutheran churches in Germany and other countries could not support the plan. This I considered as a challenge. I declared that I took it upon myself to arrange a conference at which all the European churches would participate officially.

What I thought was that my fellow European on the presidium, Dr. Baillie of Edinburgh, would issue the invitations jointly with me, and that the gathering would be a European conference in the framework of the World Council of Churches. This appeared to me the simplest thing in the world.

The project as conceived thus far had lacked any far-reaching ecumenical goal. If the only object was to facilitate contacts between the oppressed churches of the East and the churches of the West, then we did not need a European conference. International theological meetings, study groups, church music conferences could be organized, and the Gustav-Adolf Association could be activated too. There were a hundred possibilities.

The only purpose of a conference of European churches would be to assert the voices of Europe as against the American preponderance and the newly articulate churches of Asia and Africa. Europe, after all, was the continent with a two-thousand-year

270

history of Christianity. Not only the Lutherans and the Reformed, but also the Methodists and the Baptists and many others had originated in Europe. In the ecumenical movement, these European churches found themselves confronted by another world. There was a tremendous amount of American thinking, American planning in the movement. It was time for the European churches to ask themselves whether they could simply accept all this as it was offered them, whether much of it did not first have to be "translated" into European ecclesiastical terms if it was to take root in Europe, and whether the European churches did not have more to give the ecumenical world than had thus far been apparent.

That should be the function of a European conference. Naturally the great churches of Europe had to give of their best at such a conference. I refer to the churches which had been able to build up their own theology, and which had developed certain original features in their life of worship and independent methods of ecclesiastical action. These were the churches of Scandinavia, Germany, Holland, Switzerland and, if they could be brought to co-operate, the churches in England and Scotland. An important service would be rendered to the small minority churches if they were associated with the others in the context of this great ecumenical goal. But if the main emphasis was on these minority churches, then the whole conference would be dominated by political considerations.

The preparations started off well. I succeeded in persuading the British churches to agree to at least a single conference.

Then the difficulties began. First we were told that Dr. Baillie and I should not send out the invitations, because if we did so the churches of the satellite States would not be allowed to participate. Next, we were told that the conference could not take place in Switzerland, even though preparations were already under way; the hostile demonstrations in front of the Hungarian embassy in Berne after the failure of the Hungarian revolution had not been forgotten. Then we were told that the World Council of Churches must keep out of the affair, that I might not appear before the conference, and so on.

Only at the very end did it become apparent that behind all these difficulties there was none other than the Communist Minister of Churches in Budapest. He had not forgotten that at the outbreak of the Hungarian revolution, Dr. Visser 't Hooft had sent congratulations to our friends in the Hungarian church. That I personally was almost intolerable to the Communists was obvious. The Communist Minister of Churches had armed the Hungarian representatives with specific instructions which they endeavored to carry out, down to the last ridiculous detail. And of course the Czechs supported the Hungarians.

Nevertheless, the final outcome was a complete success. I went as far as I possibly could in making concessions. The project was not to break down on my account. So I left the direction of affairs to the three persons on whom we had quickly been able to agree: Dr. Emmen, representing the earlier "wildcat" conference; Archbishop Kewitt of Reval; and Dr. Lilje, whose outstanding ability saved the most difficult situations.

And now, what hardly anyone had still dared hope took place. From Madrid to Reval and Stockholm, virtually all the churches involved were represented—even the Orthodox Church of Russia and the Greek and Polish churches. Only one or two Balkan countries, such as Rumania, were unrepresented. There the atheistic attacks on the church had flared up with particular violence.

There were discussions in committee, and also in plenary, more substantive discussions than almost any I had ever experienced at ecumenical gatherings. The Hungarian opposition gradually weakened and was defeated. The conference upheld the connection with the World Council of Churches. The friends who had sought to arrange their own European conference rallied to the common position. Dr. Lilje was able to note in conclusion, with unanimous approval, that the conference had succeeded and should be repeated at a given time, even though no definite organization had been set up for this purpose.

One thing the European conference had been unable to prevent was the establishment by the Protestant churches in the eastern bloc States of a separate ecumenical movement. German pastors enthusiastically took part in this, though their church government, and I too, had most earnestly warned them against it.

Several preparatory meetings took place. In June, 1961, the first All-Christian Peace Assembly took place in Prague.

The mere fact that the conference was held in a Communist country spoke volumes. Invitations had been confined to those whose political and religious views were held to be reliable. The conference proceeded along the expected lines. Telegrams were exchanged with Khrushchev and Czech President Novotny. (A telegram to President Kennedy remained unanswered.) The Chinese Bishop Ting delivered a hate-filled speech against America. There were harsh words about the Vatican. Germany was termed responsible for the current situation—responsible not only for the Second but also for the First World War. The atheists were termed "not objects of our charity, but brethren!" And dominating everything was the theology of Professor Hromadka, which urged that the new social order of Communism should be joyfully greeted by the Christian community, and that the atheism which permeated the new regime should be regarded as nonexistent.

The repeated assurances of Professor Hromadka that this "peace" conference was not intended to create divisions within the ecumenical movements were honestly intended, I have no doubt. But a Christian should not forget the risen Christ's words to Peter—that "another" would gird him and lead him whither he would not. That "other"—at least at present—is not God, but an enemy on this earth.

The third plenary assembly of the World Council of Churches saw the end of my collaboration in the ecumenical movement in a position of responsibility.

With the Roman Catholic Church I had at first no contact worth speaking of. When I was a young man, most of the people I had worked with had been Evangelicals. The small Catholic minority had had its priests. We greeted each other in friendly fashion whenever we met, but we did not exchange visits. There were no serious difficulties. We lived together at a courteous distance.

Only in Berlin did things change.

In 1930, the Catholic diocese of Berlin was founded. The newly appointed Catholic bishops called upon me. I returned their calls. That was as far as it went. After the Second World War, when we were starting to rebuild, I visited Bishop Count Preysing. He lived rather poorly in a little room in a Catholic nursing home in the north of Berlin. His apartment, his reception rooms, his episcopal church, all had been destroyed. We had a friendly but cool conversation. I do not remember whether he ever returned my visit. He died shortly thereafter.

With his successor, Bishop Weskam, there was immediately a different, personal relationship. He came from Magdeburg where he had been a suffragan. He understood the situation which the Communist dictatorship had created, and which affected both great churches equally. From this, everything else followed automatically. We invited each other to meals and kept each other informed concerning the affairs of our churches. This relationship continued when Bishop Weskam was replaced by Bishop Döpfner, who received the cardinal's hat at an astonishingly early age.

When the Catholic rally took place in Berlin, I called upon the Evangelical population to place lodgings at the disposal of the Catholic visitors, and they responded generously. Of course I offered rooms in my house too. I was sent Bishop Wendel of Speyer, who had just been appointed Cardinal Archbishop of Munich. So far as I know, it was the first time in Germany that a Catholic bishop had stayed with an Evangelical bishop. The example was followed. A new era had dawned.

Not long after, I stopped in Rome, accompanied by my son, on my way to a meeting in Australia. The first counselor of embassy, a Catholic, who met me at the airport, asked me whether I wished to visit the Pope; he thought he could arrange it. I was surprised, but at once agreed. Could it not be of some benefit if the President of the Council of the Evangelical Church in Germany, who was at the same time one of the presidents of the World Council of Churches, took such an opportunity to visit the Pope? Had I not visited the Ecumenical Patriarch of the Orthodox Church at Istanbul?

I found out later that the Vatican bureaucracy began by making all kinds of difficulties. But when the matter was put before Pius XII, he decided immediately that he wished to see me.

The visit took place. There were no problems of ceremony such as might have embarrassed an Evangelical bishop. The conversation was informal. The present state of the church of Jesus Christ in the world, particularly in Germany, provided sufficient topics. I could tell of my experiences in Berlin. I could tell him something about the ecumenical movement. But the talk always veered back again to Germany. Pius XII loved Germany. He took especial interest in Berlin. He too was deeply concerned about the mortal threat which Communism posed to all Christian religion and Christian life in Germany.

It was a good conversation. It was difficult not to stay beyond the time prescribed by protocol.

Many of my friends in Germany shook their heads in astonishment and indignation about this visit of mine to the Pope. They read into it something like a submission to the papal claims, such as Leo XIII had once formulated in regard to the old Kaiser Wilhelm. I understood those apprehensions. Of course I understood them. They reflected the whole four-hundred-year-old history of German Protestantism.

But I did not share them. I had the impression that the upheavals of the times called for an altogether new approach. I never sought encounters with heads of State or princes of the church. But where the opportunity offered, I always grasped it, in the joyous liberty of the Christian. I never felt that I was compromising my country or my church by a courteous or a friendly conversation. On the contrary, the more significant the differences and contrasts, the more important personal contacts appear to me. For me, that applied also to the Catholic church.

The consciousness that I belonged to a different religious world from that of Eugenio Pacelli, known to the world as Pius XII, never left me for an instant during our conversation. Nothing was further from my thoughts than to seek to bridge that difference. All my life I have avoided well-intentioned but ill-considered *una sancta* talks.

But I found with thankfulness that respect and sympathy having their source in a higher world are possible among Christians, even among Christians belonging to different churches. To one who has once sat opposite him, the intelligent, friendly, ascetic face of Pius XII and his keen eyes remain unforgettable. Should it be God's last word to His children on earth that their historical heritage bars the possibility of full community?

CONCLUSION

LORD MY GOD, You are the Eternal before whom our time is but a fleeting shadow. My life is spread out before You. It has been a rich life. And yet how much of what was present has sunk into oblivion! How much of what once was important has become unimportant! How many of those who moved my heart more deeply than I could permit them to see have passed to Your eternal peace!

It only remains for me to thank You that You have done all things well. You did not allow me to set my own goals, but led me from one station in life to another, often against my will. You often humbled me, both inwardly and outwardly, most deeply when You took away my two sons, and with them so much for which I desired to live. You broke up the fatherland which I loved so dearly, and in the end, when everything within me longed for peace, You placed me in the thick of the fight against the powers of godlessness. You often led Your Church along other paths than those for which I prayed. You permitted me to find myself alone in the midst of a configuration of church and nation which I could not approve. You placed duties upon me which better men than I could have performed, and made me abundantly aware how meager can be the fruit of human labor, how modest the yield of a long life.

Nevertheless, I thank You. I thank You that despite all changes and upheavals, my life has moved in a straight line. Knowledge and opinions have changed, but my path has remained the same from youth to old age. You have preserved a family for me in which children and grandchildren are one with their elders in their faith in You. You have made Your Church my homeland.

I do not complain that Your service was often hard, and that because it was so hard I had to neglect things to which I would gladly have devoted time and energy. I do not complain that in Your service it often seemed to me that I did not live myself, but that daily and hourly the needs of others lived in me. For it was You who lived in me in all this. And if You did not always allow me to penetrate to the depths for which I longed—I had You, and You gave me what was needful to me.

Through Your Church You kept me true to Your word, and did not let me lose my way amid the temptations which assailed me from without and from within. Your word preserved me from skepticism and contempt, those characteristics of an age alienated from God. Your word sustained me when it was difficult for me to find joy in my ministry.

Your word—that is my Lord Jesus Christ. Him I thank that I was able to find my way to You and that I could always be certain of Your pardon. Him I thank that a theology of the cross should have led me to a theology of victory, which is not my victory but Yours.

And so I take leave of my life's work, which was intended as a service to You. You remain when our time is completed, and we remain eternally in You.

To You be praise and glory forever.

CHRONOLOGY

1880	Born in Berlin
1899–1903	Studied at University of Berlin
1902	Ph.D.
1904–1906	Studied at Preachers' Seminary in Wittenberg
1906	Lic. Theol. Trip to Scotland
1906–1907	Assistant pastor at Guben
1907–1909	Archdeacon at Crossen on the Oder
1909–1910	Assistant pastor at Church of SS. Peter and Paul in Danzig
1911–1915	Chief pastor at Lauenburg in Pomerania
1915–1925	Pastor of the Heilsbronnen congregation in Berlin
1918	Executive secretary of the Mutual Trust Council in the Supreme Ecclesiastical Council of the Evangelical Church (part time)
1921	Member of the Supreme Ecclesiastical Council (part time)
1925–1933	Superintendent-General of the Kurmark
1933–1945	Relieved of functions; placed in retirement
1933–1934	Pastorate at San Remo
1934–1945	Member of Councils of Brethren of the Confessing church

1945–1961   Bishop of Berlin
1949–1961   Chairman of the Council of the Evangelical Church
            in Germany (part time)
1954–1961   President of the World Council of Churches
            (part time)

Date